MARX · ENGELS · LENIN

THE ESSENTIAL LEFT

*the text of this book is printed
on 100% recycled paper*

MARX · ENGELS · LENIN

THE ESSENTIAL LEFT

*Four Classic Texts on
The Principles of Socialism*

BARNES & NOBLE BOOKS

A DIVISION OF HARPER & ROW, PUBLISHERS

New York, Evanston, San Francisco, London

First published in the United States, 1961
by Barnes & Noble, Inc.
through special arrangement with
George Allen & Unwin Ltd.
London, England

SBN 389 00240 2

Manufactured in the United States of America

CONTENTS

THE MANIFESTO OF THE COMMUNIST PARTY

KARL MARX AND FRIEDRICH ENGELS

The Communist Manifesto *has probably had a more far-reaching effect on political thought than any other single document. As Harold Laski wrote of it, 'Its character is unique, not only because of the power with which it is written, but also because of the immense scope it covers in its intense brevity. It is a philosophy of history, a critical analysis of socialist doctrines and a passionate call to revolutionary action'.*

Its joint authors, Karl Marx (1818-1883) and Friedrich Engels (1820-1895), complemented each other perfectly in their work. Marx, profound and melancholy, was the erudite thinker tenaciously seeking the heart of the problem, while Engels, friendly and optimistic, served him as the practical man in closer touch with the immediate situation. Their famous partnership, which was of such decisive influence in modern socialism, lasted for forty years.

Though the Manifesto *was first published in 1848, Engels' Preface to the English edition of 1888 has been selected as the most useful, since it gives not only an account of the genesis of the* Manifesto *but also something of its subsequent history.*

Manifesto of the Communist Party

THE *Manifesto* was published as the platform of the Communist League, a working-men's association, first exclusively German, later on international, and, under the political conditions of the Continent before 1848, unavoidably a secret society. At a Congress of the League, held in November, 1847[1], Marx and Engels were commissioned to prepare for publication a complete theoretical and practical party programme. Drawn up in German, in January, 1848, the manuscript was sent to the printer in London a few weeks before the French revolution of February 24th. A French translation was brought out in Paris shortly before the insurrection of June, 1848. The first English translation, by Miss Helen Macfarlane, appeared in George Julian Harney's *Red Republican*, London, 1850. A Danish and a Polish edition had also been published.

The defeat of the Parisian insurrection of June, 1848—the first great battle between proletariat and bourgeoisie—drove again into the background, for a time, the social and political aspirations of the European working class. Thenceforth, the struggle for supremacy was again, as it had been before the Revolution of February, solely between different sections of the propertied class; the working class was reduced to a fight for political elbow-room, and to the position of extreme wing of the middle-class Radicals. Wherever independent proletarian movements continued to show signs of life, they were ruthlessly hunted down. Thus the Prussian police hunted out the Central Board of the Communist League then located in Cologne. The members were arrested, and, after eighteen months' imprisonment, they were tried in October, 1852. This celebrated 'Cologne Communist Trial' lasted from October 4th till November 12th; seven of the prisoners were sentenced to terms of imprisonment in a fortress,

[1] In London.

varying from three to six years. Immediately after the sentence the League was formally dissolved by the remaining members. As to the *Manifesto*, it seemed thenceforth to be doomed to oblivion.

When the European working class had recovered sufficient strength for another attack on the ruling classes, the International Working Men's Association sprang up. But this association, formed with the express aim of welding into one body the whole militant proletariat of Europe and America, could not at once proclaim the principles laid down in the *Manifesto*. The International was bound to have a programme broad enough to be acceptable to the English trade unions, to the followers of Proudhon in France, Belgium, Italy, and Spain, and to the Lassalleans[1] in Germany. Marx, who drew up this programme to the satisfaction of all parties, entirely trusted to the intellectual development of the working class, which was sure to result from combined action and mutual discussion. The very events and vicissitudes of the struggle against capital, the defeats even more than the victories, could not help bringing home to men's minds the insufficiency of their various favourite nostrums, and preparing the way for a more complete insight into the true conditions of working-class emancipation. And Marx was right. The International, on its breaking up in 1874, left the workers quite different men from what it had found them in 1864. Proudhonism in France, Lassalleanism in Germany were dying out, and even the conservative English trade unions, though most of them had long since severed their connection with the International, were gradually advancing towards that point at which, last year at Swansea, their president could say in their name: 'Continental socialism has lost its terrors for us'. In fact, the principles of the *Manifesto* had made considerable headway among the working men of all countries.

The *Manifesto* itself thus came to the front again. Since 1850 the German text had been reprinted several times in Switzerland, England, and America. In 1872 it was translated into English in New York, where the translation was published in *Woodhull and*

[1] Lassalle personally, to us, always acknowledged himself to be a disciple of Marx, and, as such, stood on the ground of the *Manifesto*. But in his public agitation, 1862-64, he did not go beyond demanding co-operative workshops supported by state credit. [*Note by F. Engels.*]

Claflin's Weekly. From this English version a French one was made in *Le Socialiste* of New York. Since then at least two more English translations, more or less mutilated, have been brought out in America, and one of them has been reprinted in England. The first Russian translation, made by Bakunin, was published at Hersen's *Kolokol* office in Geneva, about 1863; a second one, by the heroic Vera Zasulich, also in Geneva, in 1882. A new Danish edition is to be found in *Socialdemokratisk Bibliothek*, Copenhagen, 1885; a fresh French translation in *Le Socialiste*, Paris, 1886. From this latter a Spanish version was prepared and published in Madrid, in 1886. The German reprints are not to be counted; there have been twelve altogether at the least. An Armenian translation, which was to be published in Constantinople some months ago, did not see the light, I am told, because the publisher was afraid of bringing out a book with the name of Marx on it, while the translator declined to call it his own production. Of further translations into other languages I have heard but have not seen. Thus the history of the *Manifesto* reflects, to a great extent, the history of the modern working-class movement; at present it is undoubtedly the most widespread, the most international production of all socialist literature, the common platform acknowledged by millions of working men from Siberia to California.

Yet, when it was written, we could not have called it a *socialist* manifesto. By Socialists, in 1847, were understood, on the one hand the adherents of the various Utopian systems: Owenites in England, Fourierists in France, both of them already reduced to the position of mere sects, and gradually dying out; on the other hand, the most multifarious social quacks, who by all manner of tinkering, professed to redress, without any danger to capital and profit, all sorts of social grievances, in both cases men outside the working-class movement, and looking rather to the 'educated' classes for support. Whatever portion of the working class had become convinced of the insufficiency of mere political revolutions, and had proclaimed the necessity of a total social change, called itself Communist. It was a crude, rough-hewn, purely instinctive sort of communism; still it touched the cardinal point and was powerful enough amongst the working class to produce the Utopian communism of Cabet in France, and of Weitling in

Germany. Thus, in 1847, socialism was a middle-class movement, communism a working-class movement. Socialism was, on the Continent at least, 'respectable'; communism was the very opposite. And as our notion, from the very beginning, was that 'the emancipation of the working class must be the act of the working class itself', there could be no doubt as to which of the two names we must take. Moreover, we have, ever since, been far from repudiating it.

The *Manifesto* being our joint production, I consider myself bound to state that the fundamental proposition which forms its nucleus belongs to Marx. That proposition is: That in every historical epoch, the prevailing mode of economic production and exchange, and the social organisation necessarily following from it, form the basis upon which is built up, and from which alone can be explained the political and intellectual history of that epoch; that consequently the whole history of mankind (since the dissolution of primitive tribal society, holding land in common ownership) has been a history of class struggles, contests between exploiting and exploited, ruling and oppressed classes; that the history of these class struggles forms a series of evolutions in which, nowadays, a stage has been reached where the exploited and oppressed class—the proletariat—cannot attain its emancipation from the sway of the exploiting and ruling class—the bourgeoisie—without, at the same time, and once and for all emancipating society at large from all exploitation, oppression, class distinction and class struggles.

This proposition, which in my opinion is destined to do for history what Darwin's theory has done for biology, we both of us had been gradually approaching for some years before 1845. How far I had independently progressed towards it is best shown by my *Conditions of the Working Class in England*.[1] But when I again met Marx at Brussels, in spring, 1845, he had it already worked out, and put it before me, in terms almost as clear as those in which I have stated it here.

From our joint preface to the German edition of 1872, I quote the following:

[1] *The Condition of the Working Class in England in* 1844. By Friederich Engels. Translated by Florence K. Wischnewetzky. London, George Allen & Unwin Ltd.

'However much the state of things may have altered during the last twenty-five years, the general principles laid down in this *Manifesto* are, on the whole, as correct today as ever. Here and there some detail might be improved. The practical application of the principles will depend, as the *Manifesto* itself states, everywhere and at all times, on the historical conditions for the time being existing, and, for that reason, no special stress is laid on the revolutionary measures proposed at the end of Section II. That passage would, in many respects, be very differently worded today. In view of the gigantic strides of modern industry since 1848, and of the accompanying improved and extended organization of the working class, in view of the practical experience gained, first in the February Revolution, and then, still more, in the Paris Commune, where the proletariat for the first time held political power for two whole months, this programme has in some details become antiquated. One thing especially was proved by the Commune, viz., that "the working class cannot simply lay hold of the ready-made state machinery, and wield it for its own purposes". (See *The Civil War in France; Address of the General Council of the International Working Men's Association*, 1871, where this point is further developed.) Further, it is self-evident that the criticism of socialist literature is deficient in relation to the present time, because it comes down only to 1847; also, that the remarks on the relation of the Communists to the various opposition parties (Section IV), although in principle still correct, yet in practice are antiquated, because the political situation has been entirely changed, and the progress of history has swept from off the earth the greater portion of the political parties there enumerated.

'But then, the *Manifesto* has become a historical document which we have no longer any right to alter.'

The present translation is by Mr Samuel Moore, the translator of the greater portion of Marx's *Capital*. We have revised it in common, and I have added a few notes explanatory of historical allusions.

FRIEDRICH ENGELS

London, January 30, 1888

Except where indicated the notes are those mentioned above.

Manifesto of the Communist Party

A SPECTRE is haunting Europe—the spectre of communism. All the powers of old Europe have entered into a holy alliance to exorcise this spectre: Pope and Tsar, Metternich and Guizot, French Radicals and German police-spies.

Where is the party in opposition that has not been decried as communistic by its opponents in power? Where is the opposition that has not hurled back the branding reproach of communism, against the more advanced opposition parties, as well as against its reactionary adversaries?

Two things result from this fact:

I. Communism is already acknowledged by all European powers to be itself a power.

II. It is high time that Communists should openly, in the face of the whole world, publish their views, their aims, their tendencies, and meet this nursery tale of the spectre of communism with a manifesto of the party itself.

To this end, Communists of various nationalities have assembled in London and sketched the following manifesto, to be published in the English, French, German, Italian, Flemish and Danish languages.

I. BOURGEOIS AND PROLETARIANS[1]

The history of all hitherto existing society[2] is the history of class struggles.

[1] By bourgeoisie is meant the class of modern capitalists, owners of the means of social production and employers of wage labour. By proletariat, the class of modern wage labourers who, having no means of production of their own, are reduced to selling their labour power in order to live.

[2] That is, all *written* history. In 1847 the pre-history of society, the social organization existing previous to recorded history, was all but unknown. Since then Haxthausen [August von, 1792-1866] discovered common ownership of land in Russia, Maurer [Georg Ludwig von] proved it to be the social foundation from which all Teutonic races

Freeman and slave, patrician and plebeian, lord and serf, guild-master[1] and journeyman, in a word, oppressor and oppressed, stood in constant opposition to one another, carried on an uninterrupted, now hidden, now open fight, a fight that each time ended, either in a revolutionary reconstitution of society at large, or in the common ruin of the contending classes.

In the earlier epochs of history, we find almost everywhere a complicated arrangement of society into various orders, a manifold gradation of social rank. In ancient Rome we have patricians, knights, plebeians, slaves; in the Middle Ages, feudal lords, vassals, guild-masters, journeymen, apprentices, serfs; in almost all of these classes, again, subordinate gradations.

The modern bourgeois society that has sprouted from the ruins of feudal society has not done away with class antagonisms. It has but established new classes, new conditions of oppression, new forms of struggle in place of the old ones.

Our epoch, the epoch of the bourgeoisie, possesses, however, this distinctive feature: It has simplified the class antagonisms. Society as a whole is more and more splitting up into two great hostile camps, into two great classes directly facing each other—bourgeoisie and proletariat.

From the serfs of the Middle Ages sprang the chartered burghers of the earliest towns. From these burgesses the first elements of the bourgeoisie were developed.

The discovery of America, the rounding of the Cape, opened up fresh ground for the rising bourgeoisie. The East-Indian and Chinese markets, the colonization of America, trade with the colonies, the increase in the means of exchange and in commodities generally, gave to commerce, to navigation, to industry,

started in history, and, by and by, village communities were found to be, or to have been, the primitive form of society everywhere from India to Ireland. The inner organization of this primitive communistic society was laid bare, in its typical form, by Morgan's [Lewis Henry, 1818-81] crowning discovery of the true nature of the *gens* and its relation to the *tribe*. With the dissolution of these primaeval communities, society begins to be differentiated into separate and finally antagonistic classes. I have attempted to retrace this process of dissolution in *Der Ursprung der Familie, des Privateigenthums und des Staats* [*The Origin of the Family, Private Property and the State*], second edition, Stuttgart 1886.

[1] Guild-master, that is a full member of a guild, a master within, not a head of a guild.

an impulse never before known, and thereby, to the revolutionary element in the tottering feudal society, a rapid development.

The feudal system of industry, in which industrial production was monopolized by closed guilds, now no longer sufficed for the growing wants of the new markets. The manufacturing system took its place. The guild-masters were pushed aside by the manufacturing middle class; division of labour between the different corporate guilds vanished in the face of division of labour in each single workshop.

Meantime the markets kept ever growing, the demand ever rising. Even manufacture no longer sufficed. Thereupon, steam and machinery revolutionized industrial production. The place of manufacture was taken by the giant, modern industry, the place of the industrial middle class by industrial millionaires, the leaders of whole industrial armies, the modern bourgeois.

Modern industry has established the world market, for which the discovery of America paved the way. This market has given an immense development to commerce, to navigation, to communication by land. This development has, in its turn, reacted on the extension of industry; and in proportion as industry, commerce, navigation, railways extended, in the same proportion the bourgeoisie developed, increased its capital, and pushed into the background every class handed down from the Middle Ages.

We see, therefore, how the modern bourgeoisie is itself the product of a long course of development, of a series of revolutions in the modes of production and of exchange.

Each step in the development of the bourgeoisie was accompanied by a corresponding political advance of that class. An oppressed class under the sway of the feudal nobility, an armed and self-governing association in the medieval commune;[1] here independent urban republic (as in Italy and Germany), there taxable 'third estate' of the monarchy (as in France); afterwards, in the period of manufacture proper, serving either the semifeudal or the absolute monarchy as a counterpoise against the

[1] 'Commune' was the name taken in France by the nascent towns even before they had conquered from their feudal lords and masters local self-government and political rights as the 'Third Estate'. Generally speaking, for the economical development of the bourgeoisie, England is here taken as the typical country, for its political development, France.

nobility, and, in fact, cornerstone of the great monarchies in general—the bourgeoisie has at last, since the establishment of modern industry and of the world market, conquered for itself, in the modern representative state, exclusive political sway. The executive of the modern state is but a committee for managing the common affairs of the whole bourgeoisie.

The bourgeoisie, historically, has played a most revolutionary part.

The bourgeoisie, wherever it has got the upper hand, has put an end to all feudal, patriarchal, idyllic relations. It has pitilessly torn asunder the motley feudal ties that bound man to his 'natural superiors', and has left no other nexus between man and man than naked self-interest, than callous 'cash payment'. It has drowned the most heavenly ecstasies of religious fervour, of chivalrous enthusiasm, of philistine sentimentalism, in the icy water of egotistical calculation. It has resolved personal worth into exchange value, and in place of the numberless indefeasible chartered freedoms, has set up that single, unconscionable freedom—Free Trade. In one word, for exploitation, veiled by religious and political illusions, it has substituted naked, shameless, direct, brutal exploitation.

The bourgeoisie has stripped of its halo every occupation hitherto honoured and looked up to with reverent awe. It has converted the physician, the lawyer, the priest, the poet, the man of science, into its paid wage labourers.

The bourgeoisie has torn away from the family its sentimental veil, and has reduced the family relation to a mere money relation.

The bourgeoisie has disclosed how it came to pass that the brutal display of vigour in the Middle Ages, which reactionaries so much admire, found its fitting complement in the most slothful indolence. It has been the first to show what man's activity can bring about. It has accomplished wonders far surpassing Egyptian pyramids, Roman aqueducts, and Gothic cathedrals; it has conducted expeditions that put in the shade all former exoduses of nations and crusades.

The bourgeoisie cannot exist without constantly revolutionizing the instruments of production, and thereby the relations of production, and with them the whole relations of society. Conservation of the old modes of production in unaltered form, was, on the contrary, the first condition of existence for all earlier industrial classes. Constant revolutionizing of production, uninterrupted disturbance of all social conditions, everlasting uncertainty and agitation distinguish the bourgeois epoch from all earlier ones. All fixed, fast frozen relations, with their train of ancient and removable prejudices and opinions, are swept away, all new-formed ones become antiquated before they can ossify. All that is solid melts into air, all that is holy is profaned, and man is at last compelled to face with sober senses his real conditions of life and his relations with his kind.

The need of a constantly expanding market for its products chases the bourgeoisie over the whole surface of the globe. It must nestle everywhere, settle everywhere, establish connections everywhere.

The bourgeoisie has through its exploitation of the world market given a cosmopolitan character to production and consumption in every country. To the great chagrin of reactionaries, it has drawn from under the feet of industry the national ground on which it stood. All old-established national industries have been destroyed or are daily being destroyed. They are dislodged by new industries, whose introduction becomes a life and death question for all civilized nations, by industries that no longer work up indigenous raw material, but raw material drawn from the remotest zones; industries whose products are consumed, not only at home, but in every quarter of the globe. In place of the old wants, satisfied by the production of the country, we find new wants, requiring for their satisfaction the products of distant lands and climes. In place of the old local and national seclusion and self-sufficiency, we have intercourse in every direction, universal inter-dependence of nations. And as in material, so also in intellectual production. The intellectual creations of individual nations become common property. National one-sidedness and narrow-mindedness become more and more impossible, and from the numerous national and local literatures there arises a world literature.

The bourgeoisie, by the rapid improvement of all instruments of production, by the immensely facilitated means of communication, draws all, even the most barbarian, nations into civilization. The cheap prices of its commodities are the heavy artillery with which it batters down all Chinese walls, with which it forces the barbarians' intensely obstinate hatred of foreigners to capitulate. It compels all nations, on pain of extinction, to adopt the bourgeois mode of production; it compels them to introduce what it calls civilization into their midst, i.e. to become bourgeois themselves. In one word, it creates a world after its own image.

The bourgeois has subjected the country to the rule of the towns. It has created enormous cities, has greatly increased the urban population as compared with the rural, and has thus rescued a considerable part of the population from the idiocy of rural life. Just as it has made the country dependent on the towns, so it has made barbarian and semi-barbarian countries dependent on the civilized ones, nations of peasants on nations of bourgeois, the East on the West.

The bourgeoisie keeps more and more doing away with the scattered state of the population, of the means of production, and of property. It has agglomerated population, centralized means of production, and has concentrated property in a few hands. The necessary consequences of this was political centralization. Independent, or but loosely connected provinces, with separate interests, laws, governments, and systems of taxation, became lumped together into one nation, with one government, one code of laws, one national class interest, one frontier and one customs tariff.

The bourgeoisie, during its rule of scarce one hundred years, has created more massive and more colossal productive forces than have all preceding generations together. Subjection of nature's forces to man, machinery, application of chemistry to industry and agriculture, steam navigation, railways, electric telegraphs, clearing of whole continents for cultivation, canalization of rivers, whole populations conjured out of the ground—what earlier century had even a presentiment that such productive forces slumbered in the lap of social labour?

We see then: the means of production and of exchange, on whose foundation the bourgeoisie built itself up, were generated in feudal society. At a certain stage in the development of these means of production and of exchange, the conditions under which feudal society produced and exchanged, the feudal organization of agriculture and manufacturing industry, in one word, the feudal relations of property became no longer compatible with the already developed productive forces; they became so many fetters. They had to be burst asunder; they were burst asunder.

Into their place stepped free competition, accompanied by a social and political constitution adapted to it, and by the economic and political sway of the bourgeois class.

A similar movement is going on before our own eyes. Modern bourgeois society with its relations of production, of exchange and of property, a society that has conjured up such gigantic means of production and of exchange, is like the sorcerer who is no longer able to control the powers of the nether world whom he has called up by his spells. For many a decade past the history of industry and commerce is but the history of the revolt of modern productive forces against modern conditions of production, against the property relations that are the conditions for the existence of the bourgeoisie and of its rule. It is enough to mention the commercial crises that by their periodical return put the existence of the entire bourgeois society on its trial, each time more threateningly. In these crises a great part not only of the existing products, but also of the previously created productive forces, are periodically destroyed. In these crises there breaks out an epidemic that, in all earlier epochs, would have seemed an absurdity—the epidemic of over-production. Society suddenly finds itself put back into a state of momentary barbarism; it appears as if a famine, a universal war of devastation had cut off the supply of every means of subsistence; industry and commerce seem to be destroyed. And why? Because there is too much civilization, too much means of subsistence, too much industry, too much commerce. The productive forces at the disposal of society no longer tend to further the development of the conditions of bourgeois property; on the contrary, they have become too powerful for these conditions, by which they are fettered, and so soon as they overcome these fetters, they bring disorder into the whole of bourgeois society, endanger the existence of bourgeois property. The conditions of bourgeois society are too narrow to comprise the wealth created by them. And how does the bourgeoisie get over these crises? On the one hand, by enforced destruction of a mass of productive forces; on the other, by the conquest of new markets, and by the more thorough exploitation of the old ones. That is to say, by paving the way for more extensive and more destructive crises, and by diminishing the means whereby crises are prevented.

The weapons with which the bourgeoisie felled feudalism to the ground are now turned against the bourgeoisie itself.

But not only has the bourgeoisie forged the weapons that bring death to itself; it has also called into existence the men who are to wield those weapons—the modern working class—the proletarians.

In proportion as the bourgeoisie, i.e. capital, is developed, in the same proportion is the proletariat, the modern working class, developed—a class of labourers, who live only so long as they find work, and who find work only so long as their labour increases capital. These labourers, who must sell themselves piecemeal, are a commodity, like every other article of commerce, and are consequently exposed to all the vicissitudes of competition, to all the fluctuations of the market.

Owing to the extensive use of machinery and to division of labour, the work of the proletarians has lost all individual character, and, consequently, all charm for the workman. He becomes an appendage of the machine, and it is only the most simple, most monotonous, and most easily acquired knack, that is required of him. Hence, the cost of production of a workman is restricted, almost entirely, to the means of subsistence that he requires for his maintenance, and for the propagation of his race. But the price of a commodity, and therefore also of labour, is equal to its cost of production. In proportion, therefore, as the repulsiveness of the work increases, the wage decreases. Nay more, in proportion as the use of machinery and division of labour increases, in the same proportion the burden of toil also increases, whether by prolongation of the working hours, by increase of the work exacted in a given time, or by increased speed of the machinery, etc.

Modern industry has converted the little workshop of the patriarchal master into the great factory of the industrial capitalist. Masses of labourers, crowded into the factory, are organized like soldiers. As privates of the industrial army they are placed under the command of a perfect hierarchy of officers and sergeants.

Not only are they slaves of the bourgeois class, and of the bourgeois state. they are daily and hourly enslaved by the machine, by the overlooker, and, above all, by the individual bourgois manufacturer himself. The more openly this despotism proclaims gain to be its end and aim, the more petty, the more hateful and the more embittering it is.

The less the skill and exertion of strength implied in manual labour, in other words, the more modern industry becomes developed, the more is the labour of men superseded by that of women. Differences of age and sex have no longer any distinctive social validity for the working class. All are instruments of labour, more or less expensive to use, according to their age and sex.

No sooner is the exploitation of the labourer by the manufacturer, so far at an end, that he receives his wages in cash, than he is set upon by the other portions of the bourgeoisie, the landlord, the shopkeeper, the pawnbroker, etc.

The lower strata of the middle class—the small tradespeople, shopkeepers, and retired tradesmen generally, the handicraftsmen and peasants—all these sink gradually into the proletariat, partly because their diminutive capital does not suffice for the scale on which modern industry is carried on, and is swamped in the competition with the large capitalists, partly because their specialized skill is rendered worthless by new methods of production. Thus the proletariat is recruited from all classes of the population.

The proletariat goes through various stages of development. With its birth begins its struggle with the bourgeoisie. At first the contest is carried on by individual labourers, then by the work people of a factory, then by the operatives of one trade, in one locality, against the individual bourgeois who directly exploits them. They direct their attacks not against the bourgeois conditions of production, but against the instruments of production themselves; they destroy imported wares that compete with their labour, they smash to pieces machinery, they set factories ablaze, they seek to restore by force the vanished status of the workman of the Middle Ages.

At this stage the labourers still form an incoherent mass scattered over the whole country, and broken up by their mutual competition. If anywhere they unite to form more compact bodies, this is not yet the consequence of their own active union, but of the union of the bourgeoisie, which class, in order to attain its own political ends, is compelled to set the whole proletariat in motion, and is moreover yet, for a time, able to do so. At this stage, therefore, the proletarians do not fight their enemies, but the enemies of their enemies, the remnants of absolute monarchy, the landowners, the non-industrial bourgeois, the petty bourgeoisie. Thus the whole historical movement is concentrated in the hands of the bourgeoisie; every victory so obtained is a victory for the bourgeoisie.

But with the development of industry the proletariat not only increases in number; it becomes concentrated in greater masses, its strength grows, and it feels that strength more. The various interests and conditions of life within the ranks of the proletariat are more and more equalized, in proportion as machinery obliterates all distinctions of labour, and nearly everywhere reduces wages to the same low level. The growing competition among the bourgeois, and the resulting commercial crises, make the wages of the workers ever more fluctuating. The unceasing improvement of machinery, ever more rapidly developing, makes their livelihood more and more precarious; the collisions between individual workmen and individual bourgeois take more and more the character of collisions between two classes. Thereupon the workers begin to form combinations (trade unions) against the bourgeois; they club together in order to keep up the rate of wages; they found permanent associations in order to make provision beforehand for these occasional revolts. Here and there the contest breaks out into riots.

Now and then the workers are victorious, but only for a time. The real fruit of their battles lies, not in the immediate result, but in the ever expanding union of the workers. This union is helped on by the improved means of communication that are created by modern industry, and that place the workers of different localities in contact with another. It was just this contact that was needed to centralize the numerous local struggles, all of the same character, into one national struggle between classes. But every class struggle is a political struggle. And that union, to attain which the burghers of the Middle Ages, with their miserable highways, required centuries, the modern proletarians, thanks to railways, achieve in a few years.

This organization of the proletarians into a class, and consequently into a political party, is continually being upset again by the competition between the workers themselves. But it ever rises up again, stronger, firmer, mightier. It compels legislative recognition of particular interests of the workers, by taking advantage of the divisions among the bourgeoisie itself. Thus the Ten-Hours Bill in England was carried.

Altogether, collisions between the classes of the old society further in many ways the course of development of the proletariat. The bourgeoisie finds itself involved in a constant battle. At first with the aristocracy; later on, with those portions of the bourgeoisie itself, whose interests have become antagonistic to the progress of industry; at all time with the bourgeoisie of foreign countries. In all these battles it sees itself compelled to appeal to the proletariat, to ask for its help, and thus, to drag it into the political arena. The bourgeoisie itself, therefore, supplies the proletariat with its own elements of political and general education, in other words, it furnishes the proletariat with weapons for fighting the bourgeoisie.

Further, as we have already seen, entire sections of the ruling classes are, by the advance of industry, precipitated into the proletariat, or are at least threatened in their conditions of existence. These also supply the proletariat with fresh elements of enlightenment and progress.

Finally, in times when the class struggle nears the decisive hour, the process of dissolution going on within the ruling class, in fact within the whole range of old society, assumes such a violent, glaring character, that a small section of the ruling class cuts itself adrift, and joins the revolutionary class, the class that holds the future in its hands. Just as, therefore, at an earlier period, a section of the nobility went over to the bourgeoisie, so now a portion of the bourgeoisie goes over to the proletariat, and in particular, a portion of the bourgeois ideologists, who have raised themselves to the level of comprehending theoretically the historical movement as a whole.

Of all the classes that stand face to face with the bourgeoisie today, the proletariat alone is a really revolutionary class. The other classes decay and finally disappear in the face of modern industry; the proletariat is its special and essential product.

The lower middle class, the small manufacturer, the shop-keeper, the artisan, the peasant, all these fight against the bourgeoisie, to save from extinction their existence as fractions of the middle class. They are therefore not revolutionary, but conservative. Nay, more, they are reactionary, for they try to roll back the wheel of history. If by chance they are revolutionary, they are so only in view of their impending transfer into the proletariat; they thus defend not their present, but their future interests; they desert their own standpoint to place themselves at that of the proletariat.

The 'dangerous class', the social scum, that passively rotting mass thrown off by the lowest layers of old society, may, here and there, be swept into the movement by a proletarian revolution; its conditions of life, however, prepare it far more for the part of a bribed tool of reactionary intrigue.

In the conditions of the proletariat, those of old society at large are already virtually swamped. The proletarian is without property; his relation to his wife and children has no longer anything in common with the bourgeois family relations; modern industrial labour, modern subjection to capital, the same in England as in France, in America as in Germany, has stripped him of every trace of national character. Law, morality, religion, are to him so many bourgeois prejudices, behind which lurk in ambush just as many bourgeois interests.

All the preceding classes that got the upper hand, sought to fortify their already acquired status by subjecting society at large to their conditions of appropriation. The proletarians cannot become masters of the productive forces of society, except by abolishing their own previous mode of appropriation, and thereby also every other previous mode of appropriation. They have nothing of their own to secure and to fortify; their mission is to destroy all previous securities for, and insurances of, individual property.

All previous historical movements were movements of minori-ties, or in the interest of minorities. The proletarian movement is the self-conscious, independent movement of the immense majority, in the interest of the immense majority. The proletariat, the lowest stratum of our present society, cannot stir, cannot raise itself up, without the whole superincumbent strata of official society being sprung into the air.

Though not in substance, yet in form, the struggle of the proletariat with the bourgeoisie is at first a national struggle. The proletariat of each country must, of course, first of all settle matters with its own bourgeoisie.

In depicting the most general phases of the development of the proletariat, we traced the more or less veiled civil war, raging within existing society, up to the point where that war breaks out into open revolution, and where the violent overthrow of the bourgeoisie lays the foundation for the sway of the proletariat.

Hitherto, every form of society has been based, as we have already seen, on the antagonism of oppressing and oppressed classes. But in order to oppress a class, certain conditions must be assured to it under which it can, at least, continue its slavish existence. The serf, in the period of serfdom, raised himself to membership in the commune, just as the petty bourgeois, under the yoke of feudal absolutism, managed to develop into a bourgeois. The modern labourer, on the contrary, instead of rising with the progress of industry, sinks deeper and deeper below the conditions of existence of his own class. He becomes a pauper, and pauperism develops more rapidly than population and wealth. And here it becomes evident that the bourgeoisie is unfit any longer to be the ruling class in society, and to impose its conditions of existence upon society as an overriding law. It is unfit to rule because it is incompetent to assure an existence to its slave within his slavery, because it cannot help letting him sink into such a state, that it has to feed him, instead of being fed by him. Society can no longer live under this bourgeoisie, in other words, its existence is no longer compatible with society.

The essential condition for the existence and for the sway of the bourgeois class is the formation and augmentation of capital; the condition for capital is wage labour. Wage labour rests exclusively on competition between the labourers. The advance of industry, whose involuntary promoter is the bourgeoisie, replaces the isolation of the labourers, due to competition, by their revolutionary combination, due to association. The development of modern industry, therefore, cuts from under its feet the very foundation on which the bourgeoisie produces and appropriates products. What the bourgeoisie therefore produces, above all, are its own grave-diggers. Its fall and the victory of the proletariat are equally inevitable.

II. PROLETARIANS AND COMMUNISTS

In what relation do the Communists stand to the proletarians as a whole?

The Communists do not form a separate party opposed to other working-class parties.

They have no interests separate and apart from those of the proletariat as a whole.

They do not set up any sectarian principles of their own, by which to shape and mould the proletarian movement.

The Communists are distinguished from the other working-class parties by this only: (1) In the national struggles of the proletarians of the different countries, they point out and bring to the front the common interests of the entire proletariat, independently of all nationality. (2) In the various stages of development which the struggle of the working class against the bourgeoisie has to pass through, they always and everywhere represent the interests of the movement as a whole.

The Communists, therefore, are on the one hand, practically, the most advanced and resolute section of the working-class parties of every country, that section which pushes forward all others; on the other hand, theoretically, they have over the great mass of the proletariat the advantage of clearly understanding the lines of march, the conditions, and the ultimate general results of the proletarian movement.

The immediate aim of the Communists is the same as that of all other proletarian parties: Formation of the proletariat into a class, overthrow of the bourgeois supremacy, conquest of political power by the proletariat.

The theoretical conclusions of the Communists are in no way based on ideas or principles that have been invented, or discovered, by this or that would-be universal reformer.

They merely express, in general terms, actual relations springing from an existing class struggle, from a historical movement going on under our very eyes. The abolition of existing property relations is not at all a distinctive feature of communism.

All property relations in the past have continually been subject to historical change consequent upon the change in historical conditions.

The French Revolution, for example, abolished feudal property in favour of bourgeois property.

The distinguishing feature of communism is not the abolition of property generally, but the abolition of bourgeois property. But modern bourgeois private property is the final and most complete expression of the system of producing and appropriating products that is based on class antagonisms, on the exploitation of the many by the few.

In this sense, the theory of the Communists may be summed up in the single sentence: Abolition of private property.

We Communists have been reproached with the desire of abolishing the right of personally acquiring property as the fruit of a man's own labour, which property is alleged to be the groundwork of all personal freedom, activity and independence.

Hard-won, self-acquired, self-earned property! Do you mean the property of the petty artisan and of the small peasant, a form of property that preceded the bourgeois form? There is no need to abolish that; the development of industry has to a great extent already destroyed it, and is still destroying it daily.

Or do you mean modern bourgeois private property?

But does wage labour create any property for the labourer? Not a bit. It creates capital, i.e. that kind of property which exploits wage labour, and which cannot increase except upon conditions of begetting a new supply of wage labour for fresh exploitation. Property, in its present form, is based on the antagonism of capital and wage labour. Let us examine both sides of this antagonism.

To be a capitalist is to have not only a purely personal, but a social, *status* in production. Capital is a collective product, and only by the united action of many members, nay, in the last resort, only by the united action of all members of society, can it be set in motion.

Capital is therefore not a personal, it is a social power.

When, therefore, capital is converted into common property, into the property of all members of society, personal property is not thereby transformed into social property. It is only the social character of the property that is changed. It loses its class character.

Let us now take wage labour.

The average price of wage labour is the minimum wage, i.e. that quantum of the means of subsistence which is absolutely requisite to keep the labourer in bare existence as a labourer. What, therefore, the wage labourer appropriates by means of his labour, merely suffices to prolong and reproduce a bare existence. We by no means intend to abolish this personal appropriation of the products of labour, an appropriation that is made for the maintenance and reproduction of human life, and that leaves no surplus wherewith to command the labour of others. All that we want to do away with is the miserable character of this appropriation, under which the labourer lives merely to increase capital, and is allowed to live only in so far as the interest of the ruling class requires it.

In bourgeois society, living labour is but a means to increase accumulated labour. In communist society, accumulated labour is but a means to widen, to enrich, to promote the existence of the labourer.

In bourgeois society, therefore, the past dominates the present; in communist society, the present dominates the past. In bourgeois society capital is independent and has individuality, while the living person is dependent and has no individuality.

And the abolition of this state of things is called by the bourgeois, abolition of individuality and freedom! And rightly so. The abolition of bourgeois individuality, bourgeois independence, and bourgeois freedom is undoubtedly aimed at.

By freedom is meant, under the present bourgeois conditions of production, free trade, free selling and buying.

But if selling and buying disappears, free selling and buying disappears also. This talk about free selling and buying, and all the other 'brave words' of our bourgeoisie about freedom in general, have a meaning, if any, only in contrast with restricted selling and buying, with the fettered traders of the Middle Ages, but have no meaning when opposed to the communist abolition of buying and selling, of the bourgeois conditions of production, and of the bourgeoisie itself.

You are horrified at our intending to do away with private property. But in your existing society, private property is already done away with for nine-tenths of the population; its existence for the few is solely due to its non-existence in the hands of those nine-tenths. You reproach us, therefore, with intending to do away with a form of property, the necessary condition for whose existence is the non-existence of any property for the immense majority of society.

In one word, you reproach us with intending to do away with your property. Precisely so; that is just what we intend.

From the moment when labour can no longer be converted into capital, money or rent, into a social power capable of being monopolized, i.e. from the moment when individual property can no longer be transformed into bourgeois property, into capital, from that moment, you say, individuality vanishes.

You must, therefore, confess that by 'individual' you mean no other person than the bourgeois, than the middle-class owner of property. This person must, indeed, be swept out of the way, and made impossible.

Communism deprives no man of the power to appropriate the products of society; all that it does is to deprive him of the power to subjugate the labour of others by means of such appropriation.

It has been objected, that upon the abolition of private property all work will cease, and universal laziness will overtake us.

According to this, bourgeois society ought long ago to have gone to the dogs through sheer idleness; for those of its members who work acquire nothing, and those who acquire anything do not work. The whole of this objection is but another expression of the tautology: There can no longer be any wage labour when there is no longer any capital.

All objections urged against the communistic mode of producing and appropriating material products, have, in the same way, been urged against the communistic modes of producing and appropriating intellectual products. Just as to the bourgeois, the disappearance of class property is the disappearance of production itself, so the disappearance of class culture is to him identical with the disappearance of all culture.

That culture, the loss of which he laments, is, for the enormous majority, a mere training to act as a machine.

But don't wrangle with us so long as you apply, to our intended abolition of bourgeois property, the standard of your bourgeois notions of freedom, culture, law, etc. Your very ideas are but the outgrowth of the conditions of your bourgeois production and bourgeois property, just as your jurisprudence is but the will of your class made into a law for all, a will whose essential character and direction are determined by the economical conditions of existence of your class.

The selfish misconception that induces you to transform into eternal laws of nature and of reason, the social forms springing from your present mode of production and form of property— historical relations that rise and disappear in the progress of production—this misconception you share with every ruling class that has preceded you. What you see clearly in the case of ancient property, what you admit in the case of feudal property, you are of course forbidden to admit in the case of your own bourgeois form of property.

Abolition of the family! Even the most radical flare up at this infamous proposal of the Communists.

On what foundation is the present family, the bourgeois family, based? On capital, on private gain. In its completely developed form this family exists only among the bourgeoisie. But this state of things finds its complement in the practical absence of the family among proletarians, and in public prostitution.

The bourgeois family will vanish as a matter of course when its complement vanishes, and both will vanish with the vanishing of capital.

Do you charge us with wanting to stop the exploitation of children by their parents? To this crime we plead guilty.

But, you will say, we destroy the most hallowed of relations, when we replace home education by social.

And your education! Is not that also social, and determined by the social conditions under which you educate, by the intervention direct or indirect, of society, by means of schools, etc.? The Communists have not invented the intervention of society in education; they do but seek to alter the character of that intervention, and to rescue education from the influence of the ruling class.

The bourgeois claptrap about the family and education, about the hallowed correlation of parent and child, becomes all the more disgusting, the more, by the action of modern industry, all family ties among the proletarians are torn asunder, and their children transformed into simple articles of commerce and instruments of labour.

But you Communists would introduce community of women, screams the whole bourgeoisie in chorus.

The bourgeois sees in his wife a mere instrument of production. He hears that the instruments of production are to be exploited in common, and, naturally, can come to no other conclusion than that the lot of being common to all will likewise fall to the women.

He has not even a suspicion that the real point aimed at is to do away with the status of women as mere instruments of production.

For the rest, nothing is more ridiculous than the virtuous indignation of our bourgeois at the community of women which, they pretend, is to be openly and officially established by the Communists. The Communists have no need to introduce community of women; it has existed almost from time immemorial.

Our bourgeois, not content with having wives and daughters of their proletarians at their disposal, not to speak of common prostitutes, take the greatest pleasure in seducing each other's wives.

Bourgeois marriage is in reality a system of wives in common and thus, at the most, what the Communists might possibly be reproached with is that they desire to introduce, in substitution for a hypocritically concealed, an openly legalized community of women. For the rest, it is self-evident that the abolition of the present system of production must bring with it the abolition of the community of women springing from that system, i.e. of prostitution both public and private.

The Communists are further reproached with desiring to abolish countries and nationality.

The working men have no country. We cannot take from them what they have not got. Since the proletariat must first of all acquire political supremacy, must rise to be the leading class of the nation, must constitute itself *the* nation, it is, so far, itself national, though not in the bourgeois sense of the word.

National differences and antagonism between peoples are daily more and more vanishing, owing to the development of the bourgeoisie, to freedom of commerce, to the world market, to uniformity in the mode of production and in the conditions of life corresponding thereto.

The supremacy of the proletariat will cause them to vanish still faster. United action of the leading civilized countries at least, is one of the first conditions for the emancipation of the proletariat.

In proportion as the exploitation of one individual by another is put an end to, the exploitation of one nation by another will also be put an end to. In proportion as the antagonism between classes within the nation vanishes, the hostility of one nation to another will come to an end.

The charges against communism made from a religious, a philosophical and, generally, from an ideological standpoint, are not deserving of serious examination.

Does it require deep intuition to comprehend that man's ideas, views, and conceptions, in one word, man's consciousness, changes with every change in the conditions of his material existence, in his social relations and in his social life?

What else does the history of ideas prove, than that intellectual production changes its character in proportion as material production is changed? The ruling ideas of each age have ever been the ideas of its ruling class.

When people speak of ideas that revolutionize society, they do but express the fact that within the old society the elements of a new one have been created, and that the dissolution of the old ideas keeps even pace with the dissolution of the old conditions of existence.

When the ancient world was in its last throes, the ancient religions were overcome by Christianity. When Christian ideas succumbed in the eighteenth century to rationalist ideas, feudal society fought its death battle with the then revolutionary bourgeoisie. The ideas of religious liberty and freedom of conscience, merely gave expression to the sway of free competition within the domain of knowledge.

'Undoubtedly,' it will be said, 'religious, moral, philosophical and juridical ideas have been modified in the course of historical development. But religion, morality, philosophy, political science, and law, constantly survived this change.'

'There are, besides, eternal truths, such as Freedom, Justice, etc., that are common to all states of society. But communism abolishes eternal truths, it abolishes all religion, and all morality, instead of constituting them on a new basis; it therefore acts in contradiction to all past historical experience.'

What does this accusation reduce itself to? The history of all past society has consisted in the development of class antagonisms, antagonisms that assumed different forms at different epochs.

But whatever form they may have taken, one fact is common to all past ages, viz., the exploitation of one part of society by the other. No wonder, then, that the social consciousness of past ages, despite all the multiplicity and variety it displays, moves within certain common forms, or general ideas, which cannot completely vanish except with the total disappearance of class antagonisms.

The communist revolution is the most radical rupture with traditional relations; no wonder that its development involves the most radical rupture with traditional ideas.

But let us have done with the bourgeois objections to communism.

We have seen above that the first step in the revolution by the working class is to raise the proletariat to the position of ruling class to win the battle of democracy.

The proletariat will use its political supremacy to wrest, by degrees, all capital from the bourgeoisie, to centralize all instruments of production in the hands of the state, i.e. of the proletariat organized as the ruling class; and to increase the total of productive forces as rapidly as possible.

Of course, in the beginning, this cannot be effected except by means of despotic inroads on the rights of property, and on the conditions of bourgeois production; by means of measures, therefore, which appear economically insufficient and untenable, but which, in the course of the movement, outstrip themselves, necessitate further inroads upon the old order, and are unavoidable as a means of entirely revolutionizing the mode of production.

These measures will of course be different in different countries.

Nevertheless, in the most advanced countries, the following will be pretty generally applicable.

1. Abolition of property in land and application of all rents of land to public purposes.

2. A heavy progressive or graduated income tax.

3. Abolition of all right of inheritance.

4. Confiscation of the property of all emigrants and rebels.

5. Centralization of credit in the hands of the state, by means of a national bank with state capital and an exclusive monopoly.

6. Centralization of the means of communication and transport in the hands of the state.

7. Extension of factories and instruments of production owned by the state; the bringing into cultivation of waste lands, and the improvement of the soil generally in accordance with a common plan.

8. Equal obligation of all to work. Establishment of industrial armies, especially for agriculture.

9. Combination of agriculture with manufacturing industries; gradual abolition of all the distinction between town and country by a more equable distribution of the population over the country.

10. Free education for all children in public schools. Abolition of children's factory labour in its present form. Combination of education with industrial production, etc.

When, in the course of development, class distinctions have disappeared, and all production has been concentrated in the hands of a vast association of the whole nation, the public power will lose its political character. Political power, properly so called, is merely the organized power of one class for oppressing another. If the proletariat during its contest with the bourgeoisie is compelled, by the force of circumstances, to organize itself as a class; if, by means of a revolution, it makes itself the ruling class, and, as such, sweeps away by force the old conditions of production, then it will, along with these conditions, have swept away the conditions for the existence of class antagonisms and of classes generally, and will thereby have abolished its own supremacy as a class.

In place of the old bourgeois society, with its classes and class antagonisms, we shall have an association in which the free development of each is the condition for the free development of all.

III. SOCIALIST AND COMMUNIST LITERATURE

I. REACTIONARY SOCIALISM

a. Feudal Socialism

Owing to their historical position it became the vocation of the aristocracies of France and England to write pamphlets against modern bourgeois society. In the French Revolution of July, 1830, and in the English reform agitation, these aristocracies again succumbed to the hateful upstart. Thenceforth a serious political struggle was altogether out of the question. A literary battle alone remained possible. But even in the domain of literature the old cries of the restoration period[1] had become impossible.

In order to arouse sympathy the aristocracy was obliged to lose sight, apparently, of its own interests, and to formulate its indictment against the bourgeoisie in the interest of the exploited working class alone. Thus the aristocracy took their revenge by singing lampoons on their new master and whispering in his ears sinister prophecies of coming catastrophe.

In this way arose feudal socialism: half lamentation, half lampoon; half echo of the past, half menace of the future; at times, by its bitter, witty and incisive criticism, striking the bourgeoisie to the very heart's core, but always ludicrous in its effect, through total incapacity to comprehend the march of modern history.

The aristocracy, in order to rally the people to them, waved the proletarian alms-bag in front for a banner. But the people, so often as it joined them, saw on their hindquarters the old feudal coats of arms, and deserted with loud and irreverent laughter.

---

[1] Not the English Restoration, 1660 to 1689, but the French Restoration, 1814 to 1830.

One section of the French Legitimists and 'Young England' exhibited this spectacle.

In pointing out that their mode of exploitation was different to that of the bourgeoisie, the feudalists forget that they exploited under circumstances and conditions that were quite different and that are now antiquated. In showing that, under their rule, the modern proletariat never existed, they forget that the modern bourgeoisie is the necessary offspring of their own form of society.

For the rest, so little do they conceal the reactionary character of their criticism that their chief accusation against the bourgeoisie amounts to this, that under the bourgeois régime a class is being developed which is destined to cut up root and branch the old order of society.

What they upbraid the bourgeoisie with is not so much that it creates a proletariat as that it creates a *revolutionary* proletariat.

In political practice, therefore, they join in all coercive measures against the working class; and in ordinary life, despite their high falutin' phrases, they stoop to pick up the golden apples dropped from the tree of industry, and to barter truth, love, and honour for traffic in wool, beetroot-sugar, and potato spirits.[1]

As the parson has ever gone hand in hand with the landlord, so has clerical socialism with feudal socialism.

Nothing is easier than to give Christian asceticism a socialist tinge. Has not Christianity declaimed against private property, against marriage, against the state? Has it not preached in the place of these, charity and poverty, celibacy and mortification of the flesh, monastic life and Mother Church? Christian socialism is but the holy water with which the priest consecrates the heart-burnings of the aristocrat.

b. Petty-Bourgeois Socialism

The feudal aristocracy was not the only class that was ruined by

[1] This applies chiefly to Germany where the landed aristocracy and squirearchy have large portions of their estates cultivated for their own account by stewards, and are, moreover, extensive beetroot-sugar manufacturers and distillers of potato spirits. The wealthier British aristocracy are, as yet, rather above that; but they, too, know how to make up for declining rents by lending their names to floaters of more or less shady joint-stock companies.

the bourgeoisie, not the only class whose conditions of existence pined and perished in the atmosphere of modern bourgeois society. The medieval burgesses and the small peasant proprietors were the precursors of the modern bourgeoisie. In those countries which are but little developed, industrially and commercially, these two classes still vegetate side by side with the rising bourgeoisie.

In countries where modern civilization has become fully developed, a new class of petty bourgeois has been formed, fluctuating between proletariat and bourgeoisie, and ever renewing itself as a supplementary part of bourgeois society. The individual members of this class, however, are being constantly hurled down into the proletariat by the action of competition, and, as modern industry develops, they even see the moment approaching when they will completely disappear as an independent section of modern society, to be replaced, in manufactures, agriculture and commerce, by overlookers, bailiffs and shopmen.

In countries like France, where the peasants constitute far more than half of the population, it was natural that writers who sided with the proletariat against the bourgeoisie should use, in their criticism of the bourgeois régime, the standard of the peasant and petty bourgeois, and from the standpoint of these intermediate classes should take up the cudgels for the working class. Thus arose petty-bourgeois socialism. Sismondi was the head of this school, not only in France but also in England.

This school of socialism dissected with great acuteness the contradictions in the conditions of modern production. It laid bare the hypocritical apologies of economists. It proved, incontrovertibly, the disastrous effects of machinery and division of labour; the concentration of capital and land in a few hands; over-production and crises; it pointed out the inevitable ruin of the petty bourgeois and peasant, the misery of the proletariat, the anarchy in production, the crying inequalities in the distribution of wealth, the industrial war of extermination between nations, the dissolution of old moral bonds, of the old family relations, of the old nationalities.

In its positive aims, however, this form of socialism aspires either to restoring the old means of production and of exchange, and with them the old property relations, and the old society, or to cramping the modern means of production and of exchange within the framework of the old property relations that have been, and were bound to be, exploded by those means. In either case it is both reactionary and utopian.

Its last words are: Corporate guilds for manufacture; patriarchal relations in agriculture.

Ultimately, when stubborn historical facts had dispersed all intoxicating effect of self-deception, this form of socialism ended in a miserable fit of the blues.

c. German or 'True' Socialism

The socialist and communist literature of France, a literature that originated under the pressure of a bourgeoisie in power, and that was the expression of the struggle against this power, was introduced into Germany at a time when the bourgeoisie in that country had just begun its contest with feudal absolutism.

German philosophers, would-be philosophers and men of letters eagerly seized on this literature, only forgetting that when these writings immigrated from France into Germany, French social conditions had not immigrated along with them. In contact with German social conditions this French literature lost all its immediate practical significance and assumed a purely literary aspect. Thus, to the German philosophers of the eighteenth century, the demands of the first French Revolution were nothing more than the demands of 'Practical Reason' in general, and the utterance of the will of the revolutionary French bourgeoisie signified in their eyes the law of pure will, of will as it was bound to be, of true human will generally.

The work of the German *literati* consisted solely in bringing the new French ideas into harmony with their ancient philosophical conscience, or rather, in annexing the French ideas without deserting their own philosophic point of view.

This annexation took place in the same way in which a foreign language is appropriated, namely, by translation.

It is well known how the monks wrote silly lives of Catholic saints *over* the manuscripts on which the classical works of ancient heathendom had been written. The German *literati* reversed this process with the profane French literature. They wrote their philosophical nonsense beneath the French original. For instance, beneath the French criticism of the economic functions of money, they wrote 'alienation of humanity', and beneath the French criticism of the bourgeois state they wrote 'dethronement of the category of the general', and so forth.

The introduction of these philosophical phrases at the back of the French historical criticisms they dubbed 'Philosophy of Action', 'True Socialism', 'German Science of Socialism', 'Philosophical Foundation of Socialism', and so on.

The French socialist and communist literature was thus completely emasculated. And, since it ceased in the hands of the German to express the struggle of one class with the other, he felt conscious of having overcome 'French one-sidedness' and of representing, not true requirements, but the requirements of truth; not the interests of the proletariat, but the interests of human nature, of man in general, who belongs to no class, has no reality, who exists only in the misty realm of philosophical phantasy.

This German socialism, which took its schoolboy task so seriously and solemnly, and extolled its poor stock-in-trade in such mountebank fashion, meanwhile gradually lost its pedantic innocence.

The fight of the German and especially of the Prussian bourgeoisie against feudal aristocracy and absolute monarchy, in other words, the liberal movement, became more earnest.

By this, the long-wished-for opportunity was offered to 'True' Socialism of confronting the political movement with the socialist demands, of hurling the traditional anathemas against liberalism, against representative government, against bourgeois competition, bourgeois freedom of the press, bourgeois legislation, bourgeois liberty and equality, and of preaching to the masses that they had nothing to gain, and everything to lose, by this bourgeois movement. German socialism forgot, in the nick of time, that the French criticism, whose silly echo it was, presupposed the existence of modern bourgeois society, with its corresponding economic conditions of existence, and the political constitution adapted thereto, the very things whose attainment was the object of the pending struggle in Germany.

To the absolute governments, with their following of parsons, professors, country squires and officials, it served as a welcome scarecrow against the threatening bourgeoisie.

It was a sweet finish after the bitter pills of floggings and bullets, with which these same governments, just at that time, dosed the German working-class risings.

While this 'True' Socialism thus served the governments as a weapon for fighting the German bourgeoisie, it, at the same time, directly represented a reactionary interest, the interest of the German philistines. In Germany the petty-bourgeois class, a relic of the sixteenth century, and since then constantly cropping up again under the various forms, is the real social basis of the existing state of things.

To preserve this class is to preserve the existing state of things in Germany. The industrial and political supremacy of the bourgeoisie threatens it with certain destruction—on the one hand, from the concentration of capital; on the other, from the rise of a revolutionary proletariat. 'True' Socialism appeared to kill these two birds with one stone. It spread like an epidemic.

The robe of speculative cobwebs, embroidered with flowers of rhetoric, steeped in the dew of sickly sentiment, this transcendental robe in which the German Socialists wrapped their sorry 'eternal truths', all skin and bone, served to wonderfully increase the sale of their goods amongst such a public. And on its part German socialism recognized, more and more, its own calling as the bombastic representative of the petty-bourgeois philistine.

It proclaimed the German nation to be the model nation, and the German petty philistine to be the typical man. To every villainous meanness of this model man it gave a hidden, higher, socialistic interpretation, the exact contrary of its real character. It went to the extreme length of directly opposing the 'brutally destructive' tendency of communism, and of proclaiming its supreme and impartial contempt of all class struggles. With very few exceptions all the so-called socialist and communist publications that now (1847) circulate in Germany belong to the domain of this foul and enervating literature.[1]

---

[1] The revolutionary storm of 1848 swept away this whole shabby tendency and cured its protagonists of the desire to dabble in socialism. The chief representative and classical type of this tendency is Mr. Karl Grün. [*Note by F. Engels to the German edition of* 1888.]

2. CONSERVATIVE OR BOURGEOIS SOCIALISM

A part of the bourgeoisie is desirous of redressing social grievances in order to secure the continued existence of bourgeois
society.

To this section belong economists, philanthropists, humani-
tarians, improvers of the condition of the working class,
organizers of charity, members of societies for the prevention of
cruelty to animals, temperance fanatics, hole-and-corner
reformers of every imaginable kind. This form of socialism has,
moreover, been worked out into complete systems.

We may cite Proudhon's *Philosophie de la Misère* [*Philosophy
of Poverty*] as an example of this form.

The socialistic bourgeois want all the advantages of modern
social conditions without the struggles and dangers necessarily
resulting therefrom. They desire the existing state of society
minus its revolutionary and disintegrating elements. They wish
for a bourgeoisie without a proletariat. The bourgeoisie naturally
conceives the world in which it is supreme to be the best; and
bourgeois socialism develops this comfortable conception into
various more or less complete systems. In requiring the proletariat to carry out such a system, and thereby to march straightway into the social New Jerusalem, it but requires in reality that
the proletariat should remain within the bounds of existing
society, but should cast away all its hateful ideas concerning the
bourgeoisie.

A second and more practical, but less systematic, form of this
socialism sought to depreciate every revolutionary movement in
the eyes of the working class by showing that no mere political
reform, but only a change in the material conditions of existence,
in economical relations, could be of any advantage to them. By
changes in the material conditions of existence, this form of
socialism, however, by no means understands abolition of the
bourgeois relations of production, an abolition that can be
effected only by a revolution, but administrative reforms, based
on the continued existence of these relations; reforms, therefore,
that in no respect affect the relations between capital and labour,
but, at the best, lessen the cost, and simplify the administrative
work of bourgeois government.

Bourgeois socialism attains adequate expression when, and only when, it becomes a mere figure of speech.

Free trade: for the benefit of the working class. Protective duties: for the benefit of the working class. Prison reform: for the benefit of the working class. This is the last word and the only seriously meant word of bourgeois socialism.

It is summed up in the phrase: the bourgeois is a bourgeois— for the benefit of the working class.

3. CRITICAL-UTOPIAN SOCIALISM AND COMMUNISM

We do not here refer to that literature which, in every great modern revolution, has always given voice to the demands of the proletariat, such as the writings of Babeuf and others.

The first direct attempts of the proletariat to attain its own ends made in times of universal excitement, when feudal society was being overthrown; these attempts necessarily failed, owing to the then undeveloped state of the proletariat, as well as to the absence of the economic conditions for its emancipation, conditions that had yet to be produced, and could be produced by the impending bourgeois epoch alone. The revolutionary literature that accompanied these first movements of the proletariat had necessarily a reactionary character. It inculcated universal asceticism and social levelling in its crudest form.

The socialist and communist systems, properly so called, those of Saint-Simon, Fourier, Owen, and others, spring into existence in the early undeveloped period, described above, of the struggle between proletariat and bourgeoisie (see Section I. Bourgeois and Proletarians).

The founders of these systems see, indeed, the class antagonisms, as well as the action of the decomposing elements in the prevailing form of society. But the proletariat, as yet in its infancy, offers to them the spectacle of a class without any historical initiative or any independent political movement.

Since the development of class antagonism keeps even pace with the development of industry, the economic situation, as they find it, does not as yet offer to them the material conditions for the emancipation of the proletariat. They therefore search after a new social science, after new social laws, that are to create these conditions.

Historical action is to yield to their personal inventive action; historically created conditions of emancipation to fantastic ones; and the gradual, spontaneous class organization of the proletariat to an organization of society especially contrived by these inventors. Future history resolves itself, in their eyes, into the propaganda and the practical carrying out of their social plans.

In the formation of their plans they are conscious of caring chiefly for the interests of the working class, as being the most suffering class. Only from the point of view of being the most suffering class does the proletariat exist for them.

The undeveloped state of the class struggle, as well as their own surroundings, causes Socialists of this kind to consider themselves far superior to all class antagonisms. They want to improve the condition of every member of society, even that of the most favoured. Hence, they habitually appeal to society at large, without distinction of class; nay, by preference, to the ruling class. For how can people, when once they understand their system, fail to see in it the best possible plan of the best possible state of society?

Hence, they reject all political, and especially all revolutionary action; they wish to attain their ends by peaceful means, and endeavour, by small experiments, necessarily doomed to failure, and by the force of example, to pave the way for the new social gospel.

Such fantastic pictures of future society, painted at a time when the proletariat is still in a very undeveloped state and has but a fantastic conception of its own position, correspond with the first instinctive yearnings of that class for a general reconstruction of society.

But these socialist and communist publications contain also a critical element. They attack every principle of existing society. Hence they are full of the most valuable materials for the enlightenment of the working class. The practical measures proposed in them—such as the abolition of the distinction between town and country, of the family, of the carrying on of industries for the account of private individuals, and of the wage system, the proclamation of social harmony, the conversion of the functions of the state into a mere superintendence of production —all these proposals point solely to the disappearance of class antagonisms which were, at that time, only just cropping up, and which, in these publications, are recognized in their earliest indistinct and undefined forms only. These proposals, therefore, are of a purely utopian character.

The significance of critical-utopian socialism and communism bears an inverse relation to historical development. In proportion as the modern class struggle develops and takes definite shape, this fantastic standing apart from the contest, these fantastic attacks on it, lose all practical value and all theoretical justification. Therefore, although the originators of these systems were, in many respects, revolutionary, their disciples have, in every case, formed mere reactionary sects. They hold fast by the original views of their masters, in opposition to the progressive historical development of the proletariat. They therefore endeavour, and that consistently, to deaden the class struggle and to reconcile the class antagonisms. They still dream of experimental realization of their social utopias, of founding isolated *phalanstères*, of establishing 'Home Colonies', or setting up a 'Little Icaria'[1]—pocket editions of the New Jerusalem—and to realize all these castles in the air they are compelled to appeal to the feelings and purses of the bourgeois. By degrees they sink into the category of the reactionary conservative socialists depicted above, differing from these only by more systematic pedantry, and by their fanatical and superstitious belief in the miraculous effects of their social science.

They therefore violently oppose all political action on the part of the working class; such action, according to them, can only result from blind unbelief in the new gospel.

The Owenites in England, and the Fourierists in France, respectively, oppose the Chartists and the *Réformistes*.

---

[1] 'Home colonies' were what Owen called his communist model societies. [*Added by F. Engels to the German edition of* 1890.] *Phalanstères* were socialist colonies on the plan of Charles Fourier; Icaria was the name given by Caber to his utopia and, later on, to his American communist colony.

IV. POSITION OF THE COMMUNISTS IN RELATION TO THE VARIOUS EXISTING OPPOSITION PARTIES

Section II has made clear the relations of the Communists to the existing working-class parties, such as the Chartists in England and the Agrarian Reformers in America.

The Communists fight for the attainment of the immediate aims, for the enforcement of the momentary interests of the working class; but in the movement of the present they also represent and take care of the future of that movement. In France the Communists ally themselves with the Social-Democrats[1] against the conservative and radical bourgeoisie, reserving, however, the right to take up a critical position in regard to phrases and illusions traditionally handed down from the Great Revolution.

In Switzerland they support the Radicals, without losing sight of the fact that this party consists of antagonistic elements, partly of Democratic Socialists, in the French sense, partly of radical bourgeois.

In Poland they support the party that insists on an agrarian revolution as the prime condition for national emancipation, that party which fomented the insurrection of Cracow in 1846.

In Germany they fight with the bourgeoisie whenever it acts in a revolutionary way, against the absolute monarchy, the feudal squirearchy, and the petty-bourgeoisie.

But they never cease, for a single instant, to instil into the working class the clearest possible recognition of the hostile antagonism between bourgeoisie and proletariat, in order that the German workers may straightway use, as so many weapons against the bourgeoisie, the social and political conditions that the bourgeoisie must necessarily introduce along with its supremacy, and in order that, after the fall of the reactionary classes in Germany, the fight against the bourgeoisie itself may immediately begin.

The Communists turn their attention chiefly to Germany,

[1] The party then represented in Parliament by Ledru-Rollin, in literature by Louis Blanc (1811-82), in the daily press by the *Réforme*. The name of Social-Democracy signifies, with these its inventors, a section of the Democratic or Republican Party more or less tinged with socialism.

because that country is on the eve of a bourgeois revolution that is bound to be carried out under more advanced conditions of European civilization and with a much more developed proletariat than that of England in the seventeenth, and of France in the eighteenth century, and because the bourgeois revolution in Germany will be but the prelude to an immediately following proletarian revolution.

In short, the Communists everywhere support every revolutionary movement against the existing social and political order of things.

In all these movements they bring to the front, as the leading question in each, the property question, no matter what its degree of development at the time.

Finally, they labour everywhere for the union and agreement of the democratic parties of all countries.

The Communists disdain to conceal their views and aims. They openly declare that their ends can be attained only by the forcible overthrow of all existing social conditions. Let the ruling classes tremble at a communist revolution. The proletarians have nothing to lose but their chains. They have a world to win.

Working men of all countries, unite!

VALUE, PRICE AND PROFIT

Addressed to Working Men

KARL MARX

Edited by his daughter
Eleanor Marx Aveling

Karl Marx was born at Trier, in the Rhineland, on May 5, 1818, the son of a lawyer who was a Jewish convert to Christianity. After studying at the universities of Bonn and Berlin he took to journalism and socialist activity in Prussia, France (where he first met Engels) and Belgium. He was expelled from Prussia in 1849, on being acquitted of high treason, and settled in London. There, often in extreme poverty, he continued his work, spending much time in the Reading Room of the British Museum. He died in 1883, and was buried in Highgate Cemetery.

His great work on political economy which became the Bible of socialism, Das Kapital, is rather too massive for most readers. The following, Value, Price and Profit, represents a simpler statement of his ideas, and an extraordinarily clear one, which he originally delivered as a paper to an international meeting of working men. It was never published during his lifetime, but was found among his papers after the death of Engels.

It was edited by Marx's daughter, Eleanor Marx Aveling, with the help of her husband, Dr Edward Aveling, and first appeared in English in 1899. Since then it has been reprinted many times.

Value, Price and Profit

CITIZENS

BEFORE entering into the subject-matter, allow me to make a few preliminary remarks.

There reigns now on the Continent a real epidemic of strikes, and a general clamour for a rise of wages. The question will turn up at our Congress.[1] You, as the head of the International Association,[2] ought to have settled convictions upon this paramount question. For my own part, I considered it therefore my duty to enter fully into the matter, even at the peril of putting your patience to a severe test.

Another preliminary remark I have to make in regard to Citizen Weston.[3] He has not only proposed to you, but has publicly defended, in the interest of the working class, as he thinks, opinions he knows to be most unpopular with the working class. Such an exhibition of moral courage all of us must highly honour. I hope that, despite the unvarnished style of my paper, at its conclusion he will find me agreeing with what appears to me the just idea lying at the bottom of his theses, which, however, in their present form, I cannot but consider theoretically false and practically dangerous.

I shall now at once proceed to the business before us.

I. PRODUCTION AND WAGES

Citizen Weston's argument rested, in fact, upon two premisses: firstly, that the *amount of national production* is a *fixed thing*, a

[1] This paper was communicated to the General International Congress held in September, 1865.

[2] The 'General Council' was the Executive of the Association.

[3] The delegate to the Congress from the International Working Men's Association.

constant quantity or magnitude, as the mathematicians would say; secondly, that the *amount of real wages*, that is to say, of wages as measured by the quantity of the commodities they can buy, is a *fixed* amount, a *constant* magnitude.

Now, his first assertion is evidently erroneous. Year after year you will find that the value and mass of production increase, that the productive powers of the national labour increase, and that the amount of money necessary to circulate this increasing production continuously changes. What is true at the end of the year, and for different years compared with each other, is true for every average day of the year. The amount or magnitude of national production changes continuously. It is not a *constant* but a *variable* magnitude, and apart from changes in population it must be so, because of the continuous change in the *accumulation of capital* and the *productive powers of labour*. It is perfectly true that if a *rise in the general rate of wages* should take place today, that rise, whatever its ulterior effects might be, would, by *itself*, not *immediately* change the amount of production. It would, in the first instance, proceed from the existing state of things. But if *before* the rise of wages the national production was *variable*, and not *fixed*, it will continue to be variable and not fixed *after* the rise of wages.

But suppose the amount of national production to be *constant* instead of *variable*. Even then, what our friend Weston considers a logical conclusion would still remain a gratuitous assertion. If I have a given number, say eight, the absolute limits of this number do not prevent its parts from changing their *relative* limits. If profits were six and wages two, wages might increase to six and profits decrease to two, and still the total amount remain eight. Thus the fixed amount of production would by no means prove the fixed amount of wages. How then does our friend Weston prove this fixity? By asserting it.

But even conceding him his assertion, it would cut both ways, while he presses it only in one direction. If the amount of wages is a constant magnitude, then it can be neither increased nor diminished. If then, in enforcing a temporary rise of wages, the working men act foolishly, the capitalists, in enforcing a temporary fall of wages, would act not less foolishly. Our friend Weston does not deny that, under certain circumstances, the working men *can* enforce a rise of wages, but their amount being naturally fixed, there must follow a reaction. On the other hand, he knows also that the capitalists *can* enforce a fall of wages, and, indeed, continuously try to enforce it. According to the principle of the constancy of wages, a reaction ought to follow in this case not less than in the former. The working men, therefore, reacting against the attempt at, or the act of, lowering wages, would act rightly. They would, therefore, act rightly in enforcing *a rise of wages*, because every *reaction* against the lowering of wages is an *action* for raising wages. According to Citizen Weston's own principle of the *constancy of wages*, the working men ought, therefore, under certain circumstances, to combine and struggle for a rise of wages.

If he denies this conclusion, he must give up the premiss from which it flows. He must not say that the amount of wages is a *constant quantity*, but that, although it cannot and must not *rise*, it can and must *fall*, whenever capital pleases to lower it. If the capitalist pleases to feed you upon potatoes instead of upon meat, and upon oats instead of upon wheat, you must accept his will as a law of political economy, and submit to it. If in one country the rate of wages is higher than in another, in the United States, for example, than in England, you must explain this difference in the rate of wages by a difference between the will of the American capitalist and the will of the English capitalist, a method which would certainly very much simplify, not only the study of economic phenomena, but of all other phenomena.

But even then, we might ask, *why* the will of the American capitalist differs from the will of the English capitalist? And to answer the question you must go beyond the domain of *will*. A person may tell me that God wills one thing in France, and another thing in England. If I summon him to explain this duality of will, he might have the brass to answer me that God wills to have one will in France and another will in England. But our friend Weston is certainly the last man to make an argument of such a complete negation of all reasoning.

The *will* of the capitalist is certainly to take as much as possible. What we have to do is not to talk about his *will*, but to enquire into his *power*, the *limits of that power*, and the *character of those limits*.

II. PRODUCTION, WAGES, PROFITS

The address Citizen Weston read to us might have been compressed into a nutshell.

All his reasoning amounted to this: If the working class forces the capitalist class to pay five shillings instead of four shillings in the shape of money wages, the capitalist will return in the shape of commodities four shillings' worth instead of five shillings' worth. The working class would have to pay five shillings for what, before the rise of wages, they bought with four shillings. But why is this the case? Why does the capitalist only return four shillings' worth for five shillings? Because the amount of wages is fixed. But why is it fixed at four shillings' worth of commodities? Why not at three, or two, or any other sum? If the limit of the amount of wages is settled by an economical law, independent alike of the will of the capitalist and the will of the working man, the first thing Citizen Weston had to do was to state that law and prove it. He ought then, moreover, to have proved that the amount of wages actually paid at every given moment always corresponds exactly to the necessary amount of wages, and never deviates from it. If, on the other hand, the given limit of the amount of wages is founded on the *mere will* of the capitalist, or the limits of his avarice, it is an arbitrary limit. There is nothing necessary in it. It may be changed *by* the will of the capitalist, and may, therefore, be changed *against* his will.

Citizen Weston illustrated his theory by telling you that when a bowl contains a certain quantity of soup, to be eaten by a certain number of persons, an increase in the broadness of the spoons would produce an increase in the amount of soup. He must allow me to find this illustration rather spoony. It reminded me somewhat of the simile employed by Menenius Agrippa. When the Roman plebeians struck against the Roman patricians, the patrician Agrippa told them that the patrician belly fed the plebeian members of the body politic. Agrippa failed to show that you feed the members of one man by filling the belly of another. Citizen Weston, on his part, has forgotten that the bowl from which the workmen eat is filled with the whole produce of the national labour, and that what prevents them fetching more out of it is neither the narrowness of the bowl nor the scantiness of its contents, but only the smallness of their spoons.

By what contrivance is the capitalist enabled to return four shillings' worth for five shillings? By raising the price of the commodity he sells. Now, does a rise and more generally a change in the prices of commodities, do the prices of commodities themselves, depend on the mere will of the capitalist? Or are, on the contrary, certain circumstances wanted to give effect to that will? If not, the ups and downs, the incessant fluctuations of market prices, become an insoluble riddle.

As we suppose that no change whatever has taken place either in the productive powers of labour, or in the amount of capital and labour employed, or in the value of the money wherein the values of products are estimated, but *only a change in the rate of wages*, how could that *rise of wages* affect the *prices of commodities*? Only by affecting the actual proportion between the demand for, and the supply of, these commodities.

It is perfectly true that, considered as a whole, the working class spends, and must spend, its income upon *necessaries*. A general rise in the rate of wages would, therefore, produce a rise in the demand for, and consequently in the *market prices of*, *necessaries*. The capitalists who produce these necessaries would be compensated for the risen wages by the rising market prices of their commodities. But how with the other capitalists who do *not* produce necessaries? And you must not fancy them a small body. If you consider that two-thirds of the national produce are consumed by one-fifth of the population—a member of the House of Commons stated it recently to be but one-seventh of the population—you will understand what an immense proportion of the national produce must be produced in the shape of luxuries, or be *exchanged* for luxuries, and what an immense amount of the necessaries themselves must be wasted upon flunkeys, horses, cats, and so forth, a waste we know from experience to become always much limited with the rising prices of necessaries.

Well, what would be the position of those capitalists who do *not* produce necessaries? For the *fall in the rate of profit*, consequent upon the general rise of wages, they could not compensate themselves by a *rise in the price of their commodities*, because the demand for those commodities would not have increased. Their income would have decreased, and from this decreased income they would have to pay more for the same amount of higher-priced necessaries. But this would not be all. As their income had diminished they would have less to spend upon luxuries, and therefore their mutual demand for their respective commodities would diminish. Consequent upon this diminished demand the prices of their commodities would fall. In these branches of industry, therefore, *the rate of profit would fall*, not only in simple proportion to the general rise in the rate of wages, but in the compound ratio of the general rise of wages, the rise in the prices of necessaries, and the fall in the prices of luxuries.

What would be the consequence of *this difference in the rates of profit* for capitals employed in the different branches of industry ? Why, the consequence that generally obtains whenever, from whatever reason, the *average rate of profit* comes to differ in different spheres of production. Capital and labour would be transferred from the less remunerative to the more remunerative branches; and this process of transfer would go on until the supply in the one department of industry would have risen proportionately to the increased demand, and would have sunk in the other departments according to the decreased demand. This change effected, the general rate of profit would again be *equalized* in the different branches. As the whole derangement originally arose from a mere change in the proportion of the demand for, and supply of, different commodities, the cause ceasing, the effect would cease, and *prices* would return to their former level and equilibrium. Instead of being limited to some branches of industry, *the fall in the rate of profit* consequent upon the rise of wages would have become general. According to our supposition, there would have taken place no change in the productive powers of labour, nor in the aggregate amount of production, but *that given amount of production would have changed its form*. A greater part of the produce would exist in the shape of necessaries, a lesser part in the shape of luxuries, or what comes to the same, a lesser part would be exchanged for foreign luxuries, and be consumed in its original form, or, what again comes to the same, a greater part of the native produce would be exchanged for foreign necessaries instead of for luxuries. The general rise in the rate of wages would, therefore, after a temporary disturbance of market prices, only result in a general fall of the rate of profit without any permanent change in the prices of commodities.

If I am told that in the previous argument I assume the whole surplus wages to be spent upon necessaries, I answer that I have made the supposition most advantageous to the opinion of Citizen Weston. If the surplus wages were spent upon articles formerly not entering into the consumption of the working men, the real increase of their purchasing power would need no proof. Being, however, only derived from an advance of wages, that increase of their purchasing power must exactly correspond to the decrease of the purchasing power of the capitalists. The *aggregate demand* for commodities would, therefore, not *increase*, but the constituent parts of that demand would *change*. The increasing demand on the one side would be counterbalanced by the decreasing demand on the other side. Thus the aggregate demand remaining stationary, no change whatever could take place in the market prices of commodities.

You arrive, therefore, at this dilemma: Either the surplus wages are equally spent upon all articles of consumption—then the expansion of demand on the part of the working class must be compensated by the contraction of demand on the part of the capitalist class—or the surplus wages are only spent upon some articles whose market prices will temporarily rise. Then the consequent rise in the rate of profit in some, and the consequent fall in the rate of profit in other branches of industry will produce a change in the distribution of capital and labour, going on until the supply is brought up to the increased demand in the one department of industry, and brought down to the diminished demand in other departments of industry. On the one supposition there will occur no change in the prices of commodities. On the other supposition, after some fluctuations of market prices, the exchangeable values of commodities will subside to the former level. On both suppositions the general rise in the rate of wages will ultimately result in nothing else but a general fall in the rate of profit.

To stir up your powers of imagination Citizen Weston requested you to think of the difficulties which a general rise of English agricultural wages from nine shillings to eighteen shillings would produce. Think, he exclaimed, of the immense rise in the demand for necessaries, and the consequent fearful rise in their prices! Now, all of you know that the average wages of the American agricultural labourer amount to more than double that of the English agricultural labourer, although the prices of agricultural produce are lower in the United States than in the United Kingdom, although the general relations of capital and labour obtain in the United States the same as in England, and although the annual amount of production is much smaller in the United States than in England. Why, then, does our friend ring this alarum bell? Simply to shift the real question before us. A sudden rise of wages from nine shillings to eighteen shillings would be a sudden rise to the amount of 100 per cent. Now, we are not at all discussing the question whether the general rate of wages in England could be suddenly increased by 100 per cent. We have nothing at all to do with the *magnitude* of the rise, which in every practical instance must depend on, and be suited to, given circumstances. We have only to inquire how a general rise in the rate of wages, even if restricted to one per cent., will act.

Dismissing friend Weston's fancy rise of 100 per cent., I propose calling your attention to the real rise of wages that took place in Great Britain from 1849 to 1859.

You are all aware of the Ten Hours Bill, or rather Ten-and-a-half Hours Bill, introduced since 1848. This was one of the greatest economical changes we have witnessed. It was a sudden and compulsory rise of wages, not in some local trades, but in the leading industrial branches by which England sways the markets of the world. It was a rise of wages under circumstances singularly unpropitious. Dr Ure, Professor Senior, and all the other official economical mouthpieces of the middle class, *proved*, and I must say upon much stronger grounds than those of our friend Weston, that it would sound the death-knell of English industry. They proved that it not only amounted to a simple rise of wages, but to a rise of wages initiated by, and based upon, a diminution of the quantity of labour employed. They asserted that the twelfth hour you wanted to take from the capitalist was exactly the only hour from which he derived his profit. They threatened a decrease of accumulation, rise of prices, loss of markets, stinting of production, consequent reaction upon wages, ultimate ruin.

In fact, they declared Maximilian Robespierre's Maximum Laws
to be a small affair compared to it; and they were right in a
certain sense. Well, what was the result? A rise in the money
wages of the factory operatives, despite the curtailing of the
working day, a great increase in the number of factory hands
employed, a continuous fall in the prices of their products, a
marvellous development in the productive powers of their
labour, an unheard-of progressive expansion of the markets for
their commodities. In Manchester, at the meeting, in 1860, of the
Society for the Advancement of Science, I myself heard Mr
Newman confess that he, Dr Ure, Senior, and all the other official
propounders of economical science had been wrong, while the
instinct of the people had been right. I mention Mr W. Newman,
not Professor Francis Newman, because he occupies an eminent
position in economical science, as the contributor to, and editor
of, Mr Thomas Tooke's *History of Prices*, that magnificent work
which traces the history of prices from 1793 to 1856. If our
friend Weston's fixed idea of a fixed amount of wages, a fixed
amount of production, a fixed degree of the productive power of
labour, a fixed and permanent will of the capitalists, and all his
other fixedness and finality were correct, Professor Senior's
woeful forebodings would have been right, and Robert Owen,
who already in 1816 proclaimed a general limitation of the working day the first preparatory step to the emancipation of the
working class, and actually in the teeth of the general prejudice
inaugurated it on his own hook in his cotton factory at New
Lanark, would have been wrong.

In the very same period during which the introduction of the
Ten Hours Bill, and the rise of wages consequent upon it,
occurred, there took place in Great Britain, for reasons which it
would be out of place to enumerate here, *a general rise in agricultural wages*.

Although it is not required for my immediate purpose, in order
not to mislead you, I shall make some preliminary remarks.

If a man got two shillings weekly wages, and if his wages rose
to four shillings, the *rate of wages* would have risen by 100 per
cent. This would seem a very magnificent thing if expressed as a
rise in the *rate of wages*, although the *actual amount of wages*, four
shillings weekly, would still remain a wretchedly small, a starva-

tion pittance. You must not, therefore, allow yourselves to be carried away by the high-sounding per cents. in the *rate* of wages. You must always ask, What was the *original* amount?

Moreover, you will understand, that if there were ten men receiving each 2s per week, five men receiving each 5s, and five men receiving 11s weekly, the twenty men together would receive 100s, or £5, weekly. If then a rise, say by twenty per cent., upon the *aggregate* sum of their weekly wages took place, there would be an advance from £5 to £6. Taking the average, we might say that the *general rate of wages* had risen by twenty-five per cent., although, in fact, the wages of the ten men had remained stationary, the wages of the one lot of five men had risen from 5s to 6s only, and the wages of the other lot of five men from 55s to 70s. One half of the men would not have improved at all their position, one quarter would have improved it in an imperceptible degree, and only one quarter would have bettered it really. Still, reckoning by the *average*, the total amount of the wages of those twenty men would have increased by twenty-five per cent., and as far as the aggregate capital that employs them, and the prices of the commodities they produce, are concerned, it would be exactly the same as if all of them had equally shared in the average rise of wages. In the case of agricultural labour, the standard wages being very different in the different counties of England and Scotland, the rise affected them very unequally.

Lastly, during the period when that rise of wages took place counteracting influences were at work, such as the new taxes consequent upon the Russian war, the extensive demolition of the dwelling-houses of the agricultural labourers, and so forth.

Having premissed so much, I proceed to state that from 1849 to 1859 there took place a *rise of about forty per cent.* in the average rate of the agricultural wages of Great Britain. I could give you ample details in proof of my assertion, but for the present purpose think it sufficient to refer you to the conscientious and critical paper read in 1860 by the late Mr John C. Morton at the London Society of Arts on 'The Forces used in Agriculture'. Mr Morton gives the returns, from bills and other authentic documents, which he had collected from about one hundred farmers, residing in twelve Scotch and thirty-five English counties.

According to our friend Weston's opinion, and taken together with the simultaneous rise in the wages of the factory operatives, there ought to have occurred a tremendous rise in the prices of agricultural produce during the period 1849 to 1859. But what is the fact? Despite the Russian war, and the consecutive unfavourable harvests from 1854 to 1856, the average price of wheat, which is the leading agricultural produce of England, fell from about £3 per quarter for the years 1838 to 1848 to about £2 10s per quarter for the years 1849 to 1859. This constitutes a fall in the price of wheat of more than sixteen per cent. simultaneously with an average rise of agricultural wages of forty per cent. During the same period, if we compare its end with its beginning, 1859 with 1849, there was a decrease of official pauperism from 934,419 to 860,470, the difference being 73,949; a very small decrease, I grant, and which in the following years was again lost, but still a decrease.

It might be said that, consequent upon the abolition of the Corn Laws, the import of foreign corn was more than doubled during the period from 1849 to 1859, as compared with the period from 1838 to 1848. And what of that? From Citizen Weston's standpoint one would have expected that this sudden, immense, and continuously increasing demand upon foreign markets must have sent up the price of agricultural produce there to a frightful height, the effect of increased demand remaining the same, whether it comes from without or from within. What was the fact? Apart from some years of failing harvests, during all that period the ruinous fall in the price of corn formed a standing theme of declamation in France; the Americans were again and again compelled to burn their surplus produce; and Russia, if we are to believe Mr Urquhart, prompted the Civil War in the United States because her agricultural exports were crippled by the Yankee competition in the markets of Europe.

Reduced to its abstract form, Citizen Weston's argument would come to this: Every rise in demand occurs always on the basis of a given amount of production. It can, therefore, *never increase the supply of the articles demanded*, but can *only enhance their money prices*. Now the most common observation shows that an increased demand will, in some instances, leave the market prices of commodities altogether unchanged, and will, in other instances, cause a temporary rise of market prices followed by an increased supply, followed by a reduction of the prices to their original level, and in many cases *below* their original level. Whether the rise of demand springs from surplus wages, or from any other cause, does not at all change the conditions of the problem. From Citizen Weston's standpoint the general phenomenon was as difficult to explain as the phenomenon occurring under the exceptional circumstances of a rise of wages. His argument had, therefore, no peculiar bearing whatever upon the subject we treat. It only expressed his perplexity at accounting for the laws by which an increase of demand produces an increase of supply, instead of an ultimate rise of market prices.

III WAGES AND CURRENCY

On the second day of the debate our friend Weston clothed his old asserions in new forms. He said: Consequent upon a general rise in money wages, more currency will be wanted to pay the same wages. The currency being *fixed*, how can you pay with this fixed currency increased money wages ? First the difficulty arose from the fixed amount of commodities accruing to the working man despite his increase of money wages; now it arises from the increased money wages, despite the fixed amount of commodities. Of course, if you reject his original dogma, his secondary grievance will disappear.

However, I shall show that this currency question has nothing at all to do with the subject before us.

In your country the mechanism of payments is much more perfected than in any other country of Europe. Thanks to the extent and concentration of the banking system, much less currency is wanted to circulate the same amount of values, and to transact the same or a greater amount of business. For example, as far as wages are concerned, the English factory operative pays his wages weekly to the shopkeeper, who sends them weekly to the banker, who returns them weekly to the manufacturer, who again pays them away to his working men, and so forth. By this contrivance the yearly wages of an operative, say of £52, may be paid by one single sovereign turning round every week in the same circle. Even in England the mechanism is less perfect than in Scotland, and is not everywhere equally perfect; and therefore we find, for example, that in some agricultural districts, as compared with the mere factory districts, much more currency is wanted to circulate a much smaller amount of values.

If you cross the Channel you will find that the *money wages* are much lower than in England, but that they are circulated in Germany, Italy, Switzerland, and France by a *much larger amount of currency*. The same sovereign will not be so quickly intercepted by the banker or returned to the industrial capitalist; and, therefore, instead of one sovereign circulating £52 yearly, you want, perhaps, three sovereigns to circulate yearly wages to the amount of £25. Thus, by comparing continental countries with England, you will see at once that low money wages may require a much larger currency for their circulation than high money wages, and that this is, in fact, a merely technical point, quite foreign to our subject.

According to the best calculations I know, the yearly income of the working class of this country may be estimated at £250,000,000. This immense sum is circulated by about three million pounds. Suppose a rise of wages of fifty per cent. to take place. Then, instead of three millions of currency, four and a half millions would be wanted. As a very considerable part of the working-man's daily expenses is laid out in silver and copper, that is to say, in mere tokens, whose relative value to gold is arbitrarily fixed by law, like that of inconvertible money paper, a rise of money wages by fifty per cent. would, in the extreme case, require an additional circulation of sovereigns, say to the amount of one million. One million, now dormant, in the shape of bullion or coin, in the cellars of the Bank of England, or of private bankers, would circulate. But even the trifling expense resulting from the additional minting or the additional wear and tear of that million might be spared, and would actually be spared, if any friction should arise from the want of the additional currency. All of you know that the currency of this country is divided into two great departments. One sort, supplied by bank-notes of different descriptions, is used in the transactions between dealers and dealers, and the larger payments from consumers to dealers, while another sort of currency, metallic coin, circulates in the retail trade. Although distinct, these two sorts of currency interwork with each other. Thus gold coin, to a very great extent, circulates even in larger payments for all the odd sums under £5. If tomorrow £4 notes, or £3 notes, or £2 notes were issued, the gold filling these channels of circulation would at once be driven out of them, and flow into those channels where they would be needed from the increase of money wages. Thus the additional million required by an advance of wages by fifty per cent, would be supplied without the addition of one single sovereign. The same effect might be produced, without one additional bank-note, by an additional bill circulation, as was the case in Lancashire for a very considerable time.

If a general rise in the rate of wages, for example, of 100 per cent, as Citizen Weston supposed it to take place in agricultural wages, would produce a great rise in the prices of necessaries, and, according to his views, require an additional amount of currency not to be procured, *a general fall in wages* must produce the same effect, on the same scale, in an opposite direction. Well! All of you know that the years 1858 to 1860 were the most prosperous years for the cotton industry, and that peculiarly the year 1860 stands in that respect unrivalled in the annals of commerce, while at the same time all other branches of industry were most flourishing. The wages of the cotton operatives and of all the other working men connected with their trade stood, in 1860, higher than ever before. The American crisis came, and those aggregate wages were suddenly reduced to about one-fourth of their former amount. This would have been in the opposite direction a rise of 400 per cent. If wages rise from five to twenty, we say that they rise by 400 per cent.; if they fall from twenty to five, we say that they fall by fifty-seven per cent.; but the amount of rise in the one and the amount of fall in the other case would be the same, namely, fifteen shillings. This, then, was a sudden change in the rate of wages unprecedented, and at the same time extending over a number of operatives which, if we count all the operatives not only directly engaged in but indirectly dependent upon the cotton trade, was larger by one-half than the number of agricultural labourers. Did the price of wheat fall? It *rose* from the annual average of 47s 8d per quarter during the three years of 1858-1860 to the annual average of 55s 10d per quarter during the three years 1861-1863. As to the currency, there were coined in the mint in 1861 £8,673,232, against £3,378,792 in 1860. That is to say, there were coined £5,294,440 more in 1861 than in 1860. It is true the bank-note circulation was in 1861 less by £1,319,000 than in 1860. Take this off. There remains still an over-plus of currency for the year 1861, as compared with the prosperity year, 1860, to the amount of £3,975,440, or about £4,000,000; but the bullion reserve in the Bank of England had simultaneously decreased, not quite to the same, but in an approximating proportion.

Compare the year 1862 with 1842. Apart from the immense increase in the value and amount of commodities circulated, in 1862 the capital paid in regular transactions for shares, loans, etc. for the railways in England and Wales amounted alone to £320,000,000, a sum that would have appeared fabulous in 1842. Still, the aggregate amounts in currency in 1862 and 1842 were pretty nearly equal, and generally you will find a tendency to a progressive diminution of currency in the face of an enormously increasing value, not only of commodities, but of monetary transactions generally. From our friend Weston's standpoint this is an unsolvable riddle.

Looking somewhat deeper into this matter, he would have found that, quite apart from wages, and supposing them to be fixed, the value and mass of the commodities to be circulated, and generally the amount of monetary transactions to be settled, vary daily; that the amount of bank-notes issued varies daily; that the amount of payments realized without the intervention of any money, by the instrumentality of bills, cheques, book-credits, clearing houses, varies daily; that, as far as actual metallic currency is required, the proportion between the coin in circulation and the coin and bullion in reserve or sleeping in the cellars of banks varies daily; that the amount of bullion absorbed by the national circulation and the amount being sent abroad for international circulation vary daily. He would have found that this dogma of a fixed currency is a monstrous error, incompatible with our everyday movement. He would have inquired into the laws which enable a currency to adapt itself to circumstances so continually changing, instead of turning his misconception of the laws of currency into an argument against a rise of wages.

IV SUPPLY AND DEMAND

Our friend Weston accepts the Latin proverb that *repetitio est mater studiorum*, that is to say, that repetition is the mother of study, and consequently he repeated his original dogma again under the new form, that the contraction of currency, resulting from an enhancement of wages, would produce a diminution of capital, and so forth. Having already dealt with his currency crotchet, I consider it quite useless to enter upon the imaginary consequences he fancies to flow from his imaginary currency mishap. I shall proceed to at once reduce his *one and the same dogma*, repeated in so many different shapes, to its simplest theoretical form.

The uncritical way in which he has treated his subject will become evident from one single remark. He pleads against a rise of wages or against high wages as the result of such a rise. Now, I ask him, What are high wages and what are low wages? Why constitute, for example, five shillings weekly low, and twenty shillings weekly high wages? If five is low as compared with twenty, twenty is still lower as compared with two hundred. If a man was to lecture on the thermometer, and commenced by declaiming on high and low degrees, he would impart no knowledge whatever. He must first tell me how the freezing-point is found out, and how the boiling-point, and how these standard points are settled by natural laws, not by the fancy of the sellers or makers of thermometers. Now, in regard to wages and profits, Citizen Weston has not only failed to deduce such standard points from economical laws, but he has not even felt the necessity to look after them. He satisfied himself with the acceptance of the popular slang terms of low and high as something having a fixed meaning, although it is self-evident that wages can only be said to be high or low as compared with a standard by which to measure their magnitudes.

He will be unable to tell me why a certain amount of money is given for a certain amount of labour. If he should answer me, 'This was settled by the law of supply and demand', I should ask him, in the first instance, by what law supply and demand are themselvse regulated. And such an answer would at once put him out of court. The relations between the supply and demand of labour undergo perpetual change, and with them the market prices of labour. If the demand overshoots the supply wages rise; if the supply overshoots the demand wages sink, although it might in such circumstances be necessary to *test* the real state of demand and supply by a strike, for example, or any other method. But if you accept supply and demand as the law regulating wages, it would be as childish as useless to declaim against a rise of wages, because, according to the supreme law you appeal to, a periodical rise of wages is quite as necessary and legitimate as a periodical fall of wages. If you do *not* accept supply and demand as the law regulating wages, I again repeat the question, why a certain amount of money is given for a certain amount of labour ?

But to consider matters more broadly: You would be altogether mistaken in fancying that the value of labour or any other commodity whatever is ultimately fixed by supply and demand. Supply and demand regulate nothing but the temporary *fluctuations* of market prices. They will explain to you why the market price of a commodity rises above or sinks below its *value*, but they can never account for that *value* itself. Suppose supply and demand to equilibrate, or, as the economists call it, to cover each other. Why, the very moment these opposite forces become equal they paralyse each other, and cease to work in the one or the other direction. At the moment when supply and demand equilibrate each other, and therefore cease to act, the *market price* of a commodity coincides with its *real value*, with the standard price round which its market prices oscillate. In inquiring into the nature of that *value*, we have therefore nothing at all to do with the temporary effects on market prices of supply and demand. The same holds true of wages and of the prices of all other commodities.

V WAGES AND PRICES

Reduced to their simplest theoretical expression, all our friend's arguments resolve themselves into this one single dogma: '*The prices of commodities are determined or regulated by wages*'.

I might appeal to practical observation to bear witness against this antiquated and exploded fallacy. I might tell you that the English factory operatives, miners, shipbuilders, and so forth, whose labour is relatively high-priced, undersell by the cheapness of their produce all other nations; while the English agricultural labourer, for example, whose labour is relatively low-priced, is undersold by almost every other nation because of the dearness of his produce. By comparing article with article in the same country, and the commodities of different countries, I might show, apart from some exceptions more apparent than real, that on an average the high-priced labour produces the low-priced, and the low-priced labour produces the high-priced commodities. This, of course, would not prove that the high price of labour in the one, and its low price in the other instance, are the respective causes of those diametrically opposed effects, but at all events it would prove that the prices of commodities are not ruled by the prices of labour. However, it is quite superfluous for us to employ this empirical method.

It might, perhaps, be denied that Citizen Weston has put forward the dogma: '*The prices of commodities are determined or regulated by wages*'. In point of fact, he has never formulated it. He said, on the contrary, that profit and rent form also constituent parts of the prices of commodities, because it is out of the prices of commodities that not only the working man's wages, but also the capitalist's profits and the landlord's rents must be paid. But how in his idea are prices formed? First by wages. Then an additional percentage is joined to the price on behalf of the capitalist, and another additional percentage on behalf of the landlord. Suppose the wages of the labour employed in the production of a commodity to be ten. If the rate of profit was 100 per cent., to the wages advanced the capitalist would add ten, and if the rate of rent was also 100 per cent. upon the wages, there would be added ten more, and the aggregate price of the commodity would amount to thirty. But such a determination of prices would be simply their determination by wages. If wages in the above case rose to twenty, the price of the commodity would rise to sixty, and so forth. Consequently all the superannuated writers on political economy who propounded the dogma that wages regulate prices, have tried to prove it by treating profit and rent *as mere additional percentages upon wages*. None of them were, of course, able to reduce the limits of those percentages to any economic law. They seem, on the contrary, to think profits settled by tradition, custom, the will of the capitalist, or by some other equally arbitrary and inexplicable method. If they assert that they are settled by the competition between the capitalists, they say nothing. That competition is sure to equalize the different rates of profit in different trades, or reduce them to one average level, but it can never determine the level itself, or the general rate of profit.

What do we mean by saying that the prices of the commodities are determined by wages ? Wages being but a name for the price of labour, we mean that the prices of commodities are regulated by the price of labour. As '*price*' is exchangeable value —and in speaking of value I speak always of exchangeable value—is exchangeable *value expressed in money*, the proposition comes to this, that 'the *value of commodities* is determined by the value of labour', or that 'the *value of labour is the general measure of value*'.

But how, then, is the '*value of labour*' itself determined ? Here we come to a standstill. Of course, to a standstill if we try reasoning logically. Yet the propounders of that doctrine make short work of logical scruples. Take our friend Weston, for example. First he told us that wages regulate the price of commodities and that consequently when wages rise prices must rise. Then he turned round to show us that a rise of wages will be no good because the prices of commodities had risen, and because wages were indeed measured by the prices of the commodities upon which they are spent. Thus we begin by saying that the value of labour determines the value of commodities, and we wind up by saying that the value of commodities determines the value of labour. Thus we move to and fro in the most vicious circle, and arrive at no conclusion at all.

On the whole, it is evident that by making the value of one commodity, say labour, corn, or any other commodity, the general measure and regulator of value, we only shift the difficulty, since we determine one value by another, which on its side wants to be determined.

The dogma that 'wages determine the price of commodities', expressed in its most abstract terms, comes to this, that 'value is determined by value,' and this tautology means that, in fact, we know nothing at all about value. Accepting this premiss, all reasoning about the general laws of political economy turns into mere twaddle. It was, therefore, the great merit of Ricardo that in his work on *The Principles of Political Economy*, published in 1817, he fundamentally destroyed the old, popular, and worn-out fallacy that 'wages determine prices', a fallacy which Adam Smith and his French predecessors had spurned in the really scientific parts of their researches, but which they reproduced in their more exoterical and vulgarizing chapters.

VI VALUE AND LABOUR

Citizens, I have now arrived at a point where I must enter upon the real development of the question. I cannot promise to do this in a very satisfactory way, because to do so I should be obliged to go over the whole field of political economy. I can, as the French would say, but *effleurer la question*, touch upon the main points.

The first question we have to put is: What is the *value* of a commodity? How is it determined?

At first sight it would seem that the value of a commodity is a thing quite *relative*, and not to be settled without considering one commodity in its relations to all other commodities. In fact, in speaking of the value, the value in exchange of a commodity, we mean the proportional quantities in which it exchanges with all other commodities. But then arises the question: How are the proportions in which commodities exchange with each other regulated?

We know from experience that these proportions vary infinitely. Taking one single commodity, wheat, for instance, we shall find that a quarter of wheat exchanges in almost countless variations of proportion with different commodities. Yet, *its value remaining always the same*, whether expressed in silk, gold, or any other commodity, it must be something distinct from, and independent of, these *different rates of exchange* with different articles. It must be possible to express, in a very different form, these various equations with various commodities.

Besides, if I say a quarter of wheat exchanges with iron in a certain proportion, or the value of a quarter of wheat is expressed in a certain amount of iron, I say that the value of wheat and its

equivalent in iron are equal to *some third thing*, which is .
wheat nor iron, because I suppose them to express the
magnitude in two different shapes. Either of them, the whea
the iron, must, therefore, independently of the other, be reduc   .c
to this third thing which is their common measure.

To elucidate this point I shall recur to a very simple geometrical
illustration. In comparing the areas of triangles of all possible
forms and magnitudes, or comparing triangles with rectangles, or
any other rectilinear figure, how do we proceed? We reduce the
area of any triangle whatever to an expression quite different
from its visible form. Having found from the nature of the
triangle that its area is equal to half the product of its base by its
height, we can then compare the different values of all sorts of
triangles, and of all rectilinear figures whatever, because all of
them may be resolved into a certain number of triangles.

The same mode of procedure must obtain with the values of
commodities. We must be able to reduce all of them to an
expression common to all, and distinguishing them only by the
proportions in which they contain that identical measure.

As the *exchangeable values* of commodities are only *social
functions* of those things, and have nothing at all to do with the
natural qualities, we must first ask, What is the common *social
substance* of all commodities? It is *Labour*. To produce a commodity a certain amount of labour must be bestowed upon it,
or worked up in it. And I say not only *Labour*, but *Social Labour*.
A man who produces an article for his own immediate use, to
consume it himself, creates a *product*, but not a *commodity*. As a
self-sustaining producer he has nothing to do with society. But
to produce a *commodity*, a man must not only produce an article
satisfying some *social* want, but his labour itself must form part
and parcel of the total sum of labour expended by society. It
must be subordinate to the *Division of Labour within Society*. It is
nothing without the other divisions of labour, and on its part is
required to *integrate* them.

If we consider *commodities as values*, we consider them exclusively under the single aspect of *realized*, *fixed*, or, if you like,
crystallized social labour. In this respect they can *differ* only by
representing greater or smaller quantities of labour, as, for
example, a greater amount of labour may be worked up in a

silken handkerchief than in a brick. But how does one measure *quantities of labour*? By the *time the labour lasts*, in measuring the labour by the hour, the day, etc. Of course, to apply this measure, all sorts of labour are reduced to average or simple labour as their unit.

We arrive, therefore, at this conclusion. A commodity has a *value*, because it is a *crystallization of social labour*. The *greatness* of its value, or its *relative* value, depends upon the greater or less amount of that social substance contained in it; that is to say, on the relative mass of labour necessary for its production. The *relative values of commodities* are, therefore, determined by the *respective quantities or amounts of labour, worked up, realized, fixed in them*. The *correlative* quantities of commodities which can be produced in the *same time of labour* are *equal*. Or the value of one commodity is to the value of another commodity as the quantity of labour fixed in the one is to the quantity of labour fixed in the other.

I suspect that many of you will ask, Does then, indeed, there exist such a vast, or any difference whatever, between determining the values of commodities by *wages*, and determining them by the *relative quantities of labour* necessary for their production? You must, however, be aware that the *reward* for labour, and *quantity* of labour, are quite disparate things. Suppose, for example, *equal quantities of labour* to be fixed in one quarter of wheat and one ounce of gold. I resort to the example because it was used by Benjamin Franklin in his first Essay published in 1721, and entitled, *A Modest Enquiry into the Nature and Necessity of a Paper Currency*, where he, one of the first, hit upon the true nature of value. Well. We suppose, then, that one quarter of wheat and one ounce of gold are *equal values* or *equivalents*, because they are *crystallizations of equal amounts of average labour*, of so many days' or so many weeks' labour respectively fixed in them. In thus determining the relative values of gold and corn, do we refer in any way whatever to the *wages* of the agricultural labourer and the miner? Not a bit. We leave it quite *indeterminate* how their day's or their week's labour was paid, or even whether wages labour was employed at all. If it was, wages may have been very unequal. The labourer whose labour is realized in the quarter of wheat may receive two bushels only, and the labourer employed in mining may receive one-half of the ounce of gold. Or, supposing their wages to be equal, they may deviate in all possible proportions from the values of the commodities produced by them. They may amount to one-half, one-third, one-fourth, one-fifth, or any other proportional part of the one quarter of corn or the one ounce of gold. Their *wages* can, of course, not *exceed*, not be *more* than the values of the commodities they produced, but they can be *less* in every possible degree. Their *wages* will be *limited* by the *values* of the products, but the *values of their products* will not be limited by the wages. And above all, the values, the relative values of corn and gold, for example, will have been settled without any regard whatever to the value of the labour employed, that is to say, to *wages*. To determine the values of commodities by the *relative quantities of labour fixed in them*, is, therefore, a thing quite different from the tautological method of determining the values of commodities by the value of labour, or by *wages*. This point, however, will be further elucidated in the progress of our inquiry.

In calculating the exchangeable value of a commodity we must add to the quantity of labour *last* employed the quantity of labour *previously* worked up in the raw material of the commodity, and the labour bestowed on the implements, tools, machinery, and buildings, with which such labour is assisted. For example, the value of a certain amount of cotton-yarn is the crystallization of the quantity of labour added to the cotton during the spinning process, the quantity of labour previously realized in the cotton itself, the quantity of labour realized in the coal, oil, and other auxiliary substances used, the quantity of labour fixed in the steam-engine, the spindles, the factory building, and so forth. Instruments of production properly so-called, such as tools, machinery, buildings, serve again and again for a longer or shorter period during repeated processes of production. If they were used up at once, like the raw material, their whole value would at once be transferred to the commodities they assist in producing. But as a spindle, for example, is but gradually used up, an average calculation is made, based upon the average time it lasts, and its average waste or wear and tear during a certain period, say a day. In this way we calculate how much of the value of the spindle is transferred to the yarn daily spun, and how much therefore, of the total amount of labour realized in a pound of yarn, for example, is due to the quantity of labour previously realized in the spindle. For our present purpose it is not necessary to dwell any longer upon this point.

It might seem that if the value of a commodity is determined by the *quantity of labour bestowed upon its production*, the lazier a man, or the clumsier a man, the more valuable his commodity, because the greater the time of labour required for finishing the commodity. This, however, would be a sad mistake. You will recollect that I used the word '*Social* labour', and many points are involved in this qualification of '*Social*'. In saying that the value of a commodity is determined by the *quantity of labour* worked up or crystallized in it, we mean *the quantity of labour necessary* for its production in a given state of society, under certain social average conditions of production, with a given social average intensity, and average skill of the labour employed. When, in England, the power-loom came to compete with the hand-loom, only half the former time of labour was wanted to convert a given amount of yarn into a yard of cotton or cloth. The poor hand-loom weaver now worked seventeen or eighteen hours daily, instead of the nine or ten hours he had worked before. Still the product of twenty hours of his labour represented now only ten social hours of labour, or ten hours of labour socially necessary for the conversion of a certain amount of yarn into textile stuffs. His product of twenty hours had, therefore, no more value than his former product of ten hours.

If then the quantity of socially necessary labour realized in commodities regulates their exchangeable values, every increase in the quantity of labour wanted for the production of a commodity must augment its value, as every diminution must lower it.

If the respective quantities of labour necessary for the production of the respective commodities remained constant, their relative values also would be constant. But such is not the case. The quantity of labour necessary for the production of a commodity changes continuously with the changes in the productive powers of the labour employed. The greater the productive powers of labour, the more produce is finished in a given time of labour; and the smaller the productive powers of labour, the less produce is finished in the same time. If, for example, in the progress of population it should become necessary to cultivate less fertile soils, the same amount of produce would be only attainable by a greater amount of labour spent, and the value of agricultural produce would consequently rise. On the other hand, if, with the modern means of production, a single spinner converts into yarn, during one working day, many thousand times the amount of cotton which he could have spun during the same time with the spinning wheel, it is evident that every single pound of cotton will absorb many thousand times less of spinning labour than it did before, and, consequently, the value added by spinning to every single pound of cotton will be a thousand times less than before. The value of yarn will sink accordingly.

Apart from the different natural energies and acquired working abilities of different peoples, the productive powers of labour must principally depend:—

Firstly. Upon the *natural* conditions of labour, such as fertility of soil, mines, and so forth.

Secondly. Upon the progressive improvement of the *Social Powers of Labour*, such as are derived from production on a grand scale, concentration of capital and combination of labour, subdivision of labour, machinery, improved methods, appliance of chemical and other natural agencies, shortening of time and space by means of communication and transport, and every other contrivance by which science presses natural agencies into the service of labour, and by which the social or co-operative character of labour is developed. The greater the productive powers of labour, the less labour is bestowed upon a given amount of produce; hence the smaller the value of the produce. The smaller the productive powers of labour, the more labour is bestowed upon the same amount of produce; hence the greater its value. As a general law we may, therefore, set it down that:—

The values of commodities are directly as the times of labour employed in their production, and are inversely as the productive powers of the labour employed.

Having till now only spoken of *Value*, I shall add a few words about *Price*, which is a peculiar form assumed by value.

Price, taken by itself, is nothing but the *monetary expression of value*. The values of all commodities of this country, for example, are expressed in gold prices, while on the Continent they are mainly expressed in silver prices. The value of gold or silver, like that of all other commodities, is regulated by the quantity of labour necessary for getting them. You exchange a certain amount of your national products, in which a certain amount of your national labour is crystallized, for the produce of the gold and silver producing countries, in which a certain quantity of *their* labour is crystallized. It is in this way, in fact by barter, that you learn to express in gold and silver the values of all commodities, that is the respective quantities of labour bestowed upon them. Looking somewhat closer into the *monetary expression of value*, or what comes to the same, the conversion of value into price, you will find that it is a process by which you give to the *values* of all commodities an *independent* and *homogeneous form*, or by which you express them as quantities of equal social labour. So far as it is but the monetary expression of value, price has been called *natural price* by Adam Smith, '*prix nécessaire*' by the French physiocrats.

What then is the relation between *value* and *market prices*, or between *natural prices* and *market prices*? You all know that the *market price* is the *same* for all commodities of the same kind, however the conditions of production may differ for the individual producers. The market price expresses only the *average amount of social labour* necessary, under the average conditions of production, to supply the market with a certain mass of a certain article. It is calculated upon the whole lot of a commodity of a certain description.

So far the *market price* of a commodity coincides with its *value*. On the other hand, the oscillations of market prices, rising now over, sinking now under the value or natural price, depend upon the fluctuations of supply and demand. The deviations of market prices from values are continual, but as Adam Smith says: 'The natural price is the central price to which the prices of commodities are continually gravitating. Different accidents may sometimes keep them suspended a good deal above it, and sometimes force them down even somewhat below it. But whatever may be the obstacles which hinder them from settling in this centre of repose and continuance, they are constantly tending towards it'.

I cannot now sift this matter. It suffices to say that *if* supply and demand equilibrate each other, the market prices of com-

modities will correspond with their natural prices, that is
with their values, as determined by the respective quanti
labour required for their production. But supply and demand
must constantly tend to equilibrate each other, although they do
so only by compensating one fluctuation by another, a rise by a
fall, and *vice versâ*. If instead of considering only the daily
fluctuations you analyse the movement of market prices for
longer periods, as Mr Tooke, for example, has done in his
History of Prices, you will find that the fluctuations of market
prices, their deviations from values, their ups and downs, paralyse and compensate each other; so that apart from the effect of
monopolies and some other modifications I must now pass by,
all descriptions of commodities are, on the average, sold at their
respective *values* or natural prices. The average periods during
which the fluctuations of market prices compensate each other
are different for different kinds of commodities, because with one
kind it is easier to adapt supply to demand than with the other.

If then, speaking broadly, and embracing somewhat longer
periods, all descriptions of commodities sell at their respective
values, it is nonsense to suppose that profit, not in individual
cases, but that the constant and usual profits of different trades
spring from the prices of commodities, or selling them at a price
over and above their *value*. The absurdity of this notion becomes
evident if it is generalized. What a man would constantly win as a
seller he would as constantly lose as a purchaser. It would not do
to say that there are men who are buyers without being sellers, or
consumers without being producers. What these people pay to the
producers, they must first get from them for nothing. If a man
first takes your money and afterwards returns that money in
buying your commodities, you will never enrich yourselves by
selling your commodities too dear to that same man. This sort of
transaction might diminish a loss, but would never help in realizing a profit.

To explain, therefore, the *general nature of profits*, you must
start from the theorem that, on an average, commodities are *sold at
their real values*, and that *profits are derived from selling them at
their values*, that is, in proportion to the quantity of labour
realized in them. If you cannot explain profit upon this supposition, you cannot explain it at all. This seems paradox and

contrary to everyday observation. It is also paradox that the earth moves round the sun, and that water consists of two highly inflammable gases. Scientific truth is always paradox, if judged by everyday experience, which catches only the delusive appearance of things.

VII LABOURING POWER[1]

Having now, as far as it could be done in such a cursory manner, analysed the nature of *Value*, of the *Value of any commodity whatever*, we must turn our attention to the specific *Value of Labour*. And here, again, I must startle you by a seeming paradox. All of you feel sure that what they daily sell is their Labour; that, therefore, Labour has a Price, and that the price of a commodity being only the monetary expression of its value, there must certainly exist such a thing as the *Value of Labour*. However, there exists no such thing as the *Value of Labour* in the common acceptance of the word. We have seen that the amount of necessary labour crystallized in a commodity constitutes its value. Now applying this notion of value, how could we define, say, the value of a ten hours' working day? How much labour is contained in that day? Ten hours labour. To say that the value of a ten hours' working day is equal to ten hours labour, or the quantity of labour contained in it, would be a tautological and, moreover, a nonsensical expression. Of course, having once found out the true but hidden sense of the expression '*Value of Labour*', we shall be able to interpret this irrational, and seemingly impossible application of value, in the same way that, having once made sure of the real movement of the celestial bodies, we shall be able to explain their apparent or merely phenomenal movements.

What the working man sells is not directly his *Labour*, but his *Labouring Power*, the temporary disposal of which he makes over to the capitalist. This is so much the case that I do not know whether by the English Laws, but certainly by some Continental Laws, the *maximum time* is fixed for which a man is allowed to sell his labouring power. If allowed to do so for any indefinite period whatever, slavery would be immediately restored. Such a

[1] 'Labour Power' in the English translation of *Das Kapital*.

sale, if it comprised his lifetime, for example, would make him at once the lifelong slave of his employer.

One of the oldest economists and most original philosophers of England—Thomas Hobbes—has already, in his *Leviathan*, instinctively hit upon this point overlooked by all his successors. He says: '*The value or worth of a man* is, as in all other things, his *price:* that is so much as would be given for the *Use of his Power*'.

Proceeding from this basis, we shall be able to determine the *Value of Labour* as that of all other commodities.

But before doing so, we might ask, how does this strange phenomenon arise, that we find on the market a set of buyers, possessed of land, machinery, raw material, and the means of subsistence, all of them, save land in its crude state, the *products of labour*, and on the other hand, a set of sellers who have nothing to sell except their labouring power, their working arms and brains? That the one set buys continually in order to make a profit and enrich themselves, while the other set continually sells in order to earn their livelihood? The inquiry into this question would be an inquiry into what the economists call '*Previous, or Original Accumulation,*' but which ought to be called *Original Expropriation*. We should find that this so-called *Original Accumulation* means nothing but a series of historical processes, resulting in a *Decomposition* of the *Original Union* existing between the Labouring Man and his Instruments of Labour. Such an inquiry, however, lies beyond the pale of my present subject. The *Separation* between the Man of Labour and the Instruments of Labour once established, such a state of things will maintain itself and reproduce itself upon a constantly increasing scale, until a new and fundamental revolution in the mode of production should again overturn it, and restore the original union in a new historical form.

What, then, is the *Value of Labouring Power?*

Like that of every other commodity, its value is determined by the quantity of labour necessary to produce it. The labouring power of a man exists only in his living individuality. A certain mass of necessaries must be consumed by a man to grow up and maintain his life. But the man, like the machine, will wear out, and must be replaced by another man. Besides the mass of necessaries required for *his own* maintenance, he wants another amount of necessaries to bring up a certain quota of children that are to replace him on the labour market and to perpetuate the race of labourers. Moreover, to develop his labouring power, and acquire a given skill, another amount of values must be spent. For our purpose it suffices to consider only *average* labour, the costs of whose education and development are vanishing magnitudes. Still I must seize upon this occasion to state that, as the costs of producing labouring powers of different quality differ, so must differ the values of the labouring powers employed in different trades. The cry for an *equality of wages* rests, therefore, upon a mistake, is an insane wish never to be fulfilled. It is an offspring of that false and superficial radicalism that accepts premisses and tries to evade conclusions. Upon the basis of the wages system the value of labouring power is settled like that of every other commodity; and as different kinds of labouring power have different values, or require different quantities of labour for their production, they *must* fetch different prices in the labour market. To clamour for *equal or even equitable retribution* on the basis of the wages system is the same as to clamour for *freedom* on the basis of the slavery system. What you think just or equitable is out of the question. The question is: What is necessary and unavoidable with a given system of production ?

After what has been said, it will be seen that the *value of labouring power* is determined by the *value of the necessaries* required to produce, develop, maintain, and perpetuate the labouring power.

VIII PRODUCTION OF SURPLUS VALUE

Now suppose that the average amount of the daily necessaries of a labouring man require *six hours of average labour* for their production. Suppose, moreover, six hours of average labour to be also realized in a quantity of gold equal to 3*s*. Then 3*s* would be the *Price*, or the monetary expression of the *Daily Value* of that man's *Labouring Power*. If he worked daily six hours he would daily produce a value sufficient to buy the average amount of his daily necessaries, or to maintain himself as a labouring man.

But our man is a wages labourer. He must, therefore, sell his labouring power to a capitalist. If he sells it at 3*s* daily, or 18*s* weekly, he sells it at its value. Suppose him to be a spinner. If he works six hours daily he will add to the cotton a value of 3*s* daily. This value, daily added by him, would be an exact equivalent for the wages, or the price of his labouring power, received daily. But in that case *no surplus value* or *surplus produce* whatever would go to the capitalist. Here, then, we come to the rub.

In buying the labouring power of the workman, and paying its value, the capitalist, like every other purchaser, has acquired the right to consume or use the commodity bought. You consume or use the labouring power of a man by making him work, as you consume or use a machine by making it run. By buying the daily or weekly value of the labouring power of the workman, the capitalist has, therefore, acquired the right to use or make that labouring power work during the *whole day or week*. The working day or the working week has, of course, certain limits, but those we shall afterwards look more closely at.

For the present I want to turn your attention to one decisive point.

The *value* of the labouring power is determined by the quantity of labour necessary to maintain or reproduce it, but the *use* of that labouring power is only limited by the active energies and physical strength of the labourer. The daily or weekly *value* of the labouring power is quite distinct from the daily or weekly exercise of that power, the same as the food a horse wants and the time it can carry the horseman are quite distinct. The quantity of labour by which the *value* of the workman's labouring power is limited forms by no means a limit to the quantity of labour which his labouring power is apt to perform. Take the example of our spinner. We have seen that, to daily reproduce his labouring power, he must daily reproduce a value of three shillings, which he will do by working six hours daily. But this does not disable him from working ten or twelve or more hours a day. But by paying the daily or weekly *value* of the spinner's labouring power the capitalist has acquired the right of using that labouring power during *the whole day or week*. He will, therefore, make him work say, daily, *twelve hours*. *Over and above* the six hours required to replace his wages, or the value of his labouring power, he will, therefore, have to work *six other hours*, which I shall call hours of *surplus labour,* which surplus labour will realize itself in a *surplus value* and a *surplus produce.* If our spinner, for example, by his daily labour of six hours, added three shillings' value to the cotton, a value forming an exact equivalent to his wages, he will, in twelve hours, add six shillings' worth to the cotton, and produce *a proportional surplus of yarn.* As he has sold his labouring power to the capitalist the whole value or produce created by him belongs to the capitalist, the owner *pro tem.* of his labouring power. By advancing three shillings, the capitalist will, therefore, realize a value of six shillings, because, advancing a value in which six hours of labour are crystallized, he will receive in return a value in which twelve hours of labour are crystallized. By repeating this same process daily, the capitalist will daily advance three shillings and daily pocket six shillings, one half of which will go to pay wages anew, and the other half of which will form *surplus value,* for which the capitalist pays no equivalent. It is this *sort of exchange between capital and labour* upon which capitalistic production, or the wages system, is founded, and which must constantly result in reproducing the working man as a working man, and the capitalist as a capitalist.

The rate of surplus value, all other circumstances remaining the same, will depend on the proportion between that part of the working day necessary to reproduce the value of the labouring power and the *surplus time* or *surplus labour* performed for the capitalist. It will, therefore, depend on the *ratio in which the working day is prolonged over and above that extent,* by working which the working man would only reproduce the value of his labouring power, or replace his wages.

IX VALUE OF LABOUR

We must now return to the expression, '*Value, or Price of Labour*'.

We have seen that, in fact, it is only the value of the labouring power, measured by the values of commodities necessary for its maintenance. But since the workman receives his wages *after* his labour is performed, and knows, moreover, that what he actually gives to the capitalist is his labour, the value or price of his labouring power necessarily appears to him as the *price* or *value of his labour itself.* If the price of his labouring power is three shillings, in which six hours of labour are realized, and if he works twelve hours, he necessarily considers these three shillings as the value or price of twelve hours of labour, although these twelve hours of labour realize themselves in a value of six shillings. A double consequence flows from this.

Firstly. The *value or price of the labouring power* takes the semblance of the *price or value of labour itself*, although, strictly speaking, value and price of labour are senseless terms.

Secondly. Although one part only of the workman's daily labour is *paid*, while the other part is *unpaid*, and while that unpaid or surplus labour constitutes exactly the fund out of which *surplus value* or *profit* is formed, it seems as if the aggregate labour was paid labour.

This false appearance distinguishes *wages labour* from other *historical* forms of labour. On the basis of the wages system even the *unpaid* labour seems to be *paid* labour. With the *slave*, on the contrary, even that part of his labour which is paid appears to be unpaid. Of course, in order to work the slave must live, and one part of his working day goes to replace the value of his own maintenance. But since no bargain is struck between him and his master, and no acts of selling and buying are going on between the two parties, all his labour seems to be given away for nothing.

Take, on the other hand, the peasant serf, such as he, I might say, until yesterday existed in the whole East of Europe. This peasant worked, for example, three days for himself on his own field or the field allotted to him, and the three subsequent days he performed compulsory and gratuitous labour on the estate of his lord. Here, then, the paid and unpaid parts of labour were sensibly separated, separated in time and space; and our Liberals overflowed with moral indignation at the preposterous notion of making a man work for nothing.

In point of fact, however, whether a man works three days of the week for himself on his own field and three days for nothing on the estate of his lord, or whether he works in the factory or the workshop six hours daily for himself and six for his employer, comes to the same, although in the latter case the paid and unpaid portions of labour are inseparably mixed up with each other, and the nature of the whole transaction is completely masked by the *intervention of a contract* and the *pay* received at

nd of the week. The gratuitous labour appears to be volun-
..ny given in the one instance, and to be compulsory in the
other. That makes all the difference.

In using the word *value of labour*, I shall only use it as a
popular slang term for *value of labouring power*.

X PROFIT IS MADE BY SELLING A COMMODITY AT ITS VALUE

Suppose an average hour of labour to be realized in a value
equal to sixpence, or twelve average hours of labour to be realized
in six shillings. Suppose, further, the value of labour to be three
shillings or the produce of six hours labour. If, then, in the raw
material, machinery, and so forth, used up in a commodity,
twenty-four hours of average labour were realized, its value
would amount to twelve shillings. If, moreover, the workman
employed by the capitalist added twelve hours of labour to those
means of production, these twelve hours would be realized in an
additional value of six shillings. The *total value of the product*
would, therefore, amount to thirty-six hours of realized labour,
and be equal to eighteen shillings. But as the value of labour, or
the wages paid to the workman, would be three shillings only,
no equivalent would have been paid by the capitalist for the six
hours of surplus labour worked by the workman, and realized in
the value of the commodity. By selling this commodity at its
value for eighteen shillings, the capitalist would, therefore,
realize a value of three shillings, for which he had paid no equivalent. These three shillings would constitute the surplus value or
profit pocketed by him. The capitalist would consequently
realize the profit of three shillings, not by selling his commodity
at a price *over and above* its value, but by selling it *at its real
value*.

The value of a commodity is determined by the *total quantity
of labour* contained in it. But part of that quantity of labour is
realized in a value, for which an equivalent has been paid in the
form of wages; part of it is realized in a value for which *no*
equivalent has been paid. Part of the labour contained in the
commodity is *paid* labour; part is *unpaid* labour. By selling,
therefore, the commodity *at its value*, that is, as the crystallization

of the *total quantity of labour* bestowed upon it, the capitalist must necessarily sell it at a profit. He sells not only what has cost him an equivalent, but he sells also what has cost him nothing, although it has cost his workman labour. The cost of the commodity to the capitalist and its real cost are different things. I repeat, therefore, that normal and average profits are made by selling commodities not *above*, but *at their real values*.

XI THE DIFFERENT PARTS INTO WHICH SURPLUS VALUE IS DECOMPOSED

The *surplus value*, or that part of the total value of the commodity in which the *surplus labour* or *unpaid labour* of the working man is realized, I call *Profit*. The whole of that profit is not pocketed by the employing capitalist. The monopoly of land enables the landlord to take one part of that *surplus value*, under the name of *rent*, whether the land is used for agricultural buildings or railways, or for any other productive purpose. On the other hand, the very fact that the possession of the *instruments of labour* enables the employing capitalist to produce a *surplus value*, or, what comes to the same, to *appropriate to himself a certain amount of unpaid labour*, enables the owner of the means of labour, which he lends wholly or partly to the employing capitalist— enables, in one word, the money-lending capitalist to claim for himself under the name of *interest* another part of that surplus value, so that there remains to the employing capitalist *as such* only what is called *industrial* or *commercial profit*.

By what laws this division of the total amount of surplus value amongst the three categories of people is regulated is a question quite foreign to our subject. This much, however, results from what has been stated.

Rent, Interest, and Industrial Profit are only *different names for* different parts of the *surplus value* of the commodity, or the *unpaid labour enclosed in it*, and they are *equally derived from this source, and from this source alone*. They are not derived from *land* as such or from *capital* as such, but land and capital enable their owners to get their respective shares out of the surplus value extracted by the employing capitalist from the labourer. For the labourer himself it is a matter of subordinate importance whether that surplus value, the result of his surplus labour, or unpaid labour, is altogether pocketed by the employing capitalist, or whether the latter is obliged to pay portions of it, under the name of rent and interest, away to third parties. Suppose the employing capitalist to use only his own capital and to be his own landlord, then the whole surplus value would go into his pocket.

It is the employing capitalist who immediately extracts from the labourer this surplus value, whatever part of it he may ultimately be able to keep for himself. Upon this relation, therefore, between the employing capitalist and the wages labourer the whole wages system and the whole present system of production hinge. Some of the citizens who took part in our debate were, therefore, wrong in trying to mince matters, and to treat this fundamental relation between the employing capitalist and the working man as a secondary question, although they were right in stating that, under given circumstances, a rise of prices might affect in very unequal degrees the employing capitalist, the landlord, the moneyed capitalist, and, if you please, the tax-gatherer.

Another consequence follows from what has been stated.

That part of the value of the commodity which represents only the value of the raw materials, the machinery, in one word, the value of the means of production used up, forms *no revenue* at all, but replaces *only capital*. But, apart from this, it is false that the other part of the value of the commodity *which forms revenue*, or may be spent in the form of wages, profits, rent, interest, is *constituted* by the value of wages, the value of rent, the value of profits, and so forth. We shall, in the first instance, discard wages, and only treat industrial profits, interest, and rent. We have just seen that the *surplus value* contained in the commodity, or that part of its value in which *unpaid labour* is realized, resolves itself into different fractions, bearing three different names. But it would be quite the reverse of the truth to say that its value is *composed* of, or *formed* by, the *addition* of the *independent values of these three constituents*.

If one hour of labour realizes itself in a value of sixpence, if the working day of the labourer comprises twelve hours, if half of this time is unpaid labour, that surplus labour will add to the commodity a *surplus value* of three shillings, that is of value for which no equivalent has been paid. This surplus value of three shillings constitutes the *whole fund* which the employing capitalist may divide, in whatever proportions, with the landlord and the money-lender. The value of these three shillings constitutes the limit of the value they have to divide amongst them. But it is not the employing capitalist who adds to the value of the commodity an arbitrary value for his profit, to which another value is added for the landlord, and so forth, so that the addition of these arbitrarily fixed values would constitute the total value. You see, therefore, the fallacy of the popular notion, which confounds the *decomposition of a given value* into three parts, with the *formation* of that value by the addition of three *independent* values, thus converting the aggregate value, from which rent, profit, and interest are derived, into an arbitrary magnitude.

If the total profit realized by a capitalist is equal to £100, we call this sum, considered as *absolute* magnitude, the *amount of profit*. But if we calculate the ratio which those £100 bear to the capital advanced, we call this *relative* magnitude, the *rate of profit*. It is evident that this rate of profit may be expressed in a double way.

Suppose £100 to be the capital *advanced in wages*. If the surplus value created is also £100—and this would show us that half the working day of the labourer consists of *unpaid* labour— and if we measured this profit by the value of the capital advanced in wages, we should say that the *rate of profit* amounted to 100 per cent., because the value advanced would be 100 and the value realized would be 200.

If, on the other hand, we should not only consider the *capital advanced in wages*, but the *total capital* advanced, say, for example, £500, of which £400 represented the value of raw materials, machinery, and so forth, we should say that the *rate of profit* amounted only to twenty per cent., because the profit of one hundred would be but the fifth part of the *total* capital advanced.

The first mode of expressing the rate of profit is the only one which shows you the real ratio between paid and unpaid labour, the real degree of the *exploitation* (you must allow me this French word) *of labour*. The other mode of expression is that in common use, and is, indeed, appropriate for certain purposes. At all events, it is very useful for concealing the degree in which the capitalist extracts gratuitous labour from the workman.

In the remarks I have still to make I shall use the word *Profit* for the whole amount of the surplus value extracted by the capitalist without any regard to the division of that surplus value between different parties, and in using the words *Rate of Profit*, I shall always measure profits by the value of the capital advanced in wages.

XII GENERAL RELATION OF PROFITS, WAGES, AND PRICES

Deduct from the value of a commodity the value replacing the value of the raw materials and other means of production used upon it, that is to say, deduct the value representing the *past* labour contained in it, and the remainder of its value will resolve into the quantity of labour added by the working man *last* employed. If that working man works twelve hours daily, if twelve hours of average labour crystallize themselves in an amount of gold equal to six shillings, this additional value of six shillings is the *only* value his labour will have created. This given value, determined by the time of his labour, is the only fund from which both he and the capitalist have to draw their respective shares or dividends, the only value to be divided into wages and profits. It is evident that this value itself will not be altered by the variable proportions in which it may be divided amongst the two parties. There will also be nothing changed if in the place of one working man you put the whole working population, twelve million working days, for example, instead of one.

Since the capitalist and workman have only to divide this limited value, that is, the value measured by the total labour of the working man, the more the one gets the less will the other get, and *vice versâ*. Whenever a quantity is given, one part of it will increase inversely as the other decreases. If the wages change, profits will change in an opposite direction. If wages fall, profits will rise; and if wages rise, profits will fall. If the working man, on our former supposition, gets three shillings, equal to one half of the value he has created, or if his whole working day consists half of paid, half of unpaid labour, the *rate of profit* will be 100 per cent., because the capitalist would also get three shillings. If the working man receives only two shillings, or works only one third of the whole day for himself, the capitalist will get four shillings, and the rate of profit will be 200 per cent. If the working man receives four shillings, the capitalist will only receive two, and the rate of profit would sink to 33⅓ per cent., but all these variations will not affect the value of the commodity. A general rise of wages would therefore result in a fall of the general rate of profit, but not affect values. But although the values of commodities, which must ultimately regulate their market prices, are exclusively determined by the total quantities of labour fixed in them, and not by the division of that quantity into paid and unpaid labour, it by no means follows that the value of the single commodities, or lots of commodities, produced during twelve hours, for example, will remain constant. The *number* or mass of commodities produced in a given time of labour, or by a given quantity of labour, depends upon the *productive power* of the labour employed and not upon its *extent* or length. With one degree of the productive power of spinning labour, for example, a working day of twelve hours may produce twelve pounds of yarn, with a lesser degree of productive power only two pounds. If then twelve hours' average labour were realized in the value of six shillings in the one case, the twelve pounds of yarn would cost six shillings, in the other case the two pounds of yarn would also cost six shillings. One pound of yarn would, therefore, cost sixpence in the one case, and three shillings in the other. The difference of price would result from the difference in the productive powers of labour employed. One hour of labour would be realized in one pound of yarn with the greater productive power, while with the smaller productive power, six hours of labour would be realized in one pound of yarn. The price of a pound of yarn would, in the one instance, be only sixpence, although wages were relatively high and the rate of profit low; it would be three shillings in the other instance, although wages were low and the rate of profit high. This would be so because the price of the pound of yarn is regulated by the *total amount of labour worked up in it*, and not by the *proportional division of that total amount into paid and unpaid labour*. The fact I have before mentioned that high-priced labour may produce cheap, and low-priced labour may produce dear commodities, loses, therefore, its paradoxical appearance. It is only the expression of the general law that the value of a commodity is regulated by the quantity of labour worked up in it, and that the quantity of labour worked up in it depends altogether upon the productive powers of the labour employed, and will, therefore, vary with every variation in the productivity of labour.

XIII MAIN CASES OF ATTEMPTS AT RAISING WAGES OR RESISTING THEIR FALL

Let us now seriously consider the main cases in which a rise of wages is attempted or a reduction of wages resisted.

1. We have seen that the *value of the labouring power*, or in more popular parlance, the *value of labour*, is determined by the value of necessaries, or the quantity of labour required to produce them. If, then, in a given country the value of the daily average necessaries of the labourer represented six hours of labour expressed in three shillings, the labourer would have to work six hours daily to produce an equivalent for his daily maintenance. If the whole working day was twelve hours, the capitalist would pay him the value of his labour by paying him three shillings. Half the working day would be unpaid labour, and the rate of profit would amount to 100 per cent. But now suppose that, consequent upon a decrease of productivity, more labour should be wanted to produce, say, the same amount of agricultural produce, so that the price of the average daily necessaries should rise from three to four shillings. In that case the *value* of labour would rise by one third, or 33⅓ per cent. Eight hours of the working day would be required to produce an equivalent for the daily maintenance of the labourer, according to his old standard of living. The surplus labour would therefore sink from six hours to four, and the rate of profit from 100 to 50 per cent. But in insisting upon a rise of wages, the labourer would only insist upon getting the *increased value of his labour*, like every other seller of a commodity, who, the costs of his commodities having increased, tries to get its increased value paid. If wages did not rise, or not sufficiently rise, to compensate for the increased values of necessaries, the *price* of labour would sink below the *value of labour*, and the labourer's standard of life would deteriorate.

But a change might also take place in an opposite direction. By virtue of the increased productivity of labour, the same amount of the average daily necessaries might sink from three to two shillings, or only four hours out of the working day, instead of six, be wanted to reproduce an equivalent for the value of the daily necessaries. The working man would now be able to buy with two shillings as many necessaries as he did before with three shillings. Indeed, the *value of labour* would have sunk, but that diminished value would command the same amount of commodities as before. Then profits would rise from three to four shillings, and the rate of profit from 100 to 200 per cent. Although the labourer's absolute standard of life would have remained the same, his *relative* wages, and therewith his *relative social position*, as compared with that of the capitalist, would have been lowered. If the working man should resist that reduction of relative wages, he would only try to get some share in the increased productive powers of his own labour, and to maintain his former relative position in the social scale. Thus, after the abolition of the Corn Laws, and in flagrant violation of the most solemn pledges given during the anti-corn law agitation, the English factory lords generally reduced wages ten per cent. The resistance of the workmen was at first baffled, but, consequent upon circumstances I cannot now enter upon, the ten per cent. lost were afterwards regained.

2. The *values* of necessaries, and consequently the *value of labour*, might remain the same, but a change might occur in their *money prices*, consequent upon a previous change in the *value of money*.

By the discovery of more fertile mines and so forth, two ounces of gold might, for example, cost no more labour to produce than one ounce did before. The *value* of gold would then be depreciated by one half, or fifty per cent. As the *values* of all other commodities would then be expressed in twice their former *money prices*, so also the same with the *value of labour*. Twelve hours of labour, formerly expressed in six shillings, would now be expressed in twelve shillings. If the working man's wages should remain three shillings, instead of rising to six shillings, the *money price of his labour* would only be equal to *half the value of his labour*, and his standard of life would fearfully deteriorate. This would also happen in a greater or lesser degree if his wages should rise, but not proportionately to the fall in the value of gold. In such a case nothing would have been changed, either in the productive powers of labour, or in supply and demand, or in values. Nothing could have changed except the money *names* of those values. To say that in such a case the workman ought not to insist upon a proportionate rise of wages, is to say that he must be content to be paid with names, instead of with things. All past history proves that whenever such a depreciation of money occurs, the capitalists are on the alert to seize this opportunity for defrauding the workman. A very large school of political economists assert that, consequent upon the new discoveries of gold lands, the better working of silver mines, and the cheaper supply of quicksilver, the value of precious metals has been again depreciated. This would explain the general and simultaneous attempts on the Continent at a rise of wages.

3. We have till now supposed that the *working day* has given limits. The working day, however, has, by itself, no constant limits. It is the constant tendency of capital to stretch it to its utmost physically possible length, because in the same degree surplus labour, and consequently the profit resulting therefrom, will be increased. The more capital succeeds in prolonging the working day, the greater the amount of other peoples' labour it will appropriate. During the seventeenth and even the first two thirds of the eighteenth century a ten hours working day was the normal working day all over England. During the anti-Jacobin war, which was in fact a war waged by the British barons against the British working masses, capital celebrated its bacchanalia, and prolonged the working day from ten to twelve, fourteen, eighteen hours. Malthus, by no means a man whom you would suspect of a maudlin sentimentalism, declared in a pamphlet, published about 1815, that if this sort of thing was to go on the life of the nation would be attacked at its very source. A few years before the general introduction of the newly-invented machinery, about 1765, a pamphlet appeared in England under the title, *An Essay on Trade*. The anonymous author, an avowed enemy of the working classes, declaims on the necessity of expanding the limits of the working day. Amongst other means to this end, he proposes *working houses*, which, he says, ought to be 'Houses of

Terror'. And what is the length of the working day he prescribes for these 'Houses of Terror'? *Twelve hours*, the very same time which in 1832 was declared by capitalists, political economists, and ministers to be not only the existing but the necessary time of labour for a child under twelve years.

By selling his labouring power, and he must do so under the present system, the working man makes over to the capitalist the consumption of that power, but within certain rational limits. He sells his labouring power in order to maintain it, apart from its natural wear and tear, but not to destroy it. In selling his labouring power at its daily or weekly value, it is understood that in one day or one week that labouring power shall not be submitted to two days' or two weeks' waste or wear and tear. Take a machine worth £1,000. If it is used up in ten years it will add to the value of the commodities in whose production it assists £100 yearly. If it is used up in five years it will add £200 yearly, or the value of its annual wear and tear is in inverse ratio to the quickness with which it is consumed. But this distinguishes the working man from the machine. Machinery does not wear out exactly in the same ratio in which it is used. Man, on the contrary, decays in a greater ratio than would be visible from the mere numerical addition of work.

In their attempts at reducing the working day to its former rational dimensions, or, where they cannot enforce a legal fixation of a normal working day, at checking overwork by a rise of wages, a rise not only in proportion to the surplus time exacted, but in a greater proportion, working men fulfil only a duty to themselves and their race. They only set limits to the tyrannical usurpations of capital. Time is the room of human development. A man who has no free time to dispose of, whose whole lifetime, apart from the mere physical interruptions by sleep, meals, and so forth, is absorbed by his labour for the capitalist, is less than a beast of burden. He is a mere machine for producing Foreign Wealth, broken in body and brutalized in mind. Yet the whole history of modern industry shows that capital, if not checked, will recklessly and ruthlessly work to cast down the whole working class to this utmost state of degradation.

In prolonging the working day the capitalist may pay *higher wages* and still lower the *value of labour*, if the rise of wages does not correspond to the greater amount of labour extracted, and the quicker decay of the labouring power thus caused. This may be done in another way. Your middle-class statisticians will tell you, for instance, that the average wages of factory families in Lancashire has risen. They forget that instead of the labour of the man, the head of the family, his wife and perhaps three or four children are now thrown under the Juggernaut wheels of capital, and that the rise of the aggregate wages does not correspond to the aggregate surplus labour extracted from the family.

Even with given limits of the working day, such as they own exist in all branches of industry subjected to the factory laws, a rise of wages may become necessary, if only to keep up the old standard *value of labour*. By increasing the *intensity* of labour, a man may be made to expend as much vital force in one hour as he formally did in two. This has, to a certain degree, been effected in the trades placed under the Factory Acts by the acceleration of machinery, and the greater number of working machines which a single individual has now to superintend. If the increase in the intensity of labour or the mass of labour spent in an hour keeps some fair proportion to the decrease in the extent of the working day, the working man will still be the winner. If this limit is overshot, he loses in one form what he has gained in another, and ten hours of labour may then become as ruinous as twelve hours were before. In checking this tendency of capital, by struggling for a rise of wages corresponding to the rising intensity of labour, the working man only resists the depreciation of his labour and the deterioration of his race.

4. All of you know that, from reasons I have not now to explain, capitalistic production moves through certain periodical cycles. It moves through a state of quiescence, growing animation, prosperity, over-trade, crisis and stagnation. The market prices of commodities, and the market rates of profit, follow these phases, now sinking below their averages, now rising above them. Considering the whole cycle, you will find that one deviation of the market price is being compensated by the other, and that, taking the average of the cycle, the market prices of commodities are regulated by their values. Well! During the phases of sinking market prices and the phases of crisis and stagnation, the working man, if not thrown out of employment altogether, is sure to have

his wages lowered. Not to be defrauded, he must, even with such a fall of market prices, debate with the capitalist in what proportional degree a fall of wages has become necessary. If, during the phases of prosperity, when extra profits are made, he did not battle for a rise of wages, he would, taking the average of one industrial cycle, not even receive his *average wages* or the *value* of his labour. It is the utmost height of folly to demand that, while his wages are necessarily affected by the adverse phases of the cycle, he should exclude himself from compensation during the prosperous phases of the cycle. Generally, the *values* of all commodities are only realized by the compensation of the continuously changing market prices, springing from the continuous fluctuations of demand and supply. On the basis of the present system labour is only a commodity like others. It must, therefore, pass through the same fluctuations to fetch an average price corresponding to its value. It would be absurd to treat it on the one hand as a commodity, and to want on the other hand to exempt it from the laws which regulate the prices of commodities. The slave receives a permanent and fixed amount of maintenance; the wages labourer does not. He must try to get a rise of wages in the one instance, if only to compensate for a fall of wages in the other. If he resigned himself to accept the will, the dictates of the capitalist as a permanent economical law, he would share in all the miseries of the slave, without the security of the slave.

5. In all the cases I have considered, and they form ninety-nine out of a hundred, you have seen that a struggle for a rise of wages follows only in the track of *previous* changes, and is the necessary offspring of previous changes in the amount of production, the productive powers of labour, the value of labour, the value of money, the extent or the intensity of labour extracted, the fluctuations of market prices, dependent upon the fluctuations of demand and supply, and consistent with the different phases of the industrial cycle; in one word, as reactions of labour against the previous action of capital. By treating the struggle for a rise of wages independently of all these circumstances, by looking only upon the change of wages, and overlooking all the other changes from which they emanate, you proceed from a false premiss in order to arrive at false conclusions.

IV THE STRUGGLE BETWEEN CAPITAL AND LABOUR, AND ITS RESULTS

1. Having shown that the periodical resistance on the part of the working men against a reduction of wages, and their periodical attempts at getting a rise of wages, are inseparable from the wages system, and dictated by the very fact of labour being assimilated to commodities, and therefore subject to the laws regulating the general movement of prices; having, furthermore, shown that a general rise of wages would result in a fall in the general rate of profit, but not affect the average prices of commodities, or their values, the question now ultimately arises, how far, in this incessant struggle between capital and labour, the latter is likely to prove successful.

I might answer by a generalization, and say that, as with all other commodities, so with labour, its *market price* will, in the long run, adapt itself to its *value;* that, therefore, despite all the ups and downs, and do what he may, the working man will, on an average, only receive the value of his labour, which resolves into the value of his labouring power, which is determined by the value of the necessaries required for its maintenance and reproduction, which value of necessaries finally is regulated by the quantity of labour wanted to produce them.

But there are some peculiar features which distinguish the *value of the labouring power, or the value of labour,* from the values of all other commodities. The value of the labouring power is formed by two elements—the one merely physical, the other historical or social. Its *ultimate limit* is determined by the *physical* element, that is to say, to maintain and reproduce itself, to perpetuate its physical existence, the working class must receive the necessaries absolutely indispensable for living and multiplying. The *value* of those indispensable necessaries forms, therefore, the ulitmate limit of the *value of labour*. On the other hand, the length of the working day is also limited by ultimate, although very elastic boundaries. Its ultimate limit is given by the physical force of the labouring man. If the daily exhaustion of his vital forces exceeds a certain degree, it cannot be exerted anew, day by day. However, as I said, this limit is very elastic. A quick succession of unhealthy and short-lived generations will keep the labour market as well supplied as a series of vigorous and long-lived generations.

Besides this mere physical element, the value of labour is in every country determined by a *traditional standard of life*. It is not mere physical life, but it is the satisfaction of certain wants springing from the social conditions in which people are placed and reared. The English standard of life may be reduced to the Irish standard; the standard of life of a German peasant to that of a Livonian peasant. The important part which historical tradition and social habitude play in this respect, you many learn from Mr Thornton's work on *Over-population*, where he shows that the average wages in different agricultural districts of England still nowadays differ more or less according to the more or less favourable circumstances under which the districts have emerged from the state of serfdom.

This historical or social element, entering into the value of labour, may be expanded, or contracted, or altogether extinguished, so that nothing remains but the *physical limit*. During the time of the anti-Jacobin war, undertaken, as the incorrigible taxeater and sinecurist, old George Rose, used to say, to save the comforts of our holy religion from the inroads of the French infidels, the honest English farmers, so tenderly handled in a former chapter of ours, depressed the wages of the agricultural labourers even beneath that *mere physical minimum*, but made up by Poor Laws the remainder necessary for the physical perpetuation of the race. This was a glorious way to convert the wages labourer into a slave, and Shakespeare's proud yeoman into a pauper.

By comparing the standard wages or values of labour in different countries, and by comparing them in different historical epochs of the same country, you will find that the *value of labour* itself is not a fixed but a variable magnitude, even supposing the values of all other commodities to remain constant.

A similar comparison would prove that not only the *market rates* of profit change, but its *average* rates.

But as to *profits*, there exists no law which determines their *minimum*. We cannot say what is the ultimate limit of their decrease. And why cannot we fix that limit? Because, although we can fix the *minimum* of wages, we cannot fix their *maximum*.

We can only say that, the limits of the working day being given, the *maximum of profit* corresponds to the *physical minimum of wages;* and that wages being given, the *maximum of profit* corresponds to such a prolongation of the working day as is compatible with the physical forces of the labourer. The maximum of profit is therefore limited by the physical minimum of wages and the physical maximum of the working day. It is evident that between the two limits of this *maximum rate of profit* an immense scale of variations is possible. The fixation of its actual degree is only settled by the continuous struggle between capital and labour, the capitalist constantly tending to reduce wages to their physical minimum, and to extend the working day to its physical maximum, while the working man constantly presses in the opposite direction.

The matter resolves itself into a question of the respective powers of the combatants.

2. As to the *limitation of the working day* in England, as in all other countries, it has never been settled except by *legislative interference*. Without the working men's continuous pressure from without that interference would never have taken place. But at all events, the result was not to be attained by private settlement between the working men and the capitalists. This very necessity of *general political action* affords the proof that in its merely economical action capital is the stronger side.

As to the *limits* of the *value of labour*, its actual settlement always depends upon supply and demand, I mean the demand for labour on the part of capital, and the supply of labour by the working men. In colonial countries the law of supply and demand favours the working man. Hence the relatively high standard of wages in the United States. Capital may there try its utmost. It cannot prevent the labour market from being continuously emptied by the continuous conversion of wages labourers into independent, self-sustaining peasants. The position of a wages labourer is for a very large part of the American people but a probational state, which they are sure to leave within a longer or shorter term. To mend this colonial state of things, the paternal British Government accepted for some time what is called the modern colonization theory, which consists in putting an artificial high price upon colonial land, in order to prevent the too quick conversion of the wages labourer into the independent peasant.

But let us now come to old civilized countries, in which capital domineers over the whole process of production. Take, for example, the rise in England of agricultural wages from 1849 to 1859. What was its consequence? The farmers could not, as our friend Weston would have advised them, raise the value of wheat, nor even its market prices. They had, on the contrary, to submit to their fall. But during these eleven years they introduced machinery of all sorts, adopted more scientific methods, converted part of arable land into pasture, increased the size of farms, and with this the scale of production, and by these and other processes diminishing the demand for labour by increasing its productive power, made the agricultural population again relatively redundant. This is the general method in which a reaction, quicker or slower, of capital against a rise of wages takes place in old, settled countries. Ricardo has justly remarked that machinery is in constant competition with labour, and can often be only introduced when the price of labour has reached a certain height, but the appliance of machinery is but one of the many methods for increasing the productive powers of labour. This very same development which makes common labour relatively redundant simplifies, on the other hand, skilled labour, amd thus depreciates it.

The same law obtains in another form. With the development of the productive powers of labour the accumulation of capital will be accelerated, even despite a relatively high rate of wages. Hence, one might infer, as Adam Smith, in whose days modern industry was still in its infancy, did infer, that the accelerated accumulation of capital must turn the balance in favour of the working man, by securing a growing demand for his labour. From this same standpoint many contemporary writers have wondered that English capital having grown in the last twenty years so much quicker than English population, wages should not have been more enhanced. But simultaneously with the progress of accumulation there takes place a *progressive change in the composition of capital*. That part of the aggregate capital which consists of fixed capital, machinery, raw materials, means of production in all possible forms, progressively increases as compared with the other part of capital, which is laid out in wages or in the purchase of labour. This law has been stated in a more or less accurate manner by Mr Barton, Ricardo, Sismondi, Professor Richard Jones, Professor Ramsey, Cherbulliez, and others.

If the proportion of these two elements of capital was originally one to one, it will, in the progress of industry, become five to one, and so forth. If of a total capital of 600, 300 is laid out in instruments, raw materials, and so forth, and 300 in wages, the total capital wants only to be doubled to create a demand for 600 working men instead of for 300. But if of a capital of 600, 500 is laid out in machinery, materials, and so forth, and 100 only in wages, the same capital must increase from 600 to 3,600 in order to create a demand for 600 workmen instead of 300. In the progress of industry the demand for labour keeps, therefore, no pace with the accumulation of capital. It will still increase, but increase in a constantly diminishing ratio as compared with the increase of capital.

These few hints will suffice to show that the very development of modern industry must progressively turn the scale in favour of the capitalist against the working man, and that consequently the general tendency of capitalistic production is not to raise, but to sink the average standard of wages, or to push the *value of labour* more or less to its *minimum limit*. Such being the tendency of *things* in this system, is this saying that the working class ought to renounce their resistance against the encroachments of capital, and abandon their attempts at making the best of the occasional chances for their temporary improvement? If they did, they would be degraded to one level mass of broken wretches past salvation. I think I have shown that their struggles for the standard of wages are incidents inseparable from the whole wages system, that in 99 cases out of 100 their efforts at raising wages are only efforts at maintaining the given value of labour, and that the necessity of debating their price with the capitalist is inherent to their condition of having to sell themselves as commodities. By cowardly giving way in their every-day conflict with capital, they would certainly disqualify themselves for the initiating of any larger movement.

At the same time, and quite apart from the general servitude involved in the wages system, the working class ought not to exaggerate to themselves the ultimate working of these every-day struggles. They ought not to forget that they are fighting with effects, but not with the cause of those effects; that they are retarding the downward movement, but not changing its direction; that they are applying palliatives, not curing the malady. They ought, therefore, not to be exclusively absorbed in these unavoidable guerilla fights incessantly springing up from the ever-ceasing encroachments of capital or changes of the market. They ought to understand that, with all the miseries it imposes upon them, the present system simultaneously engenders the *material conditions* and the *social forms* necessary for an economical reconstruction of society. Instead of the *conservative* motto, '*A fair day's wages for a fair day's work!*' they ought to inscribe on their banner the *revolutionary* watchword, '*Abolition of the wages system!*'

After this very long and, I fear, tedious exposition, which I was obliged to enter into to do some justice to the subject-matter, I shall conclude by proposing the following resolutions:—

Firstly. A general rise in the rate of wages would result in a fall of the general rate of profit, but, broadly speaking, not affect the prices of commodities.

Secondly. The general tendency of capitalist production is not to raise, but to sink the average standard of wages.

Thirdly. Trade Unions work well as centres of resistance against the encroachments of capital. They fail partially from an injudicious use of their power. They fail generally from limiting themselves to a guerilla war against the effects of the existing system, instead of simultaneously trying to change it, instead of using their organized forces as a lever for the final emancipation of the working class, that is to say, the ultimate abolition of the wages system.

SOCIALISM
UTOPIAN AND SCIENTIFIC

FRIEDRICH ENGELS

Translated by
Edward Aveling

Friedrich Engels, the son of a wealthy cotton-spinner, was born in 1820, at Barmen in the industrial area of the Rhineland. Though intended for commerce, he had a classical education and during his apprenticeship and military service he studied philosophy and mixed with radicals. He came to Manchester, where his father had a factory, in 1842, and became familiar with English conditions, with Chartism and the work of Robert Owen. He first met Marx in Paris in 1844, and found that their ideas coincided completely. From then on he devoted himself to their joint work. He died in 1895 and his ashes were scattered at sea.

In hammering out their ideas Marx and Engels were fighting, amongst other things, the sentimental idealism of much socialist thinking, especially of the German theorists. In 1875 Dr Dühring, a university professor, celebrated his conversion to socialism by bringing out a huge work in three volumes. Engels replied to it in a series of articles, later gathered into a book, from which three chapters were issued as the following pamphlet. It became one of the most widely read works on socialism.

It first appeared in English, translated by Dr Edward Aveling, in 1892, since when it has been reprinted ten times.

Socialism: Utopian and Scientific

I

MODERN Socialism is, in its essence, the direct product of the recognition, on the one hand, of the class antagonisms, existing in the society of today, between proprietors and non-proprietors, between capitalists and wage-workers; on the other hand, of the anarchy existing in production. But, in its theoretical form, modern Socialism originally appears ostensibly as a more logical extension of the principles laid down by the great French philosophers of the eighteenth century. Like every new theory, modern Socialism had, at first, to connect itself with the intellectual stock-in-trade ready to its hand, however deeply its roots lay in material economic facts.

The great men, who in France prepared men's minds for the coming revolution, were themselves extreme revolutionists. They recognized no external authority of any kind whatever. Religion, natural science, society, political institutions, everything, was subjected to the most unsparing criticism: everything must justify its existence before the judgment-seat of reason, or give up existence. Reason became the sole measure of everything. It was the time when, as Hegel says, the world stood upon its head;[1] first, in the sense that the human head, and the principles

[1] This is the passage on the French Revolution: 'Thought, the concept of law, all at once made itself felt, and against this the old scaffolding of wrong could make no stand. In this conception of law, therefore, a constitution has now been established, and henceforth everything must be based on this. Since the sun had been in the firmament, and the planets circled round him, the sight had never been seen of man standing upon his head—i.e. on the Idea—and building reality after this image. Anaxagoras first said that the Nous, reason, rules the world; but now, for the first time, had man come to recognize that the Idea must rule the mental reality. And this was a magnificent sunrise. All thinking Beings have participated in celebrating this holy day. A sublime emotion swayed men at that time, an enthusiasm of reason pervaded the world, as if now had come the

arrived at by its thought, claimed to be the basis of all human action and association; but by and by, also, in the wider sense that the reality which was in contradiction to these principles had, in fact, to be turned upside down. Every form of society and government then existing, every old traditional notion was flung into the lumber-room as irrational; the world had hitherto allowed itself to be led solely by prejudices; everything in the past deserved only pity and contempt. Now, for the first time, appeared the light of day, the kingdom of reason; henceforth superstition, injustice, privilege, oppression, were to be super-seded by eternal truth, eternal Right, equality based on Nature and the inalienable rights of man.

We know today that this kingdom of reason was nothing more than the idealized kingdom of the bourgeoisie; that this eternal Right found its realization in bourgeois justice; that this equality reduced itself to bourgeois equality before the law; that bour-geois property was proclaimed as one of the essential rights of man; and that the government of reason, the Contrat Social of Rousseau, came into being, and only could come into being, as a democratic bourgeois republic. The great thinkers of the eighteenth century could, no more than their predecessors, go beyond the limits imposed upon them by their epoch.

But, side by side with the antagonism of the feudal nobility and the burghers, who claimed to represent all the rest of society, was the general antagonism of exploiters and exploited, of rich idlers and poor workers. It was this very circumstance that made it possible for the representatives of the bourgeoisie to put them-selves forward as representing, not one special class, but the whole of suffering humanity. Still further. From its origin, the bourgeoisie was saddled with its antithesis: capitalists cannot exist without wage-workers, and, in the same proportion as the mediaeval burgher of the guild developed into the modern bour-geois, the guild journeyman and the day-labourer, outside the guilds, developed into the proletarian. And although, upon the whole, the bourgeoisie, in their struggle with the nobility, could

reconciliation of the Divine Principle with the world.' (Hegel: *Philo-sophy of History*, 1840, p. 535.) Is it not high time to set the anti-Socialist law in action against such teachings, subversive and to the common danger, by the late Professor Hegel?

claim to represent at the same time the interests of the different working-classes of that period, yet in every great bourgeois movement there were independent outbursts of that class which was the forerunner, more or less developed, of the modern proletariat. For example, at the time of the German reformation and the peasants' war, the Anabaptists and Thomas Münzer; in the great English revolution, the Levellers; in the great French revolution, Baboeuf.

There were theoretical enunciations corresponding with these revolutionary uprisings of a class not yet developed; in the sixteenth and seventeenth centuries, Utopian pictures of ideal social conditions; in the eighteenth, actual communistic theories (Morelly and Mably). The demand for equality was no longer limited to political rights; it was extended also to the social conditions of individuals. It was not simply class privileges that were to be abolished, but class distinctions themselves. A Communism, ascetic, denouncing all the pleasures of life, Spartan, was the first form of the new teaching. Then came the three great Utopians: Saint Simon, to whom the middle-class movement, side by side with the proletarian, still had a certain significance; Fourier; and Owen, who in the country where capitalist production was most developed, and under the influence of the antagonisms begotten of this, worked out his proposals for the removal of class distinction systematically and in direct relation to French materialism.

One thing is common to all three. Not one of them appears as a representative of the interests of that proletariat which historical development had, in the meantime, produced. Like the French philosophers, they do not claim to emancipate a particular class to begin with, but all humanity at once. Like them, they wish to bring in the kingdom of reason and eternal justice, but this kingdom, as they see it, is as far as heaven from earth, from that of the French philosophers.

For, to our three social reformers, the bourgeois world, based upon the principles of these philosophers, is quite as irrational and unjust, and, therefore, finds its way to the dust-hole quite as readily as feudalism and all the earlier stages of society. If pure reason and justice have not, hitherto, ruled the world, this has been the case only because men have not rightly understood them. What was wanted was the individual man of genius, who has now arisen and who understands the truth. That he has now arisen, that the truth has now been clearly understood, is not an inevitable event, following of necessity in the chain of historical development, but a mere happy accident. He might just as well have been born 500 years earlier, and might then have spared humanity 500 years of error, strife, and suffering.

We saw how the French philosophers of the eighteenth century, the forerunners of the Revolution, appealed to reason as the sole judge of all that is. A rational government, rational society, were to be founded; everything that ran counter to eternal reason was to be remorselessly done away with. We saw also that this eternal reason was in reality nothing but the idealized understanding of the eighteenth century citizen, just then evolving into the bourgeois. The French Revolution had realized this rational society and government.

But the new order of things, rational enough as compared with earlier conditions, turned out to be by no means absolutely rational. The State based upon reason completely collapsed. Rousseau's Contrat Social had found its realization in the Reign of Terror, from which the bourgeoisie, who had lost confidence in their own political capacity, had taken refuge first in the corruption of the Directorate, and, finally, under the wing of the Napoleonic despotism. The promised eternal peace was turned into an endless war of conquest. The society based upon reason had fared no better. The antagonism between rich and poor, instead of dissolving into general prosperity, had become intensified by the removal of the guild and other privileges, which had to some extent bridged it over, and by the removal of the charitable institutions of the Church. The 'freedom of property' from feudal fetters, now veritably accomplished, turned out to be, for the small capitalists and small proprietors, the freedom to sell their small property, crushed under the overmastering competition of the large capitalists and landlords, to these great lords, and thus, as far as the small capitalists and peasant proprietors were concerned, became 'freedom *from* property'. The development of industry upon a capitalistic basis made poverty and misery of the working masses conditions of existence of society. Cash payment became more and more, in Carlyle's phrase, the sole nexus between man and man. The number of crimes increased from year to year. Formerly, the feudal vices had openly stalked about in broad daylight; though not eradicated, they were now at any rate thrust into the background. In their stead, the bourgeois vices, hitherto practised in secret, began to blossom all the more luxuriantly. Trade became to a greater and greater extent cheating. The 'fraternity' of the revolutionary motto was realized in the chicanery and rivalries of the battle of competition. Oppression by force was replaced by corruption; the sword, as the first social lever, by gold. The right of the first night was transferred from the feudal lords to the bourgeois manufacturers. Prostitution increased to an extent never heard of. Marriage itself remained, as before, the legally recognized form, the official cloak of prostitution, and, moreover, was supplemented by rich crops of adultery.

In a word, compared with the splendid promises of the philosophers, the social and political institutions born of the 'triumph of reason' were bitterly disappointing caricatures. All that was wanting was the men to formulate this disappointment, and they came with the turn of the century. In 1802 Saint Simon's Geneva letters appeared; in 1808 appeared Fourier's first work, although the groundwork of his theory dated from 1799; on January 1, 1800, Robert Owen undertook the direction of New Lanark.

At this time, however, the capitalist mode of production, and with it the antagonism between the bourgeoisie and the proletariat, was still very incompletely developed. Modern Industry, which had just arisen in England, was still unknown in France. But Modern Industry develops, on the one hand, the conflicts which make absolutely necessary a revolution in the mode of production, and the doing away with its capitalistic character—conflicts not only between the classes begotten of it, but also between the very productive forces and the forms of exchange created by it. And, on the other hand, it develops, in these very gigantic productive forces, the means of ending these conflicts. If, therefore, about the year 1800, the conflicts arising from the new social order were only just beginning to take shape, this holds still more fully as to the means of ending them. The 'have-nothing' masses of Paris, during the Reign of Terror, were able for a moment to gain the mastery, and thus to lead the bourgeois revolution to victory in spite of the bourgeoisie themselves. But, in doing so, they only proved how impossible it was for their domination to last under the conditions then obtaining. The proletariat, which then for the first time evolved itself from these 'have-nothing' masses as the nucleus of a new class, as yet quite incapable of independent political action, appeared as an oppressed, suffering order, to whom, in its incapacity to help itself, help could, at best, be brought in from without, or down from above.

This historical situation also dominated the founders of Socialism. To the crude conditions of capitalistic production and the crude class conditions corresponded crude theories. The solution of the social problems, which as yet lay hidden in undeveloped economic conditions, the Utopians attempted to evolve out of the human brain. Society presented nothing but wrongs; to remove these was the task of reason. It was necessary, then, to discover a new and more perfect system of social order and to impose this upon society from without by propaganda, and, wherever it was possible, by the example of model experiments. These new social systems were foredoomed as Utopian; the more completely they were worked out in detail, the more they could not avoid drifting off into pure phantasies.

These facts once established, we need not dwell a moment longer upon this side of the question, now wholly belonging to the past. We can leave it to the literary small fry to solemnly quibble over these phantasies, which today only make us smile, and to crow over the superiority of their own bald reasoning, as compared with such 'insanity'. For ourselves, we delight in the stupendously grand thoughts and germs of thought that everywhere break out through their phantastic covering, and to which these Philistines are blind.

Saint Simon was a son of the great French Revolution, at the outbreak of which he was not yet thirty. The Revolution was the victory of the third estate, i.e. of the great masses of the nation, *working* in production and in trade, over the privileged *idle* classes, the nobles and the priests. But the victory of the third estate soon revealed itself as exclusively the victory of a small part of this 'estate', as the conquest of political power by the socially privileged section of it, i.e. the propertied bourgeoisie.

And the bourgeoisie had certainly developed rapidly during the Revolution, partly by speculation in the lands of the nobility and of the Church, confiscated and afterwards put up for sale, and partly by frauds upon the nation by means of army contracts. It was the domination of these swindlers that, under the Directorate, brought France to the verge of ruin, and thus gave Napoleon the pretext for his *coup-d'état*.

Hence, to Saint Simon the antagonism between the third estate and the privileged classes took the form of an antagonism between 'workers' and 'idlers'. The idlers were not merely the old privileged classes, but also all who, without taking any part in production or distribution, lived on their incomes. And the workers were not only the wage-workers, but also the manufacturers, the merchants, the bankers. That the idlers had lost the capacity for intellectual leadership and political supremacy had been proved, and was by the Revolution finally settled. That the non-possessing classes had not this capacity seemed to Saint Simon proved by the experiences of the Reign of Terror. Then, who was to lead and command? According to Saint Simon, science and industry, both united by a new religious bond, destined to restore that unity of religious ideas which had been lost since the time of the Reformation—a necessarily mystic and rigidly hierarchic 'new Christianity'. But science, that was the scholars; and industry, that was, in the first place, the working bourgeois, manufacturers, merchants, bankers. These bourgeoisie were, certainly, intended by Saint Simon to transform themselves into a kind of public officials, of social trustees; but they were still to hold, *vis-à-vis* of the workers, a commanding and economically privileged position. The bankers especially were to be called upon to direct the whole of social production by the regulation of credit. This conception was in exact keeping with a time in which Modern Industry in France and, with it, the chasm between bourgeoisie and proletariat was only just coming into existence. But what Saint Simon especially lays stress upon is this: what interests him first, and above all other things, is the lot of the class that is the most numerous and the most poor ('*la classe la plus nombreuse et la plus pauvre*').

Already, in his Geneva letters, Saint Simon lays down the proposition that 'all men ought to work'. In the same work he recognizes also that the Reign of Terror was the reign of the non-possessing masses. 'See,' says he to them, 'what happened in France at the time when your comrades held sway there; they brought about a famine.' But to recognize the French Revolution as a class war, and not simply one between nobility and bourgeoisie, but between nobility, bourgeoisie, and the non-possessors, was, in the year 1802, a most pregnant discovery. In 1816, he declares that politics is the science of production, and foretells the complete absorption of politics by economics. The knowledge that economic conditions are the basis of political institutions appears here only in embryo. Yet what is here already very plainly expressed is the idea of the future conversion of political rule over men into an administration of things and a direction of processes of production—that is to say, the 'abolition of the State', about which recently there has been so much noise.

Saint Simon shows the same superiority over his contemporaries, when in 1814, immediately after the entry of the allies into Paris, and again in 1815, during the Hundred Days' War, he proclaims the alliance of France with England, and then of both these countries with Germany, as the only guarantee for the prosperous development and peace of Europe. To preach to the French in 1815 an alliance with the victors of Waterloo required as much courage as historical foresight.

If in Saint Simon we find a comprehensive breadth of view, by virtue of which almost all the ideas of later Socialists, that are not strictly economic, are found in him in embryo, we find in Fourier a criticism of the existing conditions of society, genuinely French and witty, but not upon that account any the less thorough. Fourier takes the bourgeoisie, their inspired prophets before the Revolution, and their interested eulogists after it, at their own word. He lays bare remorselessly the material and moral misery of the bourgeois world. He confronts it with the earlier philosophers' dazzling promises of a society in which reason alone should reign, of a civilization in which happiness should be universal, of an illimitable human perfectibility, and with the rose-coloured phraseology of the bourgeois ideologists of his time. He points out how everywhere the most pitiful reality corresponds with the most high-sounding phrases, and he overwhelms this hopeless fiasco of phrases with his mordant sarcasm.

Fourier is not only a critic; his imperturbably serene nature makes him a satirist, and assuredly one of the greatest satirists of all time. He depicts, with equal power and charm, the swindling speculations that blossomed out upon the downfall of the Revolution, and the shopkeeping spirit prevalent in, and characteristic of, French commerce at that time. Still more masterly is his criticism of the bourgeois form of the relations between the sexes, and the position of woman in bourgeois society. He was the first to declare that in any given society the degree of woman's emancipation is the natural measure of the general emancipation.

But Fourier is at his greatest in his conception of the history of society. He divides its whole course, thus far, into four stages of evolution—savagery, barbarism, the patriarchate, civilization. This last is identical with the so-called civil, or bourgeois, society of today—i.e. with the social order that came in with the sixteenth century. He proves 'that the civilized stage raises every vice practised by barbarism in a simple fashion, into a form of existence, complex, ambiguous, equivocal, hypocritical'—that civilization moves in 'a vicious circle', in contradictions which it constantly reproduces without being able to solve them; hence it constantly arrives at the very opposite to that which it wants to attain, or pretends to want to attain, so that, e.g. 'under civilization poverty is born of superabundance itself'.

Fourier, as we see, uses the dialectic method in the same masterly way as his contemporary, Hegel. Using these same dialectics, he argues, against the talk about illimitable human perfectibility, that every historical phase has its period of ascent and also its period of descent, and he applies this observation to the future of the whole human race. As Kant introduced into natural science the idea of the ultimate destruction of the earth, Fourier introduced into historical science that of the ultimate destruction of the human race.

Whilst in France the hurricane of the Revolution swept over the land, in England a quieter, but not on that account less tremendous, revolution was going on. Steam and the new tool-making machinery were transforming manufacture into modern industry, and thus revolutionizing the whole foundation of bourgeois society. The sluggish march of development of the manufacturing period changed into a veritable storm and stress period of production. With constantly increasing swiftness the splitting-up of society into large capitalists and non-possessing proletarians went on. Between these, instead of the former stable middle-class, an unstable mass of artisans and small shopkeepers, the most fluctuating portion of the population, now led a precarious existence.

The new mode of production was, as yet, only at the beginning of its period of ascent; as yet it was the normal, regular method of production—the only one possible under existing conditions. Nevertheless, even then it was producing crying social abuses—the herding together of a homeless population in the worst quarters of the large towns; the loosening of all traditional moral bonds, of patriarchal subordination, of family relations; over-work, especially of women and children, to a frightful extent; complete demoralization of the working-class, suddenly flung into altogether new conditions, from the country into the town, from agriculture into modern industry, from stable conditions of existence into insecure ones that changed from day to day.

At this juncture there came forward as a reformer a manu-facturer twenty-nine years old—a man of almost sublime, childlike simplicity of character, and at the same time one of the few born leaders of men. Robert Owen had adopted the teaching of the materialistic philosophers: that man's character is the product, on the one hand, of heredity, on the other, of the environment of the individual during his lifetime, and especially during his period of development. In the industrial revolution most of his class saw only chaos and confusion, and the opportunity of fishing in these troubled waters and making large fortunes quickly. He saw in it the opportunity of putting into practice his favourite theory, and so of bringing order out of chaos. He had already tried it with success, as superintendent of more than 500 men in a Manchester factory. From 1800 to 1829, he directed the great cotton mill at New Lanark, in Scotland, as managing partner, along the same lines, but with greater freedom of action and with a success that made him a European reputation. A population, originally consisting of the most diverse and, for the most part, very demoralised elements, a population that gradually grew to 2,500, he turned into a model colony, in which drunkenness, police, magistrates, lawsuits, poor laws, charity, were unknown. And all this simply by placing the people in conditions worthy of human beings, and especially by carefully bringing up the rising generation. He was the founder of infant schools, and introduced them first at New Lanark. At the age of two the children came to school, where they enjoyed themselves so much that they could scarcely be got home again. Whilst his competitors worked their people thirteen or fourteen hours a day, in New Lanark the working-day was only ten and a half hours. When a crisis in cotton stopped work for four months, his workers received their full wages all the time. And with all this the business more than doubled in value, and to the last yielded large profits to its proprietors.

In spite of all this, Owen was not content. The existence which he secured for his workers was, in his eyes, still far from being worthy of human beings. 'The people were slaves at my mercy.' The relatively favourable conditions in which he had placed them were still far from allowing a rational development of the character and of the intellect in all directions, much less of the free exercise of all their faculties. 'And yet, the working part of this population of 2,500 persons was daily producing as much real wealth for society as, less than half a century before, it would have required the working part of a population of 600,000 to create. I asked myself, what became of the difference between the wealth consumed by 2,500 persons and that which would have been consumed by 600,000 ?'[1]

The answer was clear. It had been used to pay the proprietors of the establishment five per cent. on the capital they had laid out, in addition to over £300,000 clear profit. And that which held for New Lanark held to a still greater extent for all the factories in England. 'If this new wealth had not been created by machinery, imperfectly as it has been applied, the wars of Europe, in opposition to Napoleon, and to support the aristocratic principles of society, could not have been maintained. And yet this new power was the creation of the working-classes.'[2] To them, therefore, the fruits of this new power belonged. The newly-created gigantic

[1] From *The Revolution in Mind and Practice*, p. 21, a memorial addressed to all the 'red Republicans, Communists and Socialists of Europe', and sent to the provisional government of France, 1848, and also 'to Queen Victoria and her responsible advisers'.

[2] Note, l. c., p. 22.

productive forces, hitherto used only to enrich individuals and to enslave the masses, offered to Owen the foundations for a reconstruction of society; they were destined, as the common property of all, to be worked for the common good of all.

Owen's Communism was based upon this purely business foundation, the outcome, so to say, of commercial calculation. Throughout, it maintained this practical character. Thus, in 1823, Owen proposed the relief of the distress in Ireland by Communist colonies, and drew up complete estimates of costs of founding them, yearly expenditure, and probable revenue. And in his definite plan for the future, the technical working out of details is managed with such practical knowledge—ground plan, front and side and bird's-eye views all included—that the Owen method of social reform once accepted, there is from the practical point of view little to be said against the actual arrangement of details.

His advance in the direction of Communism was the turning-point in Owen's life. As long as he was simply a philanthropist, he was rewarded with nothing but wealth, applause, honour, and glory. He was the most popular man in Europe. Not only men of his own class, but statesmen and princes listened to him approvingly. But when he came out with his Communist theories, that was quite another thing. Three great obstacles seemed to him especially to block the path to social reform: private property, religion, the present form of marriage. He knew what confronted him if he attacked these—outlawry, excommunication from official society, the loss of his whole social position. But nothing of this prevented him from attacking them without fear of consequences, and what he had foreseen happened. Banished from official society, with a conspiracy of silence against him in the press, ruined by his unsuccessful Communist experiments in America, in which he sacrificed all his fortune, he turned directly to the working-class and continued working in their midst for thirty years. Every social movement, every real advance in England on behalf of the workers links itself on to the name of Robert Owen. He forced through in 1819, after five years' fighting, the first law limiting the hours of labour of women and children in factories. He was president of the first Congress at which all the Trade Unions of England united in a single great trade association. He introduced as transition measures to the complete communistic organization of society, on the one hand, co-operative societies for retail trade and production. These have since that time, at least, given practical proof that the merchant and the manufacturer are socially quite unnecessary. On the other hand, he introduced labour bazaars for the exchange of the products of labour through the medium of labour-notes, whose unit was a single hour of work; institutions necessarily doomed to failure, but completely anticipating Proudhon's bank of exchange of a much later period, and differing entirely from this in that it did not claim to be the panacea for all social ills, but only a first step towards a much more radical revolution of society.

The Utopians' mode of thought has for a long time governed the socialist ideas of the nineteenth century, and still governs some of them. Until very recently all French and English Socialists did homage to it. The earlier German Communism, including that of Weitling, was of the same school. To all these Socialism is the expression of absolute truth, reason, and justice, and has only to be discovered to conquer all the world by virtue of its own power. And as absolute truth is independent of time, space, and of the historical development of man, it is a mere accident when and where it is discovered. With all this, absolute truth, reason, and justice are different with the founder of each different school. And as each one's special kind of absolute truth, reason, and justice is again conditioned by his subjective understanding, his conditions of existence, the measure of his knowledge and his intellectual training, there is no other ending possible in this conflict of absolute truths than that they shall be mutually exclusive one of the other. Hence, from this nothing could come but a kind of eclectic, average Socialism, which, as a matter of fact, has up to the present time dominated the minds of most of the socialist workers in France and England. Hence, a mish-mash allowing of the most manifold shades of opinion; a mish-mash of such critical statements, economic theories, pictures of future society by the founders of different sects, as excite a minimum of opposition; a mish-mash which is the more easily brewed the more the definite sharp edges of the individual constituents are rubbed down in the stream of debate, like rounded pebbles in a brook.

To make a science of Socialism, it had first to be placed upon a real basis.

II

In the meantime, along with and after the French philosophy of the eighteenth century had arisen the new German philosophy, culminating in Hegel. Its greatest merit was the taking up again of dialectics as the highest form of reasoning. The old Greek philosophers were all born natural dialecticians, and Aristotle, the most encyclopaedic intellect of them, had already analysed the most essential forms of dialectic thought. The newer philosophy, on the other hand, although in it also dialectics had brilliant exponents (e.g. Descartes and Spinoza), had, especially through English influence, become more and more rigidly fixed in the so-called metaphysical mode of reasoning, by which also the French of the eighteenth century were almost wholly dominated, at all events in their special philosophical work. Outside philosophy in the restricted sense, the French nevertheless produced masterpieces of dialectic. We need only call to mind Diderot's *Le Neveu de Rameau*, and Rousseau's *Discours sur l'origine et les fondements de l'inégalité parmi les hommes*. We give here, in brief, the essential character of these two modes of thought.

When we consider and reflect upon nature at large, or the history of mankind, or our own intellectual activity, at first we see the picture of an endless entanglement of relations and reactions, permutations and combinations, in which nothing remains what, where, and as it was, but everything moves, changes, comes into being and passes away. We see, therefore, at first the picture as a whole, with its individual arts still more or less kept in the background; we observe the movements, transitions, connections, rather than the things that move, combine, and are connected. This primitive, naïve, but intrinsically correct conception of the world is that of ancient Greek philosophy, and was first clearly formulated by Heraclitus: everything is and is not, for everything is fluid, is constantly changing, constantly coming into being and passing away.

But this conception, correctly as it expresses the general character of the picture of appearances as a whole, does not suffice to explain the details of which this picture is made up, and so long as we do not understand these, we have not a clear idea of the whole picture. In order to understand these details we must detach them from their natural or historical connection and examine each one separately, its nature, special causes, effects, etc. This is, primarily, the task of natural science and historical research; branches of science which the Greeks of classical times, on very good grounds, relegated to a subordinate position, because they had first of all to collect materials for these sciences to work upon. A certain amount of natural and historical material must be collected before there can be any critical analysis, comparison, and arrangement in classes, orders, and species. The foundations of the exact natural sciences were, therefore, first worked out by the Greeks of the Alexandrian period, and later on, in the Middle Ages, by the Arabs. Real natural science dates from the second half of the fifteenth century, and thence onward it has advanced with constantly increasing rapidity. The analysis of Nature into its individual parts, the grouping of the different natural processes and objects in definite classes, the study of the internal anatomy of organized bodies in their manifold forms—these were the fundamental conditions of the gigantic strides in our knowledge of Nature that have been made during the last 400 years. But this method of work has also left us as legacy the habit of observing natural objects and processes in isolation, apart from their connection with the vast whole; of observing them in repose, not in motion; as constants, not as essentially variables; in their death, not in their life. And when this way of looking at things was transferred by Bacon and Locke from natural science to philosophy, it begot the narrow, metaphysical mode of thought peculiar to the last century.

To the metaphysician, things and their mental reflexes, ideas, are isolated, are to be considered one after the other and apart from each other, are objects of investigation fixed, rigid, given once for all. He thinks in absolutely irreconcilable antitheses. 'His communication is "yea, yea; nay, nay;" for whatsoever is more than these cometh of evil.' For him a thing either exists or does not exist; a thing cannot at the same time be itself and something else. Positive and negative absolutely exclude one another; cause and effect stand in a rigid antithesis one to the other.

At first sight this mode of thinking seems to us very luminous, because it is that of so-called sound commonsense. Only sound commonsense, respectable fellow that he is, in the homely realm of his own four walls, has very wonderful adventures directly he ventures out into the wide world of research. And the metaphysical mode of thought, justifiable and necessary as it is in a number of domains whose extent varies according to the nature of the particular object of investigation, sooner or later reaches a limit, beyond which it becomes one-sided, restricted, abstract, lost in insoluble contradictions. In the contemplation of individual things, it forgets the connection between them; in the contemplation of their existence, it forgets the beginning and end of that existence; of their repose, it forgets their motion. It cannot see the wood for the trees.

For everyday purposes we know and can say, e.g. whether an animal is alive or not. But, upon closer inquiry, we find that this is, in many cases, a very complex question, as the jurists know very well. They have cudgelled their brains in vain to discover a rational limit beyond which the killing of the child in its mother's womb is murder. It is just as impossible to determine absolutely the moment of death, for physiology proves that death in not an instantaneous, momentary phenomenon, but a very protracted process.

In like manner, every organized being is every moment the same and not the same, every moment it assimilates matter supplied from without, and gets rid of other matter; every moment some cells of its body die and others build themselves anew; in a longer or shorter time the matter of its body is completely renewed, and is replaced by other molecules of matter, so that every organized being is always itself, and yet something other than itself.

Further, we find upon closer investigation that the two poles of an antithesis, positive and negative, e.g., are as inseparable as they are opposed, and that despite all their opposition, they mutually interpenetrate. And we find, in like manner, that cause and effect are conceptions which only hold good in their application to individual cases; but as soon as we consider the individual cases in their general connection with the universe as a whole, they run into each other, and they become confounded when we contemplate that universal action and reaction in which causes and effects are eternally changing places, so that what is effect here and now will be cause there and then, and *vice versâ*.

None of these processes and modes of thought enters into the framework of metaphysical reasoning. Dialectics, on the other hand, comprehends things and their representations, ideas, in their essential connection, concatenation, motion, origin, and ending. Such processes as those mentioned above are, therefore, so many corroborations of its own method of procedure.

Nature is the proof of dialectics, and it must be said for modern science that it has furnished this proof with very rich materials increasing daily, and thus has shown that, in the last resort, Nature works dialectically and not metaphysically; that she does not move in the eternal oneness of a perpetually recurring circle, but goes through a real historical evolution. In this connection Darwin must be named before all others. He dealt the metaphysical conception of Nature the heaviest blow by his proof that all organic beings, plants, animals, and man himself, are the products of a process of evolution going on through millions of years. But the naturalists who have learned to think dialectically are few and far between, and this conflict of the results of discovery with preconceived modes of thinking explains the endless confusion now reigning in theoretical natural science, the despair of teachers as well as learners, of authors and readers alike.

An exact representation of the universe, of its evolution, of the development of mankind, and of the reflection of this evolution in the minds of men, can therefore only be obtained by the methods of dialectics with its constant regard to the innumerable actions and reactions of life and death, of progressive or retrogressive changes. And in this spirit the new German philosophy has worked. Kant began his career by resolving the stable solar system of Newton and its eternal duration, after the famous initial impulse had once been given, into the result of a historic process, the formation of the sun and all the planets out of a rotating nebulous mass. From this he at the same time drew the conclusion that, given this origin of the solar system, its future death followed of necessity. His theory half a century later was established mathematically by Laplace, and half a century after that the spectroscope proved the existence in space of such incandescent masses of gas in various stages of condensation.

This new German philosophy culminated in the Hegelian system. In this system—and herein is its great merit—for the first time the whole world, natural, historical, intellectual, is represented as a process, i.e. as in constant motion, change, transformation, development; and the attempt is made to trace out the internal connection that makes a continuous whole of all this movement and development. From this point of view the history of mankind no longer appeared as a wild whirl of sense-less deeds of violence, all equally condemnable at the judgment seat of mature philosophic reason, and which are best forgotten as quickly as possible; but as the process of evolution of man himself. It was now the task of the intellect to follow the gradual march of this process through all its devious ways, and to trace out the inner law running through all its apparently accidental phenomena.

That the Hegelian system did not solve the problem it pro-pounded is here immaterial. Its epoch-making merit was that it propounded the problem. This problem is one that no single individual will ever be able to solve. Although Hegel was—with Saint Simon—the most encyclopaedic mind of his time, yet he was limited, first, by the necessarily limited extent of his own knowledge, and, second, by the limited extent and depth of the knowledge and conceptions of his age. To these limits a third must be added. Hegel was an idealist. To him the thoughts within his brain were not the more or less abstract pictures of actual things and processes, but, conversely, things and their evolution were only the realized pictures of the 'Idea', existing somewhere from eternity before the world was. This way of thinking turned everything upside down, and completely reversed the actual connection of things in the world. Correctly and ingeniously as many individual groups of facts were grasped by Hegel, yet, for the reasons just given, there is much that is botched, artificial, laboured, in a word, wrong in point of detail. The Hegelian system, in itself, was a colossal miscarriage—but it was also the last of its kind. It was suffering, in fact, from an internal and incurable contradiction. Upon the one hand, its essential proposition was the conception that human history is a process of evolution, which, by its very nature, cannot find its intellectual final term in the discovery of any so-called absolute truth. But, on the other hand, it laid claim to being the very essence of this absolute truth. A system of natural and historical knowledge, embracing everything, and final for all time, is a contradiction to the fundamental law of dialectic reasoning. This law, indeed, by no means excludes, but, on the contrary, includes the idea that the systematic knowledge of the external universe can make giant strides from age to age.

The perception of the fundamental contradiction in German idealism led necessarily back to materialism, but *nota bene*, not to the simply metaphysical, exclusively mechanical materialism of the eighteenth century. Old materialism looked upon all previous history as a crude heap of irrationality and violence; modern materialism sees in it the process of evolution of humanity, and aims at discovering the laws thereof. With the French of the eighteenth century, and even with Hegel, the conception obtained of Nature as a whole, moving in narrow circles, and forever immutable, with its eternal celestial bodies, as Newton, and unalterable organic species, as Linnaeus, taught. Modern materialism embraces the more recent discoveries of natural science according to which Nature also has its history in time, the celestial bodies, like the organic species that, under favourable conditions, people them, being born and perishing. And even if Nature, as a whole, must still be said to move in recurrent cycles, these cycles assume infinitely larger dimensions. In both aspects, modern materialism is essentially dialectic, and no longer requires the assistance of that sort of philosophy which, queen-like, pretended to rule the remaining mob of sciences. As soon as each special science is bound to make clear its position in the great totality of things and of our knowledge of things, a special science dealing with this totality is superfluous or unnecessary. That which still survives of all earlier philosophy is the science of thought and its laws—formal logic and dialectics. Everything else is subsumed in the positive science of Nature and history.

Whilst, however, the revolution in the conception of Nature could only be made in proportion to the corresponding positive materials furnished by research, already much earlier certain historical facts had occurred which led to a decisive change in the conception of history. In 1831, the first working-class rising took place in Lyons; between 1838 and 1842, the first national working-class movement, that of the English Chartists, reached its height. The class struggle between proletariat and bourgeoisie came to the front in the history of the most advanced countries in Europe, in proportion to the development, upon the one hand, of modern industry, upon the other, of the newly-acquired political supremacy of the bourgeoisie. Facts more and more strenuously gave the lie to the teachings of bourgeois economy as to the identity of the interests of capital and labour, as to the universal harmony and universal prosperity that would be the consequence of unbridled competition. All these things could no longer be ignored, any more than the French and English Socialism, which was their theoretical, though very imperfect, expression. But the old idealist conception of history, which was not yet dislodged, knew nothing of class struggles based upon economic interests, knew nothing of economic interests; production and all economic relations appeared in it only as incidental, subordinate elements in the 'history of civilization'.

The new facts made imperative a new examination of all past history. Then it was seen that *all* past history, with the exception of its primitive stages, was the history of class struggles; that these warring classes of society are always the products of the modes of production and of exchange—in a word, of the *economic* conditions of their time; that the economic structure of society always furnishes the real basis, starting from which we can alone work out the ultimate explanation of the whole superstructure of juridical and political institutions as well as of the religious, philosophical, and other ideas of a given historical period. Hegel had freed history from metaphysics—he had made it dialectic; but his conception of history was essentially idealistic. But now idealism was driven from its last refuge, the philosophy of history; now a materialistic treatment of history was propounded, and a method of explaining man's 'knowing' by his 'being', instead of, as heretofore, his 'being' by his 'knowing'.

From that time forward Socialism was no longer an accidental discovery of this or that ingenious brain, but the necessary outcome of the struggle between two historically developed classes—the proletariat and the bourgeoisie. Its task was no longer to manufacture a system of society as perfect as possible, but to examine the historico-economic succession of events from which these classes and their antagonism had of necessity sprung, and to discover in the economic conditions thus created the means of ending the conflict. But the Socialism of earlier days was as incompatible with this materialistic conception as the conception of Nature of the French materialists was with dialectics and modern natural science. The Socialism of earlier days certainly criticised the existing capitalistic mode of production and its consequences. But it could not explain them, and, therefore, could not get the mastery of them. It could only simply reject them as bad. The more strongly this earlier Socialism denounced the exploitation of the working-class, inevitable under Capitalism, the less able was it clearly to show in what this exploitation consisted and how it arose. But for this it was necessary—(1) to present the capitalistic method of production in its historical connection and its inevitableness during a particular historical period, and therefore, also, to present its inevitable downfall; and (2) to lay bare its essential character, which was still a secret. This was done by the discovery of *surplus-value*. It was shown that the appropriation of unpaid labour is the basis of the capitalist mode of production and of the exploitation of the worker that occurs under it, that even if the capitalist buys the labour-power of his labourer at its full value as a commodity on the market, he yet extracts more value from it than he paid for; and that in the ultimate analysis this surplus-value forms those sums of value from which are heaped up the constantly increasing masses of capital in the hands of the possessing classes. The genesis of capitalist production and the production of capital were both explained.

These two great discoveries, the materialistic conception of history and the revelation of the secret of capitalistic production through surplus-value, we owe to Marx. With these discoveries Socialism became a science. The next thing was to work out all its details and relations.

III

The materialist conception of history starts from the proposition that the production of the means to support human life and next to production, the exchange of things produced, is the basis of all social structure; that in every society that has appeared in history, the manner in which wealth is distributed and society divided into classes or orders, is dependent upon what is produced, how it is produced, and how the products are exchanged. From this point of view the final causes of all social changes and political revolutions are to be sought, not in men's brains, not in man's better insight into eternal truth and justice, but in changes in the modes of production and exchange. They are to be sought, not in the *philosophy*, but in the *economics* of each particular epoch. The growing perception that existing social institutions are unreasonable and unjust, that reason has become unreason, and right wrong, is only proof that in the modes of production and exchange changes have silently taken place, with which the social order, adapted to earlier economic conditions, is no longer in keeping. From this it also follows that the means of getting rid of the incongruities that have been brought to light, must also be present, in a more or less developed condition, within the changed modes of production themselves. These means are not to be invented by deduction from fundamental principles, but are to be discovered in the stubborn facts of the existing system of production.

What is, then, the position of modern Socialism in this connexion?

The present structure of society—this is now pretty generally conceded—is the creation of the ruling class of today, of the bourgeoisie. The mode of production peculiar to the bourgeoisie, known, since Marx, as the capitalist mode of production, was incompatible with the feudal system, with the privileges it conferred upon individuals, entire social ranks and local corporations, as well as with the hereditary ties of subordination which constituted the framework of its social organization. The bourgeoisie broke up the feudal system and built upon its ruins the capitalist order of society, the kingdom of free competition, of personal liberty, of the equality, before the law, of all commodity owners, of all the rest of the capitalist blessings. Thenceforward the capitalist mode of production could develop in freedom. Since steam, machinery, and the making of machines by machinery transformed the older manufacture into modern industry, the productive forces evolved under the guidance of the bourgeoisie developed with a rapidity and in a degree unheard of before. But just as the older manufacture, in its time, and handicraft, becoming more developed under its influence, had come into collision with the feudal trammels of the guilds, so now modern industry, in its more complete development, comes into collision with the bounds within which the capitalistic mode of production holds it confined. The new productive forces have already outgrown the capitalistic mode of using them. And this conflict between productive forces and modes of production is not a conflict engendered in the mind of man, like that between original sin and divine justice. It exists, in fact, objectively, outside us, independently of the will and actions even of the men that have brought it on. Modern Socialism is nothing but the reflex, in thought, of this conflict in fact; its ideal reflection in the minds, first, of the class directly suffering under it, the working-class.

Now, in what does this conflict consist?

Before capitalistic production, i.e. in the Middle Ages, the system of petty industry obtained generally, based upon the private property of the labourers in their means of production; in the country, the agriculture of the small peasant, freeman or serf; in the towns, the handicrafts organized in guilds. The instruments of labour—land, agricultural implements, the workshop, the tool—were the instruments of labour of single individuals, adapted for the use of one worker, and, therefore, of necessity, small, dwarfish, circumscribed. But, for this very reason they belonged, as a rule, to the producer himself. To concentrate these scattered, limited means of production, to enlarge them, to turn them into the powerful levers of production of the present day—this was precisely the historic rôle of capitalist production and of its upholder, the bourgeoisie. In the fourth section of *Capital* Marx has explained in detail, how since the fifteenth century this has been historically worked out through the three phases of simple co-operation, manufacture, and modern industry. But the bourgeoisie, as is also shown there, could not transform these puny means of production into mighty productive forces, without transforming them, at the same time, from means of production of the individual into *social* means of production only workable by a collectivity of men. The spinning-wheel, the handloom, the blacksmith's hammer, were replaced by the spinning-machine, the power-loom, the steam-hammer; the individual workshop, by the factory implying the co-operation of hundreds and thousands of workmen. In like manner, production itself changed from a series of individual into a series of social acts, and the products from individual to social products. The yarn, the cloth, the metal articles that now came out of the factory were the joint product of many workers, through whose hands they had successively to pass before they were ready. No one person could say of them: 'I made that; this is *my* product'.

But where, in a given society, the fundamental form of production is that spontaneous division of labour which creeps in gradually and not upon any preconceived plan, there the products take on the form of *commodities*, whose mutual exchange, buying and selling, enable the individual producers to satisfy their manifold wants. And this was the case in the Middle Ages. The peasant, e.g., sold to the artisan agricultural products and bought from him the products of handicraft. Into this society of individual producers, of commodity-producers, the new mode of production thrust itself. In the midst of the old division of labour, grown up spontaneously and upon *no definite plan*, which had governed the whole of society, now arose division of labour upon *a definite plan*, as organized in the factory; side by side with *individual* production appeared *social* production. The products of both were sold in the same market, and, therefore, at prices at least approximately equal. But organization upon a definite plan was stronger than spontaneous division of labour. The factories working with the combined social forces of a collectivity of individuals produced their commodities far more cheaply than the individual small producers. Individual production succumbed in one department after another. Socialized production revolutionized all the old methods of production. But its revolutionary character was, at the same time, so little recognized, that it was, on the contrary, introduced as a means of increasing and developing the production of commodities. When it arose, it found ready-made, and made liberal use of, certain machinery for the production and exchange of commodities; merchants' capital, handicraft, wage-labour. Socialized production thus introducing itself as a new form of the production of commodities, it was a matter of course that under it the old forms of appropriation remained in full swing, and were applied to its products as well.

In the mediaeval stage of evolution of the production of commodities, the question as to the owner of the product of labour could not arise. The individual producer, as a rule, had, from raw material belonging to himself, and generally his own handiwork, produced it with his own tools, by the labour of his own hands or of his family. There was no need for him to appropriate the new product. It belonged wholly to him, as a matter of course. His property in the product was, therefore, based *upon his own labour*. Even where external help was used, this was, as a rule, of little importance, and very generally was compensated by something other than wages. The apprentices and journeymen of the guilds worked less for board and wages than for education, in order that they might become master craftsmen themselves.

Then came the concentration of the means of production and of the producers in large workshops and manufactories, their transformation into actual socialized means of production and socialized producers. But the socialized producers and means of production and their products were still treated, after this change, just as they had been before, i.e. as the means of production and the products of individuals. Hitherto, the owner of the instruments of labour had himself appropriated the product, because, as a rule, it was his own product and the assistance of others was the exception. Now the owner of the instruments of labour always appropriated to himself the product, although it was no longer *his* product but exclusively the product of the *labour of others*. Thus, the products now produced socially were not appropriated by those who had actually set in motion the means of production and actually produced the commodities, but by the *capitalists*. The means of production, and production itself, had become in essence socialized. But they were subjected to a form of appropriation which presupposes the private production of individuals, under which, therefore, every one owns his own product and brings it to market. The mode of production is subjected to this form of appropriation, although it abolishes the conditions upon which the latter rests.[1]

This contradiction, which gives to the new mode of production its capitalist character, *contains the germ of the whole of the social antagonisms of today*. The greater the mastery obtained by the new mode of production over all important fields of production and in all manufacturing countries, the more it reduced individual production to an insignificant residuum, *the more clearly was brought out the incompatibility of socialized production with capitalistic appropriation*.

The first capitalists found, as we have said, alongside of other forms of labour, wage-labour ready-made for them on the market. But it was exceptional, complementary, accessory, transitory wage-labour. The agricultural labourer, though, upon occasion, he hired himself out by the day, had a few acres of his own land on which he could at all events live at a pinch. The guilds were so organized that the journeyman of today became the master of tomorrow. But all this changed, as soon as the means of production became socialized and concentrated in the hands of capitalists. The means of production, as well as the product, of the individual producer became more and more worthless; there was nothing left for him but to turn wage-worker under the capitalist. Wage-labour, aforetime the exception and accessory, now became the rule and basis of all production; aforetime complementary, it now became the sole remaining function of the worker. The wage-worker for a time became a wage-worker for life. The number of these permanent wage-workers was further enormously increased by the breaking-up of the feudal system that occurred at the same time, by the disbanding of the retainers of the feudal lords, the eviction of the peasants from their homesteads, etc. The separation was made complete between the

[1] It is hardly necessary in this connexion to point out, that, even if the form of appropriation remains the same, the *character* of the appropriation is just as much revolutionized as production is by the changes described above. It is, of course, a very different matter whether I appropriate to myself my own product or that of another. Note in passing that wage-labour, which contains the whole capitalistic mode of production in embryo, is very ancient; in a sporadic, scattered form it existed for centuries alongside of slave-labour. But the embryo could duly develop into the capitalistic mode of production only when the necessary historical pre-conditions had been furnished.

means of production concentrated in the hands of the capitalists on the one side, and the producers, possessing nothing but their labour-power, on the other. *The contradiction between socialized production and capitalistic appropriation manifested itself as the antagonism of proletariat and bourgeoisie.*

We have seen that the capitalistic mode of production thrust its way into a society of commodity-producers, of individual producers, whose social bond was the exchange of their products. But every society, based upon the production of commodities, has this peculiarity: that the producers have lost control over their own social inter-relations. Each man produces for himself with such means of production as he may happen to have, and for such exchange as he may require to satisfy his remaining wants. No one knows how much of his particular article is coming on the market, nor how much of it will be wanted. No one knows whether his individual product will meet an actual demand, whether he will be able to make good his cost of production or even to sell his commodity at all. Anarchy reigns in socialized production.

But the production of commodities, like every other form of production, has its peculiar, inherent laws inseparable from it; and these laws work, despite anarchy, in and through anarchy. They reveal themselves in the only persistent form of social inter-relations, i.e. in exchange, and here they affect the individual producers as compulsory laws of competition. They are, at first, unknown to these producers themselves, and have to be discovered by them gradually and as the result of experience. They work themselves out, therefore, independently of the producers, and in antagonism to them, as inexorable natural laws of their particular form of production. The product governs the producers.

In mediaeval society, especially in the earlier centuries, production was essentially directed towards satisfying the wants of the individual. It satisfied, in the main, only the wants of the producer and his family. Where relations of personal dependence existed, as in the country, it also helped to satisfy the wants of the feudal lord. In all this there was, therefore, no exchange; the products, consequently, did not assume the character of commodities. The family of the peasant produced almost everything they wanted: clothes and furniture, as well as means of subsistence. Only when it began to produce more than was sufficient to supply its own wants and the payments in kind to the feudal lord, only then did it also produce commodities. This surplus, thrown into socialized exchange and offered for sale, became commodities.

The artisans of the towns, it is true, had from the first to produce for exchange. But they, also, themselves supplied the greatest part of their own individual wants. They had gardens and plots of land. They turned their cattle out into the communal forest, which, also, yielded them timber and firing. The women spun flax, wool, and so forth. Production for the purpose of exchange, production of commodities, was only in its infancy. Hence, exchange was restricted, the market narrow, the methods of production stable; there was local exclusiveness without, local unity within; the mark[1] in the country, in the town, the guild.

But with the extension of the production of commodities, and especially with the introduction of the capitalist mode of production, the laws of commodity-production, hitherto latent, came into action more openly and with greater force. The old bonds were loosened, the old exclusive limits broken through, the producers were more and more turned into independent, isolated producers of commodities. It became apparent that the production of society at large was ruled by absence of plan, by accident, by anarchy; and this anarchy grew to greater and greater height. But the chief means by aid of which the capitalist mode of production intensified this anarchy of socialized production, was the exact opposite of anarchy. It was the increasing organization of production, upon a social basis, in every individual productive establishment. By this, the old, peaceful, stable condition of things was ended. Wherever this organization of production was introduced into a branch of industry, it brooked no other method of production by its side. The field of labour became a battle-ground. The great geographical discoveries, and the colonization following upon them, multiplied markets and

---

[1] An association of villages that arose in Germany during the period when land was held in common, to regulate the rights and duties of the peasant. The common land itself is also known as the mark. (Publisher's note.)

quickened the transformation of handicraft into manufacture. The war did not simply break out between the individual producers of particular localities. The local struggles begat in their turn national conflicts, the commercial wars of the seventeenth and the eighteenth centuries.

Finally, modern industry and the opening of the world-market made the struggle universal, and at the same time gave it an unheard-of virulence. Advantages in natural or artificial conditions of production now decide the existence or non-existence of individual capitalists, as well as of whole industries and countries. He that falls is remorselessly cast aside. It is the Darwinian struggle of the individual for existence transferred from Nature to society with intensified violence. The conditions of existence natural to the animal appear as the final term of human development. The contradiction between socialized production and capitalistic appropriation now presents itself as *an antagonism between the organization of production in the individual workshop and the anarchy of production in society generally.*

The capitalistic mode of production moves in these two forms of the antagonism immanent to it from its very origin. It is never able to get out of that 'vicious circle', which Fourier had already discovered. What Fourier could not, indeed, see in his time is that this circle is gradually narrowing; that the movement becomes more and more a spiral, and must come to an end, like the movement of the planets, by collision with the centre. It is the compelling force of anarchy in the production of society at large that more and more completely turns the great majority of men into proletarians; and it is the masses of the proletariat again who will finally put an end to anarchy in production. It is the compelling force of anarchy in social production that turns the limitless perfectibility of machinery under modern industry into a compulsory law by which every individual industrial capitalist must perfect his machinery more and more, under penalty of ruin.

But the perfecting of machinery is the making human labour superfluous. If the introduction and increase of machinery means the displacement of millions of manual, by a few machine, workers, improvement in machinery means the displacement of more and more of the machine-workers themselves. It means, in the last instance, the production of a number of available wage-workers in excess of the average needs of capital, the formation of a complete industrial reserve army, as I called it in 1845,[1] available at the times when industry is working at high pressure, to be cast out upon the street when the inevitable crash comes, a constant dead weight upon the limbs of the working-class in its struggle for existence with capital, a regulator for the keeping of wages down to the low level that suits the interests of capital. Thus it comes about, to quote Marx, that machinery becomes the most powerful weapon in the war of capital against the working-class; that the instruments of labour constantly tear the means of subsistence out of the hands of the labourer; that the very product of the worker is turned into an instrument for his subjugation. Thus it comes about that the economising of the instruments of labour becomes at the same time, from the outset, the most reckless waste of labour-power, and robbery based upon the normal conditions under which labour functions; that machinery, 'the most powerful instrument for shortening labour-time, becomes the most unfailing means for placing every moment of the labourer's time and that of his family at the disposal of the capitalist for the purpose of expanding the value of his capital'.[2] Thus it comes about that over-work of some becomes the pre-liminary condition for the idleness of others, and that modern industry, which hunts after new consumers over the whole world, forces the consumption of the masses at home down to a starva-tion minimum, and in doing thus destroys its own home market. 'The law that always equilibrates the relative surplus population, or industrial reserve army, to the extent and energy of accumula-tion, this law rivets the labourer to capital more firmly than the wedges of Vulcan did Prometheus to the rock. It establishes an accumulation of misery, corresponding with accumulation of capital. Accumulation of wealth at one pole is, therefore, at the same time, accumulation of misery, agony of toil, slavery, ignorance, brutality, mental degradation, at the opposite pole, i.e. on the side of the class that produces *its own product in the*

[1] *The Condition of the Working-Class in England*, Sonnenschein, now George Allen & Unwin Ltd., p. 84.
[2] *Capital*, English edition, Sonnenschein, now George Allen & Unwin Ltd., p. 406.

form of capital.[1] And to expect any other division of the products from the capitalistic mode of production is the same as expecting the electrodes of a battery not to decompose acidulated water, not to liberate oxygen at the positive, hydrogen at the negative pole, so long as they are connected with the battery.

We have seen that the ever-increasing perfectibility of modern machinery is, by the anarchy of social production, turned into a compulsory law that forces the individual industrial capitalist always to improve his machinery, always to increase its productive force. The bare possibility of extending the field of production is transformed for him into a similar compulsory law. The enormous expansive force of modern industry, compared with which that of gases is mere child's play, appears to us now as a *necessity* for expansion, both qualitative and quantitative, that laughs at all resistance. Such resistance is offered by consumption, by sales, by the markets for the products of modern industry. But the capacity for extension, extensive and intensive, of the markets is primarily governed by quite different laws, that work much less energetically. The extension of the markets cannot keep pace with the extension of production. The collision becomes inevitable, and as this cannot produce any real solution so long as it does not break in pieces the capitalist mode of production, the collisons become periodic. Capitalist production has begotten another 'vicious circle'.

As a matter of fact, since 1825, when the first general crisis broke out, the whole industrial and commercial world, production and exchange among all civilized peoples and their more or less barbaric hangers-on, are thrown out of joint about once every ten years. Commerce is at a standstill, the markets are glutted, products accumulate, as multitudinous as they are unsaleable, hard cash disappears, credit vanishes, factories are closed, the mass of the workers are in want of the means of subsistence, because they have produced too much of the means of subsistence; bankruptcy follows upon bankruptcy, execution upon execution. The stagnation lasts for years; productive forces and products are wasted and destroyed wholesale, until the accumulated mass of commodities finally filter off, more or less depreciated in value, until production and exchange gradually

[1] *Ibid*, p. 661.

begin to move again. Little by little the pace quickens. It becomes a trot. The industrial trot breaks into a canter, the canter in turn grows into the headlong gallop of a perfect steeplechase of industry, commercial credit, and speculation, which finally, after breakneck leaps, ends where it began—in the ditch of a crisis. And so over and over again. We have now, since the year 1825, gone through this five times, and at the present moment (1877) we are going through it for the sixth time. And the character of these crises is so clearly defined that Fourier hit all of them off, when he described the first as '*crise pléthorique*', a crisis from plethora.

In these crises, the contradiction between socialized production and capitalist appropriation ends in a violent explosion. The circulation of commodities is, for the time being, stopped. Money, the means of circulation, becomes a hindrance to circulation. All the laws of production and circulation of commodities are turned upside down. The economic collision has reached its apogee. *The mode of production is in rebellion against the mode of exchange.*

The fact that the socialized organization of production within the factory has developed so far that it has become incompatible with the anarchy of production in society, which exists side by side with and dominates it, is brought home to the capitalists themselves by the violent concentration of capital that occurs during crises, through the ruin of many large, and a still greater number of small, capitalists. The whole mechanism of the capitalist mode of production breaks down under the pressure of the productive forces, its own creations. It is no longer able to turn all this mass of means of production into capital. They lie fallow, and for that very reason the industrial reserve army must also lie fallow. Means of production, means of subsistence, available labourers, all the elements of production and of general wealth, are present in abundance. But 'abundance becomes the source of distress and want' (Fourier), because it is the very thing that prevents the transformation of the means of production and subsistence into capital. For in capitalistic society the means of production can only function when they have undergone a preliminary transformation into capital, into the means of exploiting human labour-power. The necessity of this transformation into capital of the means of production and subsistence stands like a ghost between these and the workers. It alone prevents the coming together of the material and personal levers of production; it alone forbids the means of production to function, the workers to work and live. On the one hand, therefore, the capitalistic mode of production stands convicted of its own incapacity to further direct these productive forces. On the other, these productive forces themselves, with increasing energy, press forward to the removal of the existing contradiction, to the abolition of their quality as capital, to the *practical recognition of their character as social productive forces*.

This rebellion of the productive forces, as they grow more and more powerful, against their quality as capital, this stronger and stronger command that their social character shall be recognized, forces the capitalist class itself to treat them more and more as social productive forces, so far as this is possible under capitalist conditions. The period of industrial high pressure, with its unbounded inflation of credit, not less than the crash itself, by the collapse of great capitalist establishments, tends to bring about that form of the socialization of great masses of means of production, which we meet with in the different kinds of joint-stock companies. Many of these means of production and of distribution are, from the outset, so colossal, that, like the railroads, they include all other forms of capitalistic exploitation. At a further stage of evolution this form also becomes insufficient. The producers on a large scale in a particular branch of industry in a particular country unite in a 'Trust', a union for the purpose of regulating production. They determine the total amount to be produced, parcel it out among themselves, and thus enforce the selling price fixed beforehand. But trusts of this kind, as soon as business becomes bad, are generally liable to break up, and, on this very account, compel a yet greater concentration of association. The whole of the particular industry is turned into one gigantic joint-stock company; internal competition gives place to the internal monopoly of this one company. This has happened in 1890 with the English *alkali* production, which is now, after the fusion of forty-eight large works, in the hands of one company, conducted upon a single plan, and with a capital of £6,000,000.

In the trusts, freedom of competition changes into its very

opposite—into monopoly; and the production without any definite plan of capitalistic society capitulates to the production upon a definite plan of the invading socialistic society. Certainly this is so far still to the benefit and advantage of the capitalists. But in this case the exploitation is so palpable that it must break down. No nation will put up with production conducted by trusts, with so barefaced an exploitation of the community by a small band of dividend-mongers.

In any case, with trusts or without, the official representative of capitalist society—the State—will ultimately have to undertake the direction of production.[1] This necessity for conversion into State-property is felt first in the great institutions for intercourse and communication—the post-office, the telegraphs, the railways.

If the crises demonstrate the incapacity of the bourgeoisie for managing any longer modern productive forces, the transformation of the great establishments for production and distribution into joint-stock companies, trusts, and State property, show how unnecesary the bourgeoisie are for that purpose. All the social functions of the capitalist are now performed by salaried

[1] I say 'have to'. For only when the means of production and distribution have *actually* outgrown the form of management by joint-stock companies, and when, therefore, the taking them over by the State has become *economically* inevitable, only then—even if it is the State of today that effects this—is there an economic advance, the attainment of another step preliminary to the taking over of all productive forces by society itself. But of late, since Bismarck went in for State-ownership of industrial establishments, a kind of spurious Socialism has arisen, degenerating, now and again, into something of flunkeyism, that without more ado declares *all* State-ownership, even of the Bismarckian sort, to be socialistic. Certainly, if the taking over by the State of the tobacco industry is socialistic, then Napoleon and Metternich must be numbered among the founders of Socialism. If the Belgian State, for quite ordinary political and financial reasons, itself constructed its chief railway lines; if Bismarck, not under any economic compulsion, took over for the State the chief Prussian lines, simply to be the better able to have them in hand in case of war, to bring up the railway employees as voting cattle for the Government, and especially to create for himself a new source of income independent of parliamentary votes—this was, in no sense, a socialistic measure, directly or indirectly, consciously or unconsciously. Otherwise, the Royal Maritime Company, the Royal porcelain manufacture, and even the regimental tailor of the army would also be socialistic institutions, or even, as was seriously proposed by a sly dog in Frederick William III's reign, the taking over by the State of the brothels.

employees. The capitalist has no further social function than that of pocketing dividends, tearing off coupons, and gambling on the Stock Exchange, where the different capitalists despoil one another of their capital. At first the capitalistic mode of production forces out the workers. Now it forces out the capitalists, and reduces them, just as it reduced the workers, to the ranks of the surplus population, although not immediately into those of the industrial reserve army.

But the transformation, either into joint-stock companies and trusts, or into State-ownership, does not do away with the capitalistic nature of the productive forces. In the joint-stock companies and trusts this is obvious. And the modern State, again, is only the organization that bourgeois society takes on in order to support the external conditions of the capitalist mode of production against the encroachments, as well of the workers as of individual capitalists. The modern State, no matter what its form, is essentially a capitalist machine, the state of the capitalists, the ideal personification of the total national capital. The more it proceeds to the taking over of productive forces, the more does it actually become the national capitalist, the more citizens does it exploit. The workers remain wage-workers—proletarians. The capitalist relation is not done away with. It is rather brought to a head. But, brought to a head, it topples over. State-ownership of the productive forces is not the solution of the conflict, but concealed within it are the technical conditions that form the elements of that solution.

This solution can only consist in the practical recognition of the social nature of the modern forces of production, and therefore in the harmonizing of the modes of production, appropriation, and exchange with the socialized character of the means of production. And this can only come about by society openly and directly taking possession of the productive forces which have outgrown all control except that of society as a whole. The social character of the means of production and of the products today reacts against the producers, periodically disrupts all production and exchange, acts only like a law of Nature working blindly, forcibly, destructively. But with the taking over by society of the productive forces, the social character of the means of production and of the products will be utilized by the producers with a perfect understanding of its nature, and instead of being a source of disturbance and periodical collapse, will become the most powerful lever of production itself.

Active social forces work exactly like natural forces: blindly, forcibly, destructively, so long as we do not understand, and reckon with, them. But when once we understand them, when once we grasp their action, their direction, their effects, it depends only upon ourselves to subject them more and more to our own will, and by means of them to reach our own ends. And this holds quite especially of the mighty productive forces of today. As long as we obstinately refuse to understand the nature and the character of these social means of action—and this understanding goes against the grain of the capitalist mode of production and its defenders—so long these forces are at work in spite of us, in opposition to us, so long they master us, as we have shown above in detail.

But when once their nature is understood, they can, in the hands of the producers working together, be transformed from master demons into willing servants. The difference is as that between the destructive force of electricity in the lightning of the storm, and electricity under command in the telegraph and the voltaic arc; the difference between a conflagration, and fire working in the service of man. With this recognition at last of the real nature of the productive forces of today, the social anarchy of production gives place to a social regulation of production upon a definite plan, according to the needs of the community and of each individual. Then the capitalist mode of appropriation, in which the product enslaves first the producer and then the appropriator, is replaced by the mode of appropriation of the products that is based upon the nature of the modern means of production; upon the one hand, direct social appropriation, as means to the maintenance and extension of production—on the other, direct individual appropriation, as means of subsistence and of enjoyment.

Whilst the capitalist mode of production more and more completely transforms the great majority of the population into proletarians, it creates the power which, under penalty of its own destruction, is forced to accomplish this revolution. Whilst it forces on more and more the transformation of the vast means of production, already socialized, into State property, it shows itself the way to accomplishing this revolution. *The proletariat seizes political power and turns the means of production into State property.*

But, in doing this, it abolishes itself as proletariat, abolishes all class distinctions and class antagonisms, abolishes also the State as State. Society thus far, based upon class antagonisms, had need of the State. That is, of an organization of the particular class which was *pro tempore* the exploiting class, an organisation for the purpose of preventing any interference from without with the existing conditions of production, and therefore, especially, for the purpose of forcibly keeping the exploited classes in the condition of oppression corresponding with the given mode of production (slavery, serfdom, wage-labour). The State was the official representative of society as a whole; the gathering of it together into a visible embodiment. But it was this only in so far as it was the State of that class which itself represented, for the time being, society as a whole; in ancient times, the State of slave-owning citizens; in the middle ages, the feudal lords; in our own time, the bourgeoisie. When at last it becomes the real representative of the whole of society, it renders itself unnecessary. As soon as there is no longer any social class to be held in subjection; as soon as class rule, and the individual struggle for existence based upon our present anarchy in production, with the collisions and excesses arising from these, are removed, nothing more remains to be repressed, and a special repressive force, a State, is no longer necessary. The first act by virtue of which the State really constitutes itself the representative of the whole of society—the taking possession of the means of production in the name of society—this is, at the same time, its last independent act as a State. State interference in social relations becomes, in one domain after another, superfluous, and then dies out of itself; the government of persons is replaced by the administration of things, and by the conduct of processes of production. The State is not 'abolished'. *It dies out.* This gives the measure of the value of the phrase 'a free State', both as to its justifiable use at times by agitators, and as to its ultimate scientific insufficiency; and also of the demands of the so-called anarchists for the abolition of the State out of hand.

Since the historical appearance of the capitalist mode of

production, the appropriation by society of all the means of production has often been dreamed of, more or less vaguely, by individuals, as well as by sects, as the ideal of the future. But it could become possible, could become a historical necessity, only when the actual conditions for its realization were there. Like every other social advance, it becomes practicable, not by men understanding that the existence of classes is in contradiction to justice, equality, etc., not by the mere willingness to abolish these classes, but by virtue of certain new economic conditions. The separation of society into an exploiting and an exploited class, a ruling and an oppressed class, was the necessary consequence of the deficient and restricted development of production in former times. So long as the total social labour only yields a produce which but slightly exceeds that barely necessary for the existence of all; so long, therefore, as labour engages all or almost all the time of the great majority of the members of society —so long, of necessity, this society is divided into classes. Side by side with the great majority, exclusively bond slaves to labour, arises a class freed from directly productive labour, which looks after the general affairs of society; the direction of labour, State business, law, science, art, etc. It is, therefore, the law of division of labour that lies at the basis of the division into classes. But this does not prevent this division into classes from being carried out by means of violence and robbery, trickery and fraud. It does not prevent the ruling class, once having the upper hand, from consolidating its power at the expense of the working-class, from turning their social leadership into an intensified exploitation of the masses.

But if, upon this showing, division into classes has a certain historical justification, it has this only for a given period, only under given social conditions. It was based upon the insufficiency of production. It will be swept away by the complete development of modern productive forces. And, in fact, the abolition of classes in society presupposes a degree of historical evolution, at which the existence, not simply of this or that particular ruling class, but of any ruling class at all, and, therefore, the existence of class distinction itself has become an obsolete anachronism. It presupposes, therefore, the development of production carried out to a degree at which appropriation of the means of production and of the products, and, with this, of political domination, of the monopoly of culture, and of intellectual leadership by a particular class of society, has become not only superfluous, but economically, politically, intellectually a hindrance to development.

This point is now reached. Their political and intellectual bankruptcy is scarcely any longer a secret to the bourgeoisie themselves. Their economic bankruptcy recurs regularly every ten years. In every crisis, society is suffocated beneath the weight of its own productive forces and products, which it cannot use, and stands helpless, face to face with the absurd contradiction that the producers have nothing to consume, because consumers are wanting. The expansive force of the means of production bursts the bonds that the capitalist mode of production had imposed upon them. Their deliverance from these bonds is the one pre-condition for an unbroken, constantly-accelerated development of the productive forces, and therewith for a practically unlimited increase of production itself. Nor is this all. The socialized appropriation of the means of production does away, not only with the present artificial restrictions upon production, but also with the positive waste and devastation of productive forces and products that are at the present time the inevitable concomitants of production, and that reach their height in the crises. Further, it sets free for the community at large a mass of means of production and of products, by doing away with the senseless extravagance of the ruling classes of today, and their political representatives. The possibility of securing for every member of society, by means of socialized production, an existence not only fully sufficient materially, and becoming day by day more full, but an existence guaranteeing to all the free development and exercise of their physical and mental faculties —this possibility is now for the first time here, truly *it is here*.[1]

[1] A few figures may serve to give an approximate idea of the enormous expansive force of the modern means of production, even under capitalist pressure. According to Mr Giffen, the total wealth of Great Britain and Ireland amounted, in round numbers, in

1814 to £2,200,000,000.
1865 to £6,100,000,000.
1875 to £8,500,000,000.

As an instance of the squandering of means of production and of

With the seizing of the means of production by society, production of commodities is done away with, and, simultaneously, the mastery of the product over the producer. Anarchy in social production is replaced by systematic, definite organization. The struggle for individual existence disappears. Then for the first time, man, in a certain sense, is finally marked off from the rest of the animal kingdom, and emerges from mere animal conditions of existence into really human ones. The whole sphere of the conditions of life which environ man, and which have hitherto ruled man, now comes under the dominion and control of man, who for the first time becomes the real, conscious lord of Nature, because he has now become master of his own social organization. The laws of his own social action, hitherto standing face to face with man as laws of Nature foreign to, and dominating, him, will then be used with full understanding, and so mastered by him. Man's own social organization, hitherto confronting him as a necessity imposed by Nature and history, now becomes the result of his own free action. The extraneous objective forces that have hitherto governed history, pass under the control of man himself. Only from that time will man himself, more and more consciously, make his own history—only from that time will the social causes set in movement by him have, in the main and in a constantly growing measure, the results intended by him. It is the ascent of man from the kingdom of necessity to the kingdom of freedom.

Let us briefly sum up our sketch of historical evolution.

I. *Mediaeval Society*. Individual production on a small scale. Means of production adapted for individual use; hence primitive, ungainly, petty, dwarfed in action. Production for immediate consumption, either of the producer himself or of his feudal lord. Only where an excess of production over this consumption occurs is such excess offered for sale, enters into exchange. Production of commodities, therefore, only in its infancy. But already it contains within itself, in embryo, *anarchy in the production of society at large*.

products during a crisis, the total loss in the German iron industry alone, in the crisis 1873-78, was given at the second German Industrial Congress (Berlin, February 21, 1878) as £22,750,000.

II. *Capitalist Revolution*. Transformation of industry, at first by means of simple co-operation and manufacture. Concentration of the means of production, hitherto scattered, into great workshops. As a consequence, their transformation from individual to social means of production—a transformation which does not, on the whole, affect the form of exchange. The old forms of appropriation remain in force. The capitalist appears. In his capacity as owner of the means of production, he also appropriates the products and turns them into commodities. Production has become a *social* act. Exchange and appropriation continue to be *individual* acts, the acts of individuals. *The social product is appropriated by the individual capitalist*. Fundamental contradiction, whence arise all the contradictions in which our present day society moves, and which modern industry brings to light.

A. Severance of the producer from the means of production. Condemnation of the worker to wage-labour for life. *Antagonism between the proletariat and the bourgeoisie*.

B. Growing predominance and increasing effectiveness of the laws governing the production of commodities. Unbridled competition. *Contradiction between socialized organization in the individual factory and social anarchy in production as a whole*.

C. On the one hand, perfecting of machinery, made by competition compulsory for each individual manufacturer, and complemented by a constantly growing displacement of labourers. *Industrial reserve-army*. On the other hand, unlimited extension of production, also compulsory under competition, for every manufacturer. On both sides, unheard of development of productive forces, excess of supply over demand, over-production, glutting of the markets, crises every ten years, the vicious circle: excess here, of means of production and products—excess there, of labourers, without employment and without means of existence. But these two levers of production and of social well-being are unable to work together, because the capitalist form of production prevents the productive forces from working and the products from circulating, unless they are first turned into capital—which their very superabundance prevents. The contradiction has grown into an absurdity. *The mode of production rises in rebellion against the form of exchange.* The bourgeoisie are convicted of incapacity further to manage their own social productive forces.

D. Partial recognition of the social character of the productive forces forced upon the capitalists themselves. Taking over of the great institutions for production and communication, first by joint-stock companies, later on by trusts, then by the State. The bourgeoisie demonstrated to be a superfluous class. All its social functions are now performed by salaried employees.

III. *Proletarian Revolution.* Solution of the contradictions. The proletariat seizes the public power, and by means of this transforms the socialized means of production, slipping from the hands of the bourgeoisie, into public property. By this act, the proletariat frees the means of production from the character of capital they have thus far borne, and gives their socialized character complete freedom to work itself out. Socialized production upon a predetermined plan becomes henceforth possible. The development of production makes the existence of different classes of society thenceforth an anachronism. In proportion as anarchy in social production vanishes, the political authority of the State dies out. Man, at last the master of his own form of social organization, becomes at the same time the lord over Nature, his own master—free.

To accomplish this act of universal emancipation is the historical mission of the modern proletariat. To thoroughly comprehend the historical conditions and thus the very nature of this act, to impart to the now oppressed proletarian class a full knowledge of the conditions and of the meaning of the momentous act it is called upon to accomplish, this is the task of the theoretical expression of the proletarian movement, scientific Socialism.

THE STATE AND REVOLUTION

*Marxist Teaching on the State
and the Task of the Proletariat in the
Revolution*

V. I. ULIANOV (N. LENIN)

Lenin, the architect of the Russian revolution and first head of the Communist state, was born Vladimir Ilyitch Ulianov, the son of a college teacher, at Simbirsk, on April 22, 1870. He became a lawyer and assumed the alias Lenin on joining the socialist movement. From 1907-1917 he lived in exile in Paris, Vienna and Zurich. In April 1917 came his famous journey across Germany in a sealed carriage, arranged to embarrass the Allies. On arriving in Petrograd he took over the leadership of the Bolshevik Party and, with Trotsky, organized first the July rising, and then the successful revolution of November 7, 1917 (October 25th Russian calendar). An attempt on his life in 1922 left his health impaired and he died on January 21, 1924, exhausted by the post-revolutionary problems. His body is exhibited in a special mausoleum in Moscow.

Where Marx and Engels had fought in the realm of ideas, Lenin, fifty years younger, struggled to power in their name. The State and Revolution, *written in 1917, reflects the urgency of the time: the state was to be destroyed but what was to be put in its place? His analysis steers Marxism between the Anarchists on the one hand, who had nothing to replace it with, and the Social-Democrats and Opportunists on the other, who were as reluctant as ever to destroy anything at all. Soon after writing it Lenin saw the fulfilment of Marxist hopes. Whether or not Laski's opinion is justified, that the subsequent history of Communism shows 'what happens when the large and flexible outlook of the* Communist Manifesto *is applied in a narrow and dogmatically rigid way', is still a vexed debate in the world today.*

The State and Revolution *was first published in England in October, 1919 by George Allen & Unwin Ltd, and this text has been followed in the present edition with the addition of Section 3 of Chapter II which first appeared in the second edition.*

PREFACE

THE question of the State is acquiring at the present a particular importance, both theoretical and practical.

The Imperialist war has greatly accelerated and intensified the transformation of monopolist capitalism into State-monopoly Capitalism. The monstrous oppression of the labouring masses by the State—which is identifying itself more and more intimately with the all-powerful capitalist combines—is becoming ever more terrible. The foremost countries are being converted— we speak here of their 'rear'—into military labour prisons for the workers.

The incredible miseries and horrors of the protracted war are making the position of the masses unbearable and increasing their indignation.

It is clear an international proletarian revolution is preparing.

The question therefore of its relations to the State is acquiring a practical importance.

The accumulation of opportunist elements during the decades of comparatively peaceful development has created a predominance of Socialist Chauvinism in the official Socialist parties of the whole world: Plekhanoff, Potressoff, Breshkovskaya, Rubanovitch, and, in a slightly concealed form, Tseretelli, Tchernoff & Co., in Russia; Scheidemann, Legien, David and others in Germany; Renaudel, Guesde, Vandervelde in France and Belgium; Hyndman and the Fabians in England; and so on, and so on. Socialist in words, Chauvinist in deeds, these 'leaders of Socialism' distinguish themselves by a base, servile adaptation to the interests not only of 'their' national bourgeoisie, but also of 'their' State—for plenty of smaller, weaker nationalities have long since been exploited and enslaved by most of the so-called Great Powers. The Imperialist war is just a scramble for more division and repartition of the same kind of booty.

The struggle for the emancipation of the labouring masses from the oppression of the bourgeoisie in general, and the Imperialist bourgeoisie in particular, cannot be separated from a struggle against the opportunist superstititions concerning the State.

We first of all survey the teachings of Marx and Engels on the State, dwelling particularly fully on the forgotten parts, and on those aspects of their teachings which the opportunists have distorted. We then analyse specially the chief representative of these pervertors, Karl Kautsky, the best known leader of the Second International (1889-1914), who has suffered such a pitiful political bankruptcy during the present war. Finally, we bring forward the most important results of the experiences of the Russian revolutions of 1905, and particularly of 1917.

This last revolution is evidently completing at the present time (beginning of August, 1917) the first stage of its development; but in general the whole of this revolution can only be looked upon as a link in the chain of Socialist proletarian revolutions which will result from the imperialist war.

The question of the relation of a proletarian Socialist revolution to the State is therefore not only of practical political importance, but is an urgent need of the day, being concerned with the elucidation for the masses of what they will have to do for their liberation from the yoke of Capitalism in the very near future.

THE AUTHOR

August, 1917

CHAPTER I

Class Society and the State

―――――――――――――――――

I THE STATE AS THE PRODUCT OF THE IRRECONCILABILITY OF CLASS ANTAGONISMS

MARX'S doctrines are now undergoing the same fate, which, more than once in the course of history, has befallen the doctrines of other revolutionary thinkers and leaders of oppressed classes struggling for emancipation. During the lifetime of great revolutionaries, the oppressing classes have invariably meted out to them relentless persecution, and received their teaching with the most savage hostility, most furious hatred, and a ruthless campaign of lies and slanders. After their death, however, attempts are usually made to turn them into harmless saints, canonising them, as it were, and investing their name with a certain halo by way of 'consolation' to the oppressed classes, and with the object of duping them; while at the same time emasculating and vulgarising the real essence of their revolutionary theories and blunting their revolutionary edge. At the present time the bourgeoisie and the opportunists within the labour movement are co-operating in this work of adulterating Marxism. They omit, obliterate, and distort the revolutionary side of its teaching, its revolutionary soul, and push to the foreground and extol what is, or seems, acceptable to the bourgeoisie. All the Socialist Chauvinists are now 'Marxists'—save the mark! And more and more do German bourgeois professors, erstwhile specialists in the demolition of Marx, speak now of the 'National-German' Marx who, forsooth, has educated the splendidly organized working class for the present predatory war.

In these circumstances, when the distortion of Marxism is so widespread, our first task is to resuscitate the real nature of Marx's teaching on the subject of the State. For this purpose it will be necessary to quote copiously from the works of Marx and Engels themselves. Of course, long extracts will make our text cumbersome and will in no way add to its lucidity; but we cannot possibly avoid them. All, or at any rate, all the most essential, passages in the works of Marx and Engels on the subject of the State must be given as fully as possible, in order that the reader may form an independent and complete view of the ideas of the founders of scientific Socialism and their development, and in order that their distortions by the present predominant Kautsky school may be proved in black and white and rendered plain to all.

Let us begin with the most popular of Engels' works, *The Origin of the Family, Private Property, and the State*, the sixth edition of which was published in Stuttgart as far back as 1894. Summarising his historical analysis Engels says:—

'The State in no way constitutes a force imposed on Society from outside. Nor is the State "the reality of the Moral Idea", "the image and reality of Reason" as Hegel asserted. The State is the product of Society at a certain stage of its development. The State is tantamount to an acknowledgment that the given society has become entangled in an insoluble contradiction with itself, that it has broken up into irreconcilable antagonisms, of which it is powerless to rid itself. And in order that these antagonisms, these classes with their opposing economic interests may not devour one another and Society itself in their sterile struggle, some force standing, seemingly, above Society, becomes necessary so as to moderate the force of their collisions and to keep them within the bounds of "order." And this force arising from Society, but placing itself above it, which gradually separates itself from it—this force is the State' (pages 117-178 of 6th German Edition).

Here, we have, expressed in all its clearness, the basic idea of Marxism on the question of the historical rôle and meaning of the State. The State is the product and the manifestation of the irreconcilability of class antagonisms. When, where, and to what extent the State arises, depends directly on when, where and to what extent the class antagonisms of a given society cannot be objectively reconciled. And, conversely, the existence of the State proves that the class antagonisms *are* irreconcilable.

It is precisely on this most important and fundamental point that distortions of Marxism arise along two main lines.

On the one hand, the middle class (bourgeois) and particularly the lower middle class (petty bourgeois), ideologists, compelled by the pressure of indisputable historical facts to recognize that the State only exists where there are class antagonisms and class struggles, 'correct' Marx in such a way as to make it appear that the State is an organ for the *reconciliation* of classes. According to Marx, the State can neither arise nor maintain itself if a reconciliation of classes is possible. But with the middle class and philistine professors and publicists, the State (and this frequently on the strength of benevolent references to Marx), becomes a mediator and conciliator of classes. According to Marx, the State is the organ of class *domination*, the organ of oppression of one class by another. Its aim is the creation of order which legalizes and perpetuates this oppression by moderating the collisions between the classes. But in the opinion of the lower middle class politicians, the establishment or order is equivalent to the reconciliation of classes, and not to the oppression of one class by another. To moderate their collisions does not mean, according to them, to deprive the oppressed class of certain definite means and methods in its struggle for throwing off the yoke of the oppressors, but to conciliate it.

For instance, when, in the Revolution of 1917, the question of the real meaning and rôle of the State arose, in all its importance, as a practical question demanding immediate action on a wide mass-scale, all the Socialist-Revolutionaries and Mensheviks rattled down, suddenly and without reservation, to the lower-middle class theory of the 'conciliation of classes by the State'. Innumerable resolutions and articles by publicists of both these parties were saturated through and through with this purely middle-class and philistine theory of conciliation. That the State is the organ of domination of a definite class which *cannot* be reconciled to its social antipodes—this the lower middle-class democracy is never able to understand. Their attitude towards the State is one of the most telling proofs that our Socialist-Revolutionaries and Mensheviks are not Socialists at all (which we, Bolsheviks, have always maintained), but only lower middle-class democrats, with a phraseology very nearly Socialist.

On the other hand, the distortion of Marx by the Kautsky school is far more subtle. 'Theoretically,' there is no denial that the State is the organ of class domination, or that the class antagonisms are irreconcilable. But what is forgotten or over-looked is this:—If the State is the product of the irreconcilable character of class antagonisms, if it is a force standing above society and 'separating itself gradually from it', then it is clear that the liberation of the oppressed class is impossible without a violent revolution, and without the destruction of the machinery of State power, which has been created by the governing class and in which this 'separation' is embodied. This inference, theoretically quite self-evident, was drawn by Marx, as we shall see later, with the greatest precision from a concrete historical analysis of the problems of Revolution. And it is exactly this inference which Kautsky—we shall show this fully in our subsequent remarks—has 'forgotten' and distorted.

2 THE SPECIAL BODIES OF ARMED MEN, PRISONS, ETC.

Engels continues:—

'As compared with the ancient gentilic (tribal or clan) organization, the State is distinguished, first of all, by the grouping of the subjects of the State according to territorial divisions.'

Such a grouping seems 'natural' to us, but it came after a prolonged and costly struggle against the old form of tribal, gentilic Society.

'The second distinguishing feature is the establishment of a public power which is no longer identical with the population and which is organized as an armed force.

'This distinct public power is necessary, because a self-acting armed organization of the population has become impossible with the break up of Society into classes. . . . This public authority exists in every State. It consists not only of armed men, but also of material additions in the shape of prisons and repressive institutions of all kinds which were unknown in the gentilic (clan) form of Society.'

Engels develops the conception of that 'force' which is termed the State—a force arising from Society, but placing itself above it and becoming more and more divorced from it. What does this force consist of, in the main? It consists of special bodies of armed men who have at their command prisons, etc.

We are justified in speaking of special bodies of armed men, because the public power peculiar to every State 'is not identical' with the armed population, with its 'self-acting armed organization'. Like all revolutionary thinkers, Engels tries to draw the attention of the class-conscious workers to that very fact which to prevailing philistinism appears least of all worthy of attention, most common and sanctified by solid, indeed, one might say, petrified prejudices. A standing army and police are the chief instruments of force of the State authority: but can it, then, be otherwise?

From the point of view of the vast majority of Europeans at the end of the 19th century to whom Engels addressed himself and who had neither lived through nor observed at close quarters a single important revolution, this could not be otherwise. They could not understand what was meant by this 'self-acting armed organization of the population'.

To the question, whence arose the necessity for forming special bodies of armed men (police, and standing army) standing above Society and becoming divorced from it, the Western European and Russian philistines are inclined to answer with a few phrases, borrowed from Spencer, about the complexity of social life, the differentiation of functions, and so forth.

Such a reference seems 'scientific' and effectively dulls the senses of the average man, obscuring the most important and basic fact, viz.: the break up of Society into irreconcilably antagonistic classes. Without such a split the 'self-acting armed organization of the population' might have differed from the primitive organization of a herd of monkeys merely grasping sticks, or of primitive man, or races united in a clan form of society, by its complexity, its high technique, and so forth, but would still have been possible. It cannot, however, exist now, because Society, in the period of Civilization, is broken up into antagonistic and, indeed, *irreconcilably* antagonistic classes, the 'self-acting' arming of which would lead to armed struggles between them. The State is therefore formed, a special force is created in the form of special bodies of armed men, and every revolution, in shattering the State machinery, demonstrates to us how the governing class aims at the restoration of the special bodies of armed men at *its* service, and how the oppressed class tries to create a new organization of a similar nature, capable of serving not the exploiting, but the exploited class.

In the above discussion, Engels poses theoretically the very same question which is presented to us in a practical, palpable form, on a mass-scale, by every great revolution, viz.: the question of the relation between 'special bodies of armed men' and the 'self-acting armed organization of the population'. We shall see how this question is illustrated concretely by the experience of the European and Russian revolutions.

But let us return to Engels.

He points out that sometimes (for instance, here and there in North America) this public power is weak (he has in mind here rare exceptions in capitalist society and parts of North America in its pre-Imperialist days, where the free colonist predominated), but that in general, it tends to become stronger:—

'The above-mentioned public force increases with the intensification of class antagonisms within the State, and with the growth in size and population of the adjacent States. One has but to glance at present-day Europe in which the class-struggle and rivalry in conquests have screwed up that public force to such a pitch that it threatens to swallow up the whole of Society and even the State itself. . . .'

This was written as far back as the beginning of the 'nineties of last century, Engles' last Preface being dated June 16, 1891. The turn towards Imperialism, in the shape both of a complete domination of the Trusts and of the all-powerful large banks, and of a colonial policy on a grand scale and so forth, had only just begun in France, and was even weaker in North America and in Germany. Since then the 'rivalry in conquests' has made gigantic advances—especially as, by the beginning of the second decade of the twentieth century, the whole world had been finally divided up between these 'rival conquerors', that is, between the great Predatory Powers. Military and naval armaments then grew to monstrous proportions, and the predatory war of 1914-17 for the domination of the world by England or Germany, for the division of the spoils, bids fair to bring about the 'swallowing up' of all the forces of Society by the rapacious State power, and lead to a complete catastrophe.

Already in 1891 Engels was able to point to 'rivalry in

conquests' as one of the most important features of the foreign policy of the Great Powers, but in 1914-1917, when this rivalry, many times intensified, had given birth to an Imperialist war, the rascally Social-Chauvinists cover up their defence of the policy of grab of 'their' capitalist classes by phrases about the 'defence of the Fatherland', or 'the defence of the Republic and the Revolution' and so on, and so on!

3 THE STATE AS AN INSTRUMENT OF EXPLOITATION OF THE OPPRESSED CLASS

For the maintenance of a special public force standing above Society, taxes and State loans are indispensable.

'Wielding public power and the right to exact taxes, the officials [Engels writes] are raised as organs of Society, *above* Society. The free, voluntary respect enjoyed by the organs of the tribal (clan) society is no longer sufficient for them, even could they win it.'

Special laws are enacted regarding the sanctity and the inviolability of the officials. 'The most insignificant police servant' has more authority than the representative of the clan, but even the head of a civilized State might well envy the Elder of a clan in respect of the 'spontaneous, unforced regard on the part of Society' enjoyed by that Elder.

Here is the question raised of the privileged position of the officials as organs of the State power, and the fundamental problem that has to be answered is this:—What is it that places them above Society? We shall see how this theoretical problem was solved practically by the Paris Commune in 1871 and how it was slurred over in a reactionary manner in 1912 by Kautsky.

'Since the State arose out of the need of keeping in check the antagonisms of classes; since at the same time it arose as a *result* of the collisions of these classes, it is, as a general rule, the State of the most powerful and economically predominant class, which by means of the State also becomes the predominant class politically, thereby obtaining new means for the oppression and exploitation of the oppressed class.'

It was not only the ancient and feudal States which were organs of exploitation of the slaves and serfs, but the '. . .

modern representative State, too, is the means of exploitation of wage labour by capital. By way of exceptions, however, there are periods when the warring classes attain such an equilibrium of strength that the State power for a time becomes, to an extent, independent of both classes and appears as a mediator between them. . . .'

Such, for instance, were the absolute monarchies of the seventeenth and eighteenth centuries, the Bonapartism of the First and Third Empires in France, and the Bismarck regime in Germany.

Such, we may add, is now the Kerensky Government in Republican Russia after it has initiated the persecution of the revolutionary proletariat, at a moment when the Soviets, thanks to the leadership of the lower middle-class democrats, have already become impotent whilst the capitalist class is not yet strong enough to dissolve them.

'In a democratic Republic [Engels continues] wealth uses its power indirectly, but so much the more effectively, first, by means of direct bribery of officials [as in America]; second, by means of an alliance between the Government and the Stock Exchange [as in France and America].'

At the present time, Imperialism and the domination of the banks have reduced to a fine art both these methods of defending and practically asserting the omnipotence of wealth in democratic Republics of all descriptions. If, for instance, in the very first months of the Russian Democratic Republic—one might say during the honeymoon of the union of the 'Socialist'-Revolutionaries and Mensheviks with the bourgeoisie in the Coalition Ministry, M. Paltchinski obstructed every measure of restraint against the capitalists and war-profiteering, or the plunder of the public treasury by army contractors; and if, after his resignation, M. Paltchinski (replaced, of course, by an exactly similar Paltchinski) was 'rewarded' by the capitalists with a 'cushy' little job carrying a salary of 120,000 roubles (£12,000) per annum, what was this? Direct or indirect bribery? A league of the Government with the capitalist syndicates, or 'only' friendly relations? What is the precise rôle played by Tchernoff, Tseretelli, Avksentieff and Skobeleff? Are they the 'direct', or 'only' the indirect, allies of the millionaire thieves who are plundering the public treasury? The omnipotence of 'wealth' is also more 'secure' in a democratic republic, because it does not depend on the bad political form of capitalism. The democratic Republic is the best possible political form for capitalism, and, therefore, once capital has gained control (through the Paltchinskis, Tchernoffs, Tseretellis & Co.) of this very best form, it establishes its power so securely, so firmly that no change of persons, or institutions, or parties, in the bourgeois republic can shake it.

We must also note that Engels quite definitely regards universal suffrage as a means of capitalist domination. Universal suffrage, he says (summing up obviously the long experience of German Social Democracy), is 'an index of the maturity of the working class; it cannot, and never will, give anything more in the present state'. The lower middle-class democrats such as our Socialist-Revolutionaries and Mensheviks and also their twin brothers, the Social-Chauvinists and opportunists of Western Europe, all expect a 'great deal' from this universal suffrage. They themselves think and instil into the minds of the people the wrong idea that universal suffrage in the 'present state' is really capable of expressing the will of the majority of the labouring masses and of securing its realization.

Here we can only note this wrong idea, and point out that this perfectly clear, exact, and concrete statement by Engels is distorted at every step in the propaganda and agitation of the 'official' (that is, opportunist) Socialist parties. A detailed exposure of all the falseness of this idea, which Engels simply brushes aside, is given in our further account of the views of Marx and Engels on the 'modern' State.

A general summary of his views is given by Engels in the most popular of his works in the following words:—

'Thus, the State has not always existed. There were societies which did without it, which had no idea of the State or of State power. At a given stage of economic development, which was necessarily bound up with the break up of society into classes, the State became a necessity, as a result of this division. We are now rapidly approaching a stage in the development of production, in which the existence of these classes is not only no longer necessary, but is becoming a direct impediment to production. Classes will vanish as inevitably as they inevitably arose in the past. With the disappearance of classes the State, too, will inevitably disappear. When organizing production anew on the basis of a free and equal association of the producers, Society will banish the whole State machine to a place which will then be the most proper one for it—to the museum of antiquities side by side with the spinning-wheel and the bronze axe.'

It is not often that we find this passage quoted in the propagandist literature of contemporary Social Democracy. But even when we do come across it, it is generally quoted as some sacred or ritual formula, that is, merely to show official respect for Engels, without any attempt to gauge the width and the depth of the revolutionary act presupposed by this 'banishment of the whole State machine to the museum of antiquities'. And often one cannot even trace the least comprehension of what Engels calls the State machine.

4 THE WITHERING AWAY OF THE STATE AND REVOLUTION BY FORCE

Engels' words regarding the 'withering away' of the State enjoy such a popularity, are so often quoted, and reveal so clearly the essence of the common adulteration of Marxism in an opportunist sense that we must examine them in detail. Let us give the whole argument from which they are taken.

'The proletariat takes control of the State authority and, first of all, converts the means of production into State property. But by this very act it destroys itself, as a proletariat, destroying at the same time all class differences and class antagonisms, and with this, also, the State. Past and present Society, which moved amidst class antagonisms, had to have the State, that is, an organization of the exploiting class for the support of its external conditions of production, therefore, in particular, for the forcible retention of the exploited class in such conditions of oppression (such as slavery, serfdom, wage-labour), as are determined by the given methods of production. The State was the official representative of the whole of Society, its embodiment in a visible corporation; but it was such only in so far as it was the State of that class which, in the given epoch, alone represented the whole of Society. In ancient times it was the State of the slave-owners—the only citizens of the State; in the middle ages it was the State of the feudal nobility: in our own times it is the State of the capitalists. When, ultimately, the State really becomes the representative of the whole of Society, it will make itself superfluous. From the time when, together with class domination and the struggle for individual existence, resulting from the present anarchy in production, those conflicts and excesses which arise from this struggle will all disappear—from that time there will be nobody to be oppressed; there will, therefore, be no need for any special force of oppression—no need for the State. The first act of the State, in which it really acts as the representative of the whole of Society, namely, the assumption of control over the means of production on behalf of Society, is also its last independent act as a State. The interference of the authority of the State with social relations will then become superfluous in one field after another, and finally will cease of itself. The authority of the Government over persons will be replaced by the administration of things and the direction of the processes of production. The State will not be "abolished"; it will wither away. It is from this point of view that we must appraise the phrase, "a free popular State"—a phrase which, for a time, had a right to be employed as a purely propaganda slogan, but which in the long run is scientifically untenable. It is also from this point of view that we must appraise the demand of the so-called anarchists that the State "should be abolished overnight".' (*Herr Eugen Dührings Umwälzung der Wissenschaft*, p. 302, 303, 3rd German Edition.)

Without fear of committing an error, it can be said that the only point in this argument by Engels, so singularly rich in ideas, which has become an integral part of Socialist thought among modern Socialist parties has been that, according to Marx, the State 'withers away' in contradiction to the Anarchist teaching of the 'abolition' of the State. To emasculate Marxism in such a manner is simply to reduce it to opportunism, for such an 'interpretation' only leaves the semi-articulate conception of a slow, even, continuous change, free from leaps and storms, free from Revolution. The current popular conception, if one may say so, of the 'withering away' of the State undoubtedly means a quenching, if not negation, of Revolution. Yet, such an 'interpretation' is a most vulgar distortion of Marxism, advantageous only to the capitalist classes and based theoretically on the neglect of the most important conditions and considerations pointed out in the very passage summarizing Engels' ideas, which we have just quoted in full.

In the first place, at the very outset of his argument, Engels says that in assuming State power, the proletariat 'by that very act destroys the State as such'. It is not the custom to reflect on what this really means. Generally, it is either ignored altogether or it is considered as a piece of 'Hegelian weakness' on Engels' part. As a matter of fact, however, these words express succinctly the experience of one of the greatest proletarian revolutions—the Paris Commune of 1871, of which we shall speak in greater detail in its own place. In reality, Engels speaks here of the *destruction* of the capitalist State by the proletarian revolution, while the words about its withering away refer to the remains of a *proletarian* State *after* the Socialist revolution. The capitalist State does not wither away, according to Engels, but is *destroyed* by the proletariat in the course of the revolution. Only the proletarian State or semi-State withers away after the revolution.

Second, the State is a 'particular power of suppression.' This splendid and extremely profound definition of Engels is given by him here with complete lucidity. It follows therefrom that the 'particular power of suppression' of the proletariat by the capitalist class, of the millions of workers by a handful of rich, must be replaced by a 'particular power of suppression' of the capitalist class by the proletariat (the dictatorship of the proletariat). It is just this that constitutes the destruction of the State as such. It is just this that constitutes the 'act' of taking possession of the means of production on behalf of Society. And it is obvious that such a substitution of one (capitalist) 'particular power' by another (proletarian) 'particular power' could in no way take place in the form of a 'withering away'.

Third, in using the term, 'withering away', Engels refers quite clearly and definitely to the period *after* 'the taking over of the means of production by the State on behalf of the whole of Society', that is, after the Socialist Revolution. We all know that the proletarian form of the 'State' is then an absolutely complete democracy. But it never enters the head of any of the opportunists who shamelessly distort Marx that Engels deals here with the withering away of the Democracy. At first sight this seems very strange. But it will only be unintelligible to one who has not reflected on the fact that Democracy is also a State and that, consequently, Democracy will also disappear when the State disappears. Only a revolution can 'destroy' the capitalist State. The State in general, that is, most complete Democracy, can only wither away.

Fourth, having formulated his famous proposition that 'the State withers away,' Engels at once explains concretely that this proposition is directed equally against the opportunists and the anarchists. In doing this, however, Engels draws, in the first place, that deduction from his proposition, which is directed against the opportunists.

One can wager that out of every 10,000 persons who have read or heard of the 'withering away' of the State 9,990 do not know at all, or do not remember that Engels did not direct his conclusions from this proposition against the anarchists alone. And out of the remaining ten, nine do not know the meaning of a 'free popular State' nor the reason why an attack on this watchword contains an attack on the opportunists. This is how history is written! This is how a great revolutionary doctrine is imperceptibly adulterated and adapted to current philistinism! The reference to the anarchists has been repeated thousands of times, has been vulgarized in the crudest fashion possible until it has acquired the strength of a prejudice, whereas the reference to the opportunists has been hushed up and 'forgotten'.

'A free popular State' was the demand and current watchword in the programme of the German Social Democrats of the 'seventies. There is no political substance in this watchword other than a pompous middle-class circumlocution of the idea of Democracy. In so far as it pointed in 'lawful' manner at a democratic Republic, Engels was prepared 'for a time' to justify it from a propaganda point of view. But this watchword was really opportunist, for it not only took an exaggerated view of the attractiveness of bourgeois democracy, but also implied a lack of understanding of the Socialist criticism of the State in general. We are in favour of a democratic Republic as the best form of the State for the proletariat under Capitalism, but we have no right to forget that wage slavery is the lot of the people even in the most democratic middle-class Republic. Furthermore, every State is a 'particular power of suppression' of the oppressed class. Consequently, no State is either 'free' or 'popular.' Marx and Engels explained this repeatedly to their party comrades in the 'seventies.

Fifth, in the same work of Engels, from which everyone remembers his argument on 'withering away' of the State, there is also a disquisition on the nature of a violent revolution; and the historical appreciation of its rôle becomes, with Engels, a veritable panegyric of a revolution by force. This, of course, no one remembers. To talk or even to think of the importance of this idea, is not considered respectable by our modern Socialist parties, and in the daily propaganda and agitation among the masses it plays no part whatever. Yet is is indissolubly bound up with the 'withering away' of the State in one harmonious whole. Here is Engels' argument:

'That force also plays another part in history (other than that of a perpetuation of evil), namely, a *revolutionary* part; that, as Marx says, it is the midwife of every old society when it is pregnant with a new one; that force is the instrument and the means by which social movements hack their way through and break up the dead and fossilized political forms—of all this not a word by Herr Dühring. Duly, with sighs and groans, does he admit the possibility that for the overthrow of the system of exploitation force may, perhaps, be necessary, but most unfortunate if you please, because all use of force, forsooth, demoralises its user! And this is said in face of the great moral and intellectual advance which has been the result of every victorious revolution! And this is said in Germany where a violent collision—which might, perhaps, be forced on the people—should have, at the very least, this advantage that it would destroy the spirit of subservience which has been permeating the national mind ever since the degradation and humiliation of the Thirty Years' War. And this turbid, flabby, impotent, parson's mode of thinking dares offer itself for acceptance to the most revolutionary party history has ever known!' (p. 193, 3rd German Edition).

How can this eulogy of a revolution by force, which Engels used to propound to the German Social Democrats between 1878-94, that is, up to the very day of his death, be reconciled with the theory of the 'withering away' of the State, and combined into one doctrine? Usually the two views are combined by a process of eclecticism, by an unprincipled, sophistic, arbitrary selection sometimes of passages here and there (to oblige the powers that be)—and in ninety-nine cases out of a hundred (if not more often), it is the idea of the withering away of the State that is specially emphasized. Dialectics is replaced by eclectics— this is the most usual, the most widespread method used in the official Social Democratic literature of our day in respect of Marxist teachings. Such a substitution is, of course, not new; one can see it even in the history of classic Greek philosophy. In the process of camouflaging Marxism as Opportunism the substitution of eclecticism for dialectics is the best method of deceiving the masses. It gives an illusory satisfaction. It seems to take into account all sides of the process, all the tendencies of development, all the contradictory factors and so forth, whereas, in reality, it offers no consistent revolutionary view of the process of social development at all.

We have already said above and shall show more fully at a later stage that the teaching of Marx and Engels regarding the inevitability of a violent revolution refers to the capitalist State. It cannot be replaced by the proletarian State (the dictatorship of the proletariat) through mere 'withering away', but, in accordance with the general rule, can only be brought about by a violent revolution. The hymn of praise sung in its honour by Engels and fully corresponding to the repeated declarations of Marx (see the concluding passages of the *Poverty of Philosophy* and the *Communist Manifesto*, with its proud and open declaration of the inevitability of a violent revolution; also Marx's *Criticism of the Gotha Programme of* 1875, in which, thirty years after, he mercilessly castigates its opportunist character)—this praise is by no means a mere 'impulse', a mere declamation, or a mere polemical sally. The necessity of systematically fostering among the masses this and only this point of view about violent revolution lies at the root of the whole of Marx's and Engels' teaching, and it is just the neglect of such propaganda and agitation both by the present predominant Social-Chauvinists and the Kautskian schools that brings their betrayal of it into prominent relief.

The substitution of a proletarian for the capitalist State is impossible without a violent revolution, while the abolition of the proletarian State, that is, of all States, is only possible through 'withering away'.

Marx and Engels gave a full and concrete illustration of these views in their study of each revolutionary situation separately, by an analysis of the lessons of the experience of each individual revolution. To this, undoubtedly the most important part of their work, we shall now pass.

CHAPTER II

The Experience of 1848-51

_____

I THE EVE OF REVOLUTION

THE first production of mature Marxism—*The Poverty of Philosophy* and *The Communist Manifesto*—date from the very eve of the revolution of 1848. As a result of this fact, we have in them, side by side with a statement of the general principles of Marxism, a reflection, to a certain degree, of the concrete revolutionary situation at that moment. Consequently, it will possibly be more to the point to examine what the authors of these works had written of the State immediately before they drew conclusions from their experience of the years 1848-51.

'The working class,' wrote Marx in *The Poverty of Philosophy*, 'will in the course of its development, replace the old bourgeois society by a society which will exclude classes and their antagonisms: there will no longer be any political authority in the proper sense of the word, since political authority is the official expression of the antagonism of classes within bourgeois society' (German Edition, 1885, p. 182).

It is instructive to compare, side by side with this general statement of the idea of the disappearance of the State with the disappearance of classes, the statement contained in the *Communist Manifesto*, written by Marx and Engels a few months later—to be precise, in November, 1847:

'Tracing the most general phases of the development of the proletariat, we followed up the more or less hidden civil war within existing society to the point at which it is transformed into open revolution, and the proletariat establishes its rule by means of the violent overthrow of the capitalist class. . . . We have already seen that the first step in the Workers' revolution is the transformation [literally 'the promotion'] of the proletariat into the ruling class, the conquest of democracy. . . . The proletariat will use its political supremacy in order gradually to wrest the whole of capital from the capitalist class, to centralise all the instruments of production in the hands of the State, i.e. of the proletariat organized as the ruling class, and to increase as quickly as possible the total of productive forces' (7th German Edition, 1906, pp. 31-37).

Here we have a formulation of one of the most remarkable and most important ideas of Marxism on the subject of the State—namely, the idea of 'the dictatorship of the proletariat' (as Marx and Engels began to write after the Paris Commune); and also a definition of the State, in the highest degree interesting, but nevertheless also belonging to the category of forgotten thoughts of Marxism: '*The State, that is, the proletariat organized as the ruling class.*'

This definition of the State, so far from having ever been explained in the current propagandist and agitation literature of the official Social-Democratic parties, has been deliberately forgotten, as it is quite irreconcilable with Reformism, strikes straight at the heart of the common opportunist prejudices and middle-class illusions about the 'peaceful development of democracy'.

'The proletariat needs the State', a phrase repeated by all the Opportunists, Social-Chauvinists and Kautskians, who assure us that this is what Marx taught. They 'forget', however, to add that, in the first place, the proletariat, according to Marx, needs only a withering away State—a State, that is, so constituted that it begins to wither away immediately, and cannot but wither away; and, secondly, the workers 'need' a State, 'that is, the proletariat organized as the ruling class'.

The State is a particular form of organization of force; it is the organization of violence for the purpose of holding down some class. What is the class which the proletariat must hold down? It can only be, naturally, the exploiting class, i.e. the bourgeoisie. The toilers need the State only to overcome the resistance of the exploiters, and only the proletariat can guide this suppression and bring it to fulfilment—the proletariat, the only class revolutionary to the finish, the only class which can unite all the toilers and the exploited in the struggle against the capitalist class for its complete displacement from power.

The exploiting classes need political supremacy in order to maintain exploitation, i.e. in the selfish interests of a tiny minority, and against the vast majority of the community. The exploited classes need political supremacy in order completely to abolish all exploitation, i.e. in the interests of the enormous majority of the people, and against the tiny minority constituted by the slave-owners of modern times—the landlords and the capitalists. The lower middle-class democrats, these sham Socialists who have replaced the class-war by dreams of harmony between classes, have imagined even the transition to Socialism, in a dream, as it were—that is, not in the form of the overthrow of the supremacy of the exploiting class, but in the form of the peaceful submission of the minority to the fully enlightened majority. This lower middle-class Utopia, indissolubly connected with the vision of a State above classes, in practice led to the betrayal of the interests of the toiling classes, as was shown, for example, in the history of the Revolutions of 1848 and 1871, and in that of 'Socialist' participation in bourgeois Ministries in England, France, Italy, and other countries, at the end of the nineteenth and the beginning of the twentieth centuries.

Marx fought all his life against this lower middle-class Socialism—now re-born in Russia in the Menshevik and S.R. parties. He carried his analysis of the class-war logically, right up to the doctrine on political power and the State.

The overthrow of capitalist supremacy can be accomplished only by the proletariat, as the particular class, which is being prepared for this work, and is provided both with the opportunity and the power to perform it, by the economic conditions of its existence. While the capitalist class breaks up and dissolves the peasantry and all the lower middle classes, it welds together, unites and organizes the town proletariat. Only the proletariat— on account of its economic rôle in production on a large scale— is capable of leading *all* the toiling and exploited masses, who are exploited, oppressed, crushed by the capitalists often more, not less, than the town proletariat, but who are incapable of carrying on the struggle for freedom unaided.

The doctrine of the class-war, as applied by Marx to the question of the State and of the Socialist revolution, leads inevitably to the recognition of the *political supremacy* of the proletariat, of its dictatorship, i.e. of an authority shared with none else and relying directly upon the armed force of the masses. The overthrow of the capitalist class is feasible only by the transformation of the proletariat into the *ruling class*, able to crush the inevitable and desperate resistance of the bourgeoisie, and to organize, for the new settlement of economic order, *all* the toiling and exploited masses.

The proletariat needs the State, the centralized organization of force and violence, both for the purpose of crushing the resistance of the exploiters and for the purpose of guiding the great mass of the population—the peasantry, the lower middle-class, the semi-proletariat—in the work of economic Socialist reconstruction.

By educating a workers' party, Marxism educates also the advance-guard of the proletariat, capable of assuming power and of *leading the whole community* to Socialism, fit to direct and organize the new order, to be the teacher, guide, leader of all the toiling and exploited in the task of building up their common life without capitalists and against capitalists. As against this, the Opportunism predominant at present breeds in the labour movement a class of representatives of the better-paid workers, who lose touch with the rank and file, 'get-on' fairly well under Capitalism, and sell their birthright for a mess of pottage, i.e. renounce the rôle of revolutionary leaders of the people against the capitalist class.

'The State, i.e. the proletariat organized as the ruling class'—this theory of Marx's is indissolubly connected with all his teaching concerning the revolutionary part to be played in history by the proletariat. The fulfilment of this part is proletarian dictatorship, the political supremacy of the proletariat.

But, if the proletariat needs the State, as a particular form of organization of force *against* the capitalist class, the question almost spontaneously forces itself upon us: Is it thinkable that such an organization can be created without a preliminary breaking-up and destruction of the machinery of government created for *its own* use by the capitalist class? The *Communist Manifesto* leads us straight to this conclusion, and it is of this conclusion that Marx wrote when summing up the practical results of the revolutionary experience gained between 1848 and 1851.

2 THE RESULTS OF REVOLUTION

On this question of the State with which we are concerned, Marx sums up his conclusions from the revolutions of the years 1848-51 in the following way (in his work *The Eighteenth Brumaire of Louis Bonaparte*):—

'Nevertheless, the Revolution is thorough. It is still passing through its purgatory. It is doing its work systematically. By December 2, 1851 [the day of Louis Bonaparte's *coup d'état*] it had fulfilled half of its programme; now it is fulfilling the other half. First, it perfected parliamentary power, in order to be able to overthrow it. Now, when this has been accomplished, it is drawing the *executive power* through the perfecting process; it reduces that power to its simplest terms, isolates it, sets it up against itself as its own sole reproach—all in order to *concentrate against it all the forces of destruction* [the italics are ours]. And when the revolution has completed this second part of its preliminary work, Europe will rise to exclaim in triumph, "Well grubbed, old mole!" . . . This executive power with its enormous bureau-cratic and military organization, with its multiform and artificial machinery of government, with this army of half a million officials, side by side with a military force of another half million, this frightful parasitic organism covering as with a net the whole body of French society and blocking up all its pores, had arisen in the period of absolute monarchy, at the time of the fall of Feudalism: a fall which this organism had helped to hasten.'

The first French Revolution developed centralization 'but at the same time increased the scope, the attributes, the number of servants of the central Government. Napoleon completed this Government machinery.' The Legitimist and the July monarchies 'contributed nothing but a greater division of labour'. . . . 'Finally, the Parliamentary Republic found itself compelled, in its struggle against the Revolution, along with its repressive measures, to increase the resources and the centralization of the State. *Every Revolution brought this machine to greater perfection instead of breaking it up* [the italics are ours]. The political parties, which alternately struggled for supremacy, looked upon the capture of this gigantic governmental structure as the principal spoils of victory.' (*Eighteenth Brumaire of Louis Bonaparte*, 1907 German Edition, pp. 98, 99.)

In this remarkable passage Marxism makes a great step forward in comparison with the position of the *Communist Manifesto*. There the question of the State is dealt with still extremely in the abstract, and most general ideas and expressions are employed. Here the question becomes concrete, and the conclusions are most precise, definite, practical: all former revolutions helped to perfect the machinery of Government, whereas now we must shatter it, break it to pieces.

This conclusion is the chief and fundamental point in the Marxist theory of the State, yet it is exactly this fundamental point which has been not merely completely 'forgotten' by the dominant official Social-Democratic parties, but absolutely distorted (as we shall see later) by the foremost theoretician of the Second International, K. Kautsky.

In the *Communist Manifesto* are set out the general lessons of history, which force us to see in the State the organ of class domination, and bring us to the necessary conclusion that the proletariat cannot overthrow the capitalist class without, as a preliminary step, winning political power, without obtaining political supremacy, without transforming the State into the 'proletariat organized as the ruling class'; and that this proletarian State must begin to wither away immediately after its victory, because in a community without class antagonisms, the State is unnecessary and impossible. At this stage the problem is not yet considered as to what form, from the point of view of historical development, this replacement of the capitalist State by the proletarian State is to assume.

It is precisely this problem that is stated and solved by Marx in 1852. True to his philosophy of dialectical materialism, Marx takes as his basis the experience of the great revolutionary years 1848-51. Here, as everywhere, his teaching is the summing-up of practical experience, illuminated by a profound philosophical world-conception and a great knowledge of history.

The problem of the State is put concretely: how, in actual fact, the capitalist State arose, that is, the governmental machine necessary for capitalist supremacy? What have been its changes, what has been its evolution in the course of the bourgeois revolutions and in the face of the spontaneous risings of the oppressed classes ? What are the problems confronting the proletariat in respect of this government machine ?

The centralized power of the State, peculiar to capitalist society, grew up in the period of the fall of Feudalism. Two institutions are especially characteristic of this machine: the bureaucracy and the standing army. More than once, in the works of Marx and Engels, we find mention of the thousand threads which connect these institutions with the capitalist class; and the experience of every worker illustrates this connection with extraordinary clearness and impressiveness. The working class learns to recognize this connection by its own bitter experience; that is why it so easily acquires, so firmly absorbs the idea of its inevitability—an idea which the lower middle-class democrats either ignorantly and superficially deny, or, still more superficially admit 'in theory', forgetting to draw the corresponding practical conclusions.

The bureaucracy and the standing army constitute a 'parasite' on the body of capitalist society—a parasite born of the internal struggles which tear that society asunder, but essentially a parasite, 'blocking up' the pores of existence. The Kautskian Opportunism prevalent at present amongst the official Social-Democratic parties considers this view of the State as *a parasitic organism* to be the peculiar and exclusive property of Anarchism. Naturally, this distortion of Marxism is extremely useful to those philistines who have brought Socialism to the unheard-of disgrace of trying to justify and gloss over an Imperialist war on the pretext of 'defence of the fatherland'; but none the less it is an absolute distortion.

The development, perfection, strengthening of the bureaucratic and military apparatus has been going on during all those bourgeois revolutions of which Europe has seen so many since the decay of Feudalism.

In particular, the lower middle-classes are attracted to the side of the capitalists and to their allegiance, largely by means of this very apparatus, which provides the upper sections of the peasantry, artisans and tradesmen with a number of comparatively comfortable, quiet and respectable posts, and thereby raises their holders above the general mass. Consider what happened in Russia during the six months following February 27 (March 12), 1917. The Government posts, which hitherto had been given by preference to members of the Black Hundreds, now became the booty of Cadets, Mensheviks and Socialist-Revolutionaries. Nobody really thought of any serious reforms. They were to be put off 'till the Constituent Assembly', which, in its turn, was gradually put off until the end of the war! But there was no delay, no waiting for a Constituent Assembly in the matter of dividing the spoils, of capturing snug places like Ministries, Under-Secretaryships, Governor-Generalships, etc., etc.! The game of permutations and combinations that went on in connection with the composition of the Provisional Government was, in reality, merely the expression of this division and re-division of the spoils, as it was going on high and low, up and down the country, in all departments of the central and local government. The concrete, practical result of the six months between February 27 (March 12) and August 27 (September 9), 1917, is beyond all dispute: reforms shelved, distribution of the official places accomplished, and 'mistakes' in the distribution corrected by a few re-shufflings. But the longer the process of re-shuffling the posts goes on among the various capitalist and middle-class parties (among the Cadets, S.R.s and Mensheviks, if we take the case of Russia), the more clearly the oppressed classes, with the proletariat at their head, begin to realize the irreconcilable opposition of their interests to the *whole* of capitalist society. Hence arises the necessity for the bourgeois parties, even for the most democratic and 'revolutionary democratic' sections, to increase their repressive measures against the revolutionary proletariat, to strengthen the machinery of repression, that is, the power of the State. Such a course of events compels the Revolution '*to concentrate all the forces of destruction*' against the State, and to regard the problem as one not of perfecting the machinery of the State, but of *breaking up and annihilating it.*

It was not logical theorizing, but the practical course of events, the living experience of the years 1848-51, that produced such a statement of the problem. We can see to what extent Marx held strictly to the solid ground of historical experience from the fact that, in 1852, he did not as yet deal concretely with the question of what was to replace this State machinery that had to be destroyed. Experience had not as yet yielded material data sufficient for the solution of such a problem: history placed it on the order of the day later on, in 1871. In 1852 it could only be laid down, with the accuracy that comes of scientific historical observation, that the proletarian revolution *had arrived* at the stage when it must consider the problem of 'concentrating all the forces of destruction' against the State, of 'breaking' the Governmental machine.

Here the question may arise: is it correct to generalize the experience, observation and conclusions of Marx, and to apply them to a wider scene of action that that of France during three years (1848-51)? In the discussion of this point, let us recall, first of all, a remark of Engels, and then proceed to examine our facts.

'France,' wrote Engels in his introduction to the 3rd Edition of the *Eighteenth Brumaire*, 'France is a country in which the historical struggle of classes, more than in any other, was carried each time to a decisive conclusion. In France were hammered into most definite shapes those changing political forms within which that class struggle went on, and through which its results found expression. The centre of Feudalism during the Middle Ages; the model country, with the most centralized monarchy, based on rigid ranks and orders after the Renaissance, France shattered Feudalism during the Great Revolution, and founded the undiluted supremacy of the middle class with such classical clearness as was to be found in no other European country. And the struggle of the revolting proletariat against the capitalist tyranny is in its turn taking here an acute form which is unknown elsewhere' (Edition 1907, p. 4).

The last sentence is out of date, inasmuch as there has been a lull in the revolutionary struggle of the French proletariat since 1871; though, long as this lull may be, it in no way excludes the possibility that, in the oncoming proletarian revolution, France may once more reveal itself as the traditional home of the class-war to a finish.

Let us, however, cast a general glance over the history of the more advanced nations during the end of the nineteenth and beginning of the twentieth centuries. We shall see that the same process has been going on more slowly, in more varied forms, on a much wider field. On the one hand, there has been a development of 'parliamentary Government' not only in the republican countries (France, America, Switzerland), but also in the monarchies (England, Germany to a certain extent, Italy, the Scandinavian countries, etc.). On the other hand, there has been the struggle for power of the various middle and lower middle-class parties distributing and re-distributing the 'plunder' of official appointments, the foundations of capitalist society remaining all the while unchanged. Finally, there has been the perfecting and strengthening of the 'Executive' and of its bureaucratic and military apparatus.

There can be no doubt that these are the general features of the latest stage in the evolution of all capitalist States generally. In the three years, 1848-51, France had shown in a swift, sharp, concentrated form, all those processes of development which are inherent in the whole capitalist world.

Imperialism in particular, the era of financial capital, the era of gigantic capitalist monopolies, the era of the transformation of *simple* trust-capitalism into *State* trust-capitalism, shows an unprecedented strengthening of the 'State' and an unheard of development of its bureaucratic and military apparatus, side by side with the increase of oppression of the proletariat, alike in the Monarchical and the freest republican countries.

World-history is undoubtedly leading up at the present moment, on an incomparably larger scale than in 1852, to the 'concentration of all the forces' of the proletarian revolution for the purpose of 'breaking up' the machinery of the State.

As to what the proletariat will put in its place, instructive data on the subject were given us by the Paris Commune.

3 THE PRESENTATION OF THE QUESTION BY MARX IN 1852[1]

In 1907, Mehring, in the magazine *Neue Zeit*[2] (Vol. XXV, 2, p. 164), published extracts from a letter from Marx to

---

[1] This section was added by Lenin in the second Russian edition of *The State and Revolution*, 1918.—*Ed.*

[2] *New Times*, the theoretical organ of the Social Democratic Party of Germany.—*Ed.*

Weydemeyer dated March 5, 1852. This letter, among other things, contains the following remarkable observation:

'And now as to myself, no credit is due to me for discovering the existence of classes in modern society, nor yet the struggle between them. Long before me, bourgeois historians had described the historical development of this class struggle, and bourgeois economists the economic anatomy of the classes. What I did that was new was to prove: (1) that the *existence of classes* is only bound up with *particular historical phases in the development of production* [*historische Entwicklungsphasen der Produktion*]; (2) that the class struggle necessarily leads to the *dictatorship of the proletariat;* (3) that this dictatorship itself only constitutes the transition to the *abolition of all classes and to a classless society.*'[1]

In these words Marx succeeded in expressing with striking clarity, first, the chief and radical difference between his doctrine and those of the most advanced and most profound thinkers of the bourgeoisie; and, second, the essence of his doctrine of the state.

It is often said and written that the core of Marx's theory is the class struggle, but it is not true. And from this error, very often, springs the opportunist distortion of Marxism, its falsification to make it acceptable to the bourgeoisie. The theory of the class struggle was *not* created by Marx, but by the bourgeoisie *before* Marx, and generally speaking it is *acceptable* to the bourgeoisie. Those who recognize *only* the class struggle are not yet Marxists; those may be found to have gone no further than the boundaries of bourgeois reasoning and bourgeois politics. To limit Marxism to the theory of the class struggle means curtailing Marxism, distorting it, reducing it to something which is acceptable to the bourgeoisie. A Marxist is one who *extends* the acceptance of the class struggle to the acceptance of the *dictatorship of the proletariat*. This is where the profound difference lies between a Marxist and an ordinary petty (and even big) bourgeois. This is the touchstone on which the *real* understanding and acceptance of Marxism should be tested. And it is not surprising that when the history of Europe brought the working class face to face with this question in a *practical* way, not only all the opportunists and reformists, but all the Kautskyists (those who

[1] *The Correspondence of Marx and Engels.—Ed. Eng. ed.*

vacillate between reformism and Marxism) proved to be miserable Philistines and petty-bourgeois democrats who *repudiated* the dictatorship of the proletariat. Kautsky's pamphlet, *The Dictatorship of the Proletariat*, published in August, 1918, i.e. long after the first edition of the present pamphlet, is an example of the petty-bourgeois distortion of Marxism and base renunciation of it *in practice*, while hypocritically recognizing it *in words* (see my pamphlet, *The Proletarian Revolution and the Renegade Kautsky*, Petrograd and Moscow, 1918).

Present-day opportunism in the person of its principal representative, the ex-Marxist, K. Kautsky, fits in completely with Marx's characterization of the *bourgeois* position as quoted above, for this opportunism limits the field of recognition of the class struggle to the realm of bourgeois relationships. (Within this realm, within its framework, not a single educated liberal will refuse to recognize the class struggle 'in principle'!) Opportunism *does not carry* the recognition of class struggle to the main point, to the period of *transition* from capitalism to communism, to the period of the *overthrow* and complete abolition of the bourgeoisie. In reality, this period inevitably becomes a period of unusually violent class struggles in their sharpest possible forms and, therefore, during this period, the state must inevitably be a state that is democratic *in a new way* (for the proletariat and the propertyless in general) and dictatorial *in a new way* (against the bourgeoisie).

To proceed. The essence of Marx's doctrine of the state is assimilated only by those who understand that the dictatorship of a *single* class is necessary not only for class society in general, not only for the *proletariat* which has overthrown the bourgeoisie, but for the entire *historical period* between capitalism and 'classless society', communism. The forms of the bourgeois state are extremely varied, but in essence they are all the same: in one way or another, in the last analysis, all these states are inevitably the *dictatorship of the bourgeoisie*. The transition from capitalism to communism will certainly create a great variety and abundance of political forms, but in essence there will inevitably be only one: *the dictatorship of the proletariat*.

CHAPTER III

The Experience of the Paris Commune of 1871: Marx's Analysis

I IN WHAT LAY THE HEROISM OF THE COMMUNARDS?

IT is known that in the autumn of 1870, a few months before the Commune, Marx warned the Paris workers, proving to them that an attempt to overthrow the Government would be the folly of despair. But when, in March, 1871, a decisive battle was forced upon the workers and they accepted it, when the rising had become an accomplished fact, Marx welcomed the proletarian revolution with the greatest enthusiasm, in spite of unfavourable auguries. Marx did not fall back upon an attitude of pedantic condemnation of an 'untimely' movement: unlike the all-too-famous Russian renegade from Marxism Plekhanoff, who, in November, 1905, wrote in the sense of encouraging the workers' and peasants' struggle, but, after December, 1905, took up the liberal cry of 'You should not have resorted to arms'.

Marx, however, was not only enthusiastic about the heroism of the Communards—'storming Heaven', as he said. In the mass revolutionary movement, although it did not attain its objective, he saw a historic experiment of gigantic importance, a certain advance of the world proletarian revolution, a practical step more important than hundreds of programmes and discussions. To analyse this experiment, to draw from it lessons in tactics, to re-examine his theory in the new light it afforded—such was the problem as it presented itself to Marx. The only 'correction' which Marx thought it necessary to make in the *Communist Manifesto* was made by him on the basis of the revolutionary experience of the Paris Communards.

The last preface to a new German edition of the *Communist Manifesto* signed by both its authors is dated June 24, 1872. In this preface the authors, Karl Marx and Friedrich Engels, say that the programme of the *Communist Manifesto* is now 'in places out of date'.

'*Especially,*' they continue, '*did the Commune demonstrate that the "working class cannot simply seize the available ready machinery of the State and set it going for its own ends".*'

The words within the second inverted commas of this passage are borrowed by its authors from Marx's book on *The Civil War in France*. One fundamental and principal lesson of the Paris Commune, therefore, was considered by Marx and Engels to be of such enormous importance that they introduced it as a vital correction into the *Communist Manifesto*.

It is most characteristic that it is precisely this correction which has been distorted by the opportunists, and its meaning, probably, is not clear to nine-tenths, if not ninety-nine hundredths, of the readers of the *Communist Manifesto*. We shall deal with it more fully further on, in a chapter devoted specially to distortions. It will be sufficient here to remark that the current, vulgar, 'interpretation' of the famous formula of Marx here adduced consists in that Marx, it is said, is here emphasising the idea of gradual development, in contradistinction to a sudden seizure of power, and so on.

As a matter of fact, *exactly the reverse is the case*. What Marx says is that the working class must *break up, shatter* the 'available ready machinery of the State', and not confine itself merely to taking possession of it.

On April 12, 1871—that is, just at the time of the Commune—Marx wrote to Kugelmann:

'If you look at the last chapter of my *Eighteenth Brumaire*, you will see that I declare the next attempt of the French Revolution to be: not merely to hand over, from one set of hands to another, the bureaucratic and military machine—as has occurred hitherto —but to *shatter* it [Marx's italics—the original is *zerbrechen*]; and it is this that is the preliminary condition of any real people's revolution on the Continent. It is exactly this that constitutes the attempt of our heroic Parisian comrades' (*Neue Zeit*, xx. i., 1901-2, p. 709).

In these words, 'to shatter the bureaucratic and military machinery of the State', is to be found, tersely expressed, the principal teaching of Marxism on the subject of the problems concerning the State, facing the proletariat in a revolution. And it is just this teaching which has not only been forgotten, but has also been completely distorted, by the prevailing Kautskian 'interpretation' of Marxism!

As for Marx's reference to the *Eighteenth Brumaire*, we have quoted the corresponding passage in full above.

It is interesting particularly to notice two points in the passage quoted. First, he confines his conclusions to the Continent. This was natural in 1871, when England was still the pattern of a purely capitalist country, without a military machine and, in large measure, without a bureaucracy.

Hence Marx excluded England, where a revolution, even a people's revolution, could be imagined, and was then possible, *without* the preliminary condition of the destruction 'of the available ready machinery of the State'.

Today in 1917, in the epoch of the first great imperialist war, this distinction of Marx's becomes unreal, and England and America, the greatest and last representatives of Anglo-Saxon 'liberty', in the sense of the absence of militarism and bureaucracy, have today completely rolled down into the dirty, bloody morass of military-bureaucratic institutions common to all Europe, subordinating all else to themselves, crushing all else under themselves. Today, both in England and in America, the 'preliminary condition of any real people's revolution' is the break-up, the shattering of the 'available ready machinery of the State' (perfected in those countries between 1914 and 1917, up to the 'European', general imperialist standard).

Secondly, this extremely pregnant remark of Marx is worth particular attention in that it states that the destruction of the military and bureaucratic machinery of the State is 'the preliminary condition of any real *people's* revolution'. This idea of a 'people's' revolution seems strange on Marx's lips. And the Russian Plekhanovists and Mensheviks, those followers of Struve who wish to be considered Marxists, might possibly consider such an expression a slip of the tongue. They have reduced Marxism to such a state of meagre 'liberal' distortion that nothing exists for them beyond the distinction between capitalist and proletarian revolutions: and even that distinction becomes for them a lifeless doctrine.

If we take examples from the revolutions of the twentieth century, we shall, of course, have to recognize both the Portuguese and the Turkish revolutions to be middle-class. Neither, however, is a 'people's' revolution, inasmuch as the mass of the people, the enormous majority, does not make its appearance actively, independently, with its own economic and political demands, in either the one or the other. On the other hand, the Russian middle-class revolution of 1905-7, although it presented no such 'brilliant' successes as at times fell to the lot of the Portuguese and Turkish revolutions, was undoubtedly a 'real people's' revolution, since the masses of the people, the majority, the lowest social 'depths', crushed down by oppression and exploitation, rose up independently, impressed on all the course of the revolution the stamp of *their* demands, *their* attempts to build up a new order on their own lines in place of the old shattered order.

On the Continent of Europe, in 1871, the proletariat did not in a single country constitute the majority of the people. A 'people's' revolution, actually sweeping the majority into its current, could be such only if embracing both the proletariat and the peasantry. Both classes then constituted the 'people'. Both classes are united by the circumstance that the 'military and bureaucratic machinery of the State' oppresses, crushes, exploits them. *To shatter* this machinery, *to break it up*—this is the true interest of the 'people', of its majority—the workers, and most of the peasants—this is the 'preliminary condition' of a union of the poorest peasantry with the proletarians: while, without such a union, democracy is unstable and Socialist reconstruction is impossible. Towards such a union, as is well known, the Paris Commune was making its way; though it did not reach its goal, by reason of a number of circumstances, internal and external.

Consequently, when speaking of 'a real people's revolution,' Marx did not in the least forget the peculiar characteristics of the lower middle classes (he spoke of them much and often), and was very carefully taking into account the actual relationship of classes in most of the continental European States in 1871. From another standpoint, also, he laid it down that the 'shattering' of the machinery of the State is demanded by the interests both of the workers and of the peasants, unites them, places before them the common task of destroying the 'parasite' and replacing it by something new.

By what exactly?

2 WHAT IS TO REPLACE THE MACHINERY OF THE STATE?

In 1847, in the *Communist Manifesto*, Marx was as yet only able to answer this question entirely in an abstract manner, stating the problem rather than its solution. To replace this machinery by 'the proletariat organized as the ruling class', 'by the conquest of Democracy'—such was the answer of the *Communist Manifesto*.

Refusing to plunge into Utopia, Marx waited for the experience of a mass movement to produce the answer to the problem as to the exact forms which this organization of the proletariat as the dominant class will assume and exactly in what manner this organization will embody the most complete, most consistent, 'conquest of Democracy.' Marx subjected the experiment of the Commune, although it was so meagre, to a most minute analysis in his *Civil War in France*. Let us bring before the reader the most important passages of this work.

In the nineteenth century took place the development of 'the centralized State power, originating from the Middle Ages, with its ubiquitous organs: a standing army, police, bureaucracy, clergy and judges'. With the development of class antagonism between capital and labour, 'the State assumed more and more the character of a public organization for the oppression of labour, that is, of a machine for class domination. After every revolution marking a certain advance in the class struggle, the purely oppressive character of the power of the State became more and more apparent.' The State, after the revolution of 1848-9, becomes 'the national weapon of capital in its war against labour.' The Second Empire consolidates this.

'The Commune was the direct antithesis of the Empire. It was a definite form . . . of a Republic which was to abolish, not only the monarchial form of class rule, but also class rule itself.'

What was this 'definite' form of the proletarian Socialist Republic? What was the State it was beginning to create?

'The first decree of the Commune was the abolition of the

standing army and its replacement by the nation in arms.' This demand now figures in the programme of every party calling itself Socialist. But the value of these programmes is best shown by the behaviour of our Socialist-Revolutionaries and Mensheviks, who refused to put their theories into practice even after the Revolution of March 12, 1917!

'The Council of the Commune consisted of municipal representatives elected by universal suffrage in the various districts of Paris. They were responsible and could be recalled at any time. The majority were, naturally, working men or acknowledged representatives of the working class. . . .'

' . . . The police, until then merely an instrument of the Government, was immediately stripped of all its political functions, and turned into the responsible and at any time replaceable organ of the Commune. . . .'

' . . . The same was applied to the officials of all other branches of the administration. From the members of the Council of the Commune down to the humblest worker, everybody in the public services was paid at the same rates as ordinary working men. All privileges and representation allowances attached to the high offices of the State disappeared along with the offices themselves. . . . Having got rid of the standing army and police, the material weapons of the old Government, the Commune turned its attention, without delay, to breaking the weapons of spiritual oppression, the power of the priests. . . . The judicial functionaries lost their sham independence. . . . In future, they were to be elected openly and to be responsible and revocable. . . .'

And so the Commune would seem to have replaced the broken machinery of the State, 'only' by a fuller democracy: the abolition of the standing army and the transformation of all officials into elective and revocable agents of the State. But, as a matter of fact, this 'only' represents a gigantic replacement of one type of institutions by others of a fundamentally different order. Here we see precisely a case of the 'transformation of quantity into quality'. Democracy, carried out with the fullest imaginable completeness and consistency, is transformed from capitalist democracy into proletarian democracy: from the State (that is, a special force for the suppression of a particular class) to something which is no longer really a form of the State.

It is still necessary to suppress the capitalist class and crush its resistance. This was particularly necessary for the Commune; and one of the reasons of its defeat was that it did not do this with sufficient determination. But the organ of suppression is now the majority of the population, and not a minority, as was always the case under slavery, serfdom and wage-labour. And, once the majority of the nation *itself* suppresses its oppressors, a '*special*' force for suppression *is no longer necessary*. In this sense the State begins to disappear. Instead of the special institutions of a privileged minority (privileged officials and chiefs of a standing army), the majority can itself directly fulfil all these functions; and the more the discharge of the functions of the State devolves upon the masses of the people, the less need is there for the existence of the State itself.

In this connection the special measures adopted by the Commune and emphasized by Marx, are particularly noteworthy: the abolition of all representative allowances, and of all special salaries in the case of officials; and the lowering of the payment of *all* servants of the State to the level of the *workmen's wages*. Here is shown, more clearly than anywhere else, the *break*— from a bourgeois democracy to a proletarian democracy; from the democracy of the oppressors to the democracy of the oppressed; from the domination of a 'special force' for the suppression of a given class to the suppression of the oppressors by the whole force of the majority of the nation—the proletariat and the peasants. And it is precisely on this most obvious point, perhaps the most important so far as the problem of the State is concerned, that the teachings of Marx have been forgotten. It is entirely neglected in all the innumerable popular commentaries. It is not 'proper' to speak about it as if it were a piece of old-fashioned '*naïveté*'; just as the Christians, having attained the position of a State religion 'forget' the '*naïveté*' of primitive Christianity, with its revolutionary democratic .spirit.

The lowering of the pay of the highest State officials seems simply a naïve, primitive demand of democracy. One of the 'founders' of the newest Opportunism, the former Social-Democrat, E. Bernstein, has more than once exercised his talents in the repetition of the vulgar capitalist jeers at 'primitive'

Democracy. Like all opportunists, like the present followers of Kautsky, he quite failed to understand that, first of all, the transition from Capitalism to Socialism is impossible without 'return', in a measure, to 'primitive' Democracy. How can we otherwise pass on to the discharge of all the functions of Government by the majority of the population and by every individual of the population? And, secondly, he forgets that 'primitive Democracy' on the basis of Capitalism and capitalist culture is not the same primitive Democracy as in pre-historic or pre-capitalist times. Capitalist culture has created industry on a large scale in the shape of factories, railways, posts, telephones and so forth: and *on this basis* the great majority of functions of 'the old State' have become enormously simplified and reduced, in practice, to very simple operations such as registration, filing and checking. Hence they will be quite within the reach of every literate person, and it will be possible to perform them for the usual 'working man's wage'. This circumstance ought, and will, strip them of all their former glamour as 'Government' and, therefore, privileged service.

The control of all officials, without exception, by the unreserved application of the principle of election and, *at any time*, re-call; and the approximation of their salaries to the 'ordinary pay of the workers'—these are simple and 'self-evident' democratic measures, which harmonize completely the interests of the workers and the majority of peasants; and, at the same time, serve as a bridge, leading from Capitalism to Socialism. These measures refer to the State, that is, to the purely political reconstruction of society; but, of course, they only acquire their full meaning and importance when accompanied by the 'expropriation of the expropriators' or at least by the preliminary steps towards it, that is, by the passage from capitalist private ownership of the means of production to social ownership.

'The Commune [wrote Marx] realized that ideal of all bourgeois revolutions, cheap Government, by eliminating the two largest items of expenditure—the army and the bureaucracy.'

From the peasantry, as from other sections of the lower middle class, only an insignificant minority 'rise to the top', and 'enter society', make a career in a bourgeois sense, that is, become transformed either into propertied members of the upper middle class, or into secure and privileged officials. The great majority of peasants in all capitalist countries where the peasant class does exist (and the majority of capitalist countries are of this kind) are oppressed by the Government and long for its overthrow, in the hope of a 'cheap' Government. This hope can only be realized by the proletariat; and by the fact of realizing it, the proletariat makes a step forward at the same time towards the Socialist reconstruction of the State.

3 THE DESTRUCTION OF PARLIAMENTARISM

'The Commune [wrote Marx] was to have been not a parliamentary, but a working corporation, legislative and executive at one and the same time. Instead of deciding once in three or six years which member of the ruling class was to "represent" and repress the people in Parliament, universal suffrage was to serve the people, organized in communes, as a means of securing the necessary workers, controllers, clerks and so forth for its business in the same way as individual suffrage serves any individual employer in his.'

This remarkable criticism of parliamentarism in 1871 is also one of those of Marx's dicta which have been conveniently 'forgotten,' thanks to the prevalence of Socialist Chauvinism and Opportunism. Ministers and professional politicians, 'practical' Socialists and traitors of the proletariat of today have left all criticism of parliamentarism to the anarchists, and, on this wonderfully intelligent ground, denounce all criticism of parliamentarism as 'anarchism'. It is indeed not surprising that the proletariat of the most 'advanced' parliamentary countries, being disgusted with such 'Socialists' as Messrs Scheidemann, David, Legien, Sembat, Renaudel, Henderson, Vandervelde, Stauning, Branting, Bissolati & Co., have been giving their sympathies more and more to Anarcho-Syndicalism, in spite of the fact that it is the twin brother of Opportunism.

But to Marx revolutionary dialectics was never the empty fashionable phrase, the toy rattle, which Plekhanoff, Kautsky and the others have made of it. Marx knew how to castigate Anarchism pitilessly for its inability to make use at least of the 'sty' of capitalist parliamentarism when the situation is not revolutionary, but at the same time he knew how to subject parliamentarism to a really revolutionary proletarian criticism.

To decide once every few years which member of the ruling class is to repress and oppress the people through parliament—this is the real essence of middle class parliamentarism, not only in parliamentary and constitutional Monarchies, but also in the most democratic Republics.

But if, in connection with the question of the State, parliamentarism is to be regarded as one of its institutions, what, from the point of view of those tasks which the proletariat has to face in this field, is to be the way out of parliamentarism? How can we do without it?

Again and again we must repeat: The teaching of Marx, based on the study of the Commune, has been so completely forgotten that any criticism of parliamentarism other than anarchist or reactionary is quite unintelligible to the 'Social-Democrats' (read—traitors to Socialism) of today.

The way out of parliamentarism is to be found, of course, not in the abolition of the representative institutions and the elective principle, but in the conversion of the representative institutions from mere 'talking shops' into working bodies: 'The Commune was to have been not a parliamentary institution, but a working corporation, legislative and executive at one and the same time.'

'Not a parliamentary, but a working' institution—this is directly aimed, as it were, at present-day parliamentarians and at the parliamentary Social-Democratic 'lap-dogs'. Take any parliamentary country, from America to Switzerland, from France to England, Norway and so forth; the actual work of the State is done behind the scenes and is carried out by the departments, the chancelleries and the staffs. Parliament itself is given up to talk for the special purpose of fooling the 'common people'. This is so true that even in the Russian Republic, in our middle-class democratic Republic, parliamentarism has already revealed its real purpose, though a real parliament has not yet come into existence. Such heroes of putrid philistinism as the Skobeleffs and the Tseretellis, Tchernoffs and Avksentieffs have managed to pollute even the Soviets, after the model of the most despicable middle-class parliamentarism, by turning them into hollow talking shops. In the Soviets the Right Honourable 'Socialist' Ministers are fooling the confiding peasants with phrases and resolutions. In the Government itself a sort of incessant quadrille is going on in order that, on the one hand, as many Socialist-Revolutionaries and Mensheviks as possible may get at the 'pie', that is, the 'cushy' jobs, and that, on the other hand, the attention of the people may be occupied. All the while the real 'State' business is being done in the chancelleries and the departments.

Dielo Naroda, the organ of the ruling party, the Socialist-Revolutionaries, recently admitted, in an editorial article, with the incomparable candour of people of 'good society' in which 'all' are engaged in political prostitution, that even in those Ministerial departments which belong to the 'Socialists' (pray, excuse the term) the whole official apparatus remains essentially the same as of old, working as before, and obstructing every revolutionary initiative without let or hindrance. And indeed, even if we did not have this admission, would not the actual history of the participation of the Socialist-Revolutionaries and Mensheviks in the Government prove this? It is only characteristic that, while in Ministerial company with the Cadets, Messrs Tchernoff, Roussanoff, Zenzinoff and others of the *Dielo Naroda* staff have so completely lost all shame that they un-blushingly proclaim, as if it were a mere bagatelle, that in 'their' Ministries everything remains as of old. Revolutionary and democratic phrases to gull the Simple Simons; bureaucracy and red tape in the Government departments for the 'benefit' of the capitalists—here you have the *essence* of the present 'honourable' coalition.

For the mercenary and corrupt parliamentarism of capitalist society, the Commune substitutes institutions in which freedom of opinion and discussion does not become a mere delusion, for the representatives must themselves work, must themselves execute their own laws, must themselves verify their results in actual practice, must themselves be directly responsible to their electorate. Representative institutions remain, but parliamentarism as a special system, as a division of labour between the legislative and the executive functions, as creating a privileged position for its deputies, *no longer exists*. Without representative institutions we cannot imagine a Democracy, even a proletarian Democracy; but we can and *must* think of democracy without parliamentarism, if our criticism of capitalist society is not mere empty words, if to overthrow the supremacy of the capitalists is for us a serious and sincere aim, and not a mere 'election cry' for catching working men's votes—as it is with the Mensheviks and Socialist-Revolutionaries, the Scheidemanns, the Legiens, the Sembats and the Vanderveldes.

It is most instructive to notice that, in speaking of the functions of what officials are still necessary both in the Commune and in the proletarian Democracy, Marx compares them with the workers of 'any other employer', that is, of the usual capitalist concern, with its workers, foremen and clerks. There is no trace of Utopian thinking in Marx, in the sense of inventing or imagining a 'new' society. No, he studies, as a scientific historical process, the *birth* of the new society from the old, the forms of transition from the latter to the former. He takes the actual experience of a mass proletarian movement and tries to draw from it practical lessons. He 'learns' from the Commune, as all great revolutionary thinkers have not been afraid to learn from the experience of great movements of the oppressed classes; never preaching them pedantic 'sermons' (such as Plekhanoff's, 'They should not have resorted to arms', or Tseretelli's, 'A class must know where to limit itself').

To destroy officialism immediately, everywhere, completely— of this there can be no question. That is a utopia. But to *break up* at once the old bureaucratic machine and to start immediately the construction of a new one, enabling us gradually to abolish bureaucracy—this is not a utopia, it is the experience of the Commune, it is the direct and necessary task of the revolutionary proletariat. Capitalism simplifies the functions of 'the Government'. It makes it possible to throw off autocratic methods and to bring it all down to a matter of the organization of the proletariat (as the ruling class) hiring 'workers and clerks' in the name of the whole of society. We are not utopians, we do not indulge in 'dreams' of how best to do away *immediately* with all management, with all subordination: these are anarchist dreams based upon a want of understanding of the tasks of a proletarian dictatorship. They are foreign in their essence to Marxism, and, as a matter of fact, they serve but to put off the Socialist revolution 'until human nature is different'. No, we want the Socialist revolution with human nature as it is now; human nature itself cannot do without subordination, without control, without managers and clerks.

But there must be submission to the armed vanguard of all the exploited and labouring classes—to the proletariat. The specific 'bossing' methods of the State officials can and must begin to be replaced—immediately, within twenty-four hours—by the simple functions of managers and clerks—functions which are now already quite within the capacity of the average townsman and can well be performed for a working man's wage.

We must organize production on a large scale, starting from what has already been done by Capitalism. By *ourselves*, we workers, relying on our own experience as workers, must create an unshakable and iron discipline supported by the power of the armed workers; we must reduce the rôle of the State officials to that of simply carrying out our instructions; they must be responsible, revocable, moderately paid 'managers and clerks' (of course, with technical knowledge of all sorts, types and degrees). This is *our* proletarian task. With this we can and must begin when we have accomplished the proletarian revolution. Such a beginning, on the basis of large scale industry, will of itself lead to the gradual decay of all bureaucracy, to the gradual creation of a new order, an order without inverted commas, an order bearing no similarity to wage slavery, an order in which the constant simplification of the functions of inspection and registration will admit of their being performed by each in turn, will then become a habit, and will finally die out as *special* functions of a special class.

A witty German Social-Democrat of the 'seventies of last century called the *post office* an example of the Socialist system. This is very true. At present the post office is a business organized on the lines of a State capitalist monopoly. Imperialism is gradually transforming all trusts into organizations of a similar type. Above the 'common' workers, who are overloaded with work and yet starve, there stands the same bourgeois bureaucracy. But the mechanism of social management is here already to hand. We have but to overthrow the capitalists, to crush with the iron hand of the armed workers the resistance of these exploiters, to break the bureaucratic machine of the modern State—and we have before us a highly technically-fashioned machine freed of its parasites, which can quite well be set going by the united workers themselves, hiring their own technical advisers, their own inspectors, their own clerks, and paying them all, as, indeed, every 'State' official, with the usual workers' wage. Here is a concrete task immediately practicable and realizable as regards all trusts, which would rid the workers of exploitation and which would make practical use of the experience (especially in the task of the reconstruction of the State) which the Commune has given us. To organize our whole national economy like the postal system, but in such a way that the technical experts, inspectors, clerks and indeed, all persons employed, should receive no higher wage than the working man, and the whole under the management of the armed proletariat—this is our immediate aim. This is the kind of State and the economic basis we need. This is what will produce the destruction of Parliamentarism, while retaining representative institutions. This is what will free the labouring classes from the prostitution of these institutions by the capitalist class.

4 THE ORGANIZATION OF THE UNITY
OF THE NATION

'In the short sketch of national organization which the Commune had had no time to develop, it was stated quite clearly that the Commune was to become . . . the political form of even the smallest village.' . . . From these Communes would be elected the 'National' Delegation at Paris. . . .

'The few but very important functions which would still remain for a Central Government were not to be abolished—such a statement was a deliberate falsehood—but were to be discharged by communal, that is, strictly responsible agents. . . .'

'The unity of the nation was not to be destroyed, but, on the contrary, organized by means of the communal structure. The unity of the nation was to become a reality by the destruction of the State, which claimed to be the embodiment of that unity and yet desired to be independent of, and superior to, the nation. In reality, this State was but a parasitic excrescence on the body of the nation. . . .'

'The problem consisted in this: Whilst amputating the purely repressive organs of the old Government power, to wrest its legitimate functions from an authority which claims to be above society, and to hand them over to the responsible servants of society.'

To what extent the Opportunists of contemporary Social-Democracy have failed to understand—or perhaps it would be more true to say, did not want to understand—these words of Marx, is best shown by the book, as famous or infamous as the work of Herostratus, of the renegade Bernstein—*The Fundamentals of Socialism and the Problems of Social-Democracy*. It is just in connection with the above passage from Marx that Bernstein wrote saying that this programme 'in its political content displays, in all its essential features, the greatest similarity to the Federalism of Proudhon. . . . In spite of all the other points of difference between Marx and the "petty shopkeeper" Proudhon [Bernstein places the words "petty shopkeeper" in inverted commas in order to make them sound ironical], on these points their currents of thought resemble one another as closely as could be.' Of course, Bernstein continues, the importance of the municipalities is growing, but 'it seems to me doubtful whether the first task of the democracy would be such a dissolution (*Auflösung*) of modern forms of the State, and such a complete transformation (*Umwandlung*) of their organization as is imagined by Marx and by Proudhon, that is, the formation of a national assembly from delegates of the provincial or district assemblies, which, in their turn, would consist of delegates from the Communes, so that the whole previous mode of national representation would vanish completely.' (Bernstein, *Fundamentals*, pp. 134-136, German Edition, 1899.)

It is really monstrous thus to confuse Marx's views on the 'destruction of the State as parasite' with the federalism of Proudhon. But this is no accident, for it never occurs to the Opportunist that Marx is not speaking here at all of Federalism as opposed to Centralism, but of the destruction of the old capitalist machinery of government which exists in all bourgeois countries.

The Opportunist cannot see further than the 'municipalities' which he finds around him in a society of middle-class philistinism and 'reformist' stagnation. As for a proletarian revolution, the

Opportunist has forgotten even how to imagine it. It is amusing. But it is remarkable that this point of Bernstein's has not been disputed. Bernstein has been refuted often enough especially by Plekhanoff in Russian literature and by Kautsky in European, but neither made any remark upon this perversion of Marx by Bernstein.

The Opportunist has forgotten to such an extent how to think in a revolutionary way and how to reflect on revolution, that he attributes 'Federalism' to Marx, mixing him up with the founder of Anarchism, Proudhon; and, although they are anxious to be orthodox Marxists and to defend the teaching of revolutionary Marxism, Kautsky and Plekhanoff are nevertheless silent on this point. Herein lies one of the roots of those banalities and platitudes about the difference between Marxism and Anarchism, which are common to both Kautskians and Opportunists, and which we shall have to discuss later.

There is no trace of Federalism in Marx's discussion of the experience of the Commune, quoted above. Marx agrees with Proudhon precisely on that point which has quite escaped the Opportunist Bernstein; while he differs from Proudhon just on the point where Bernstein sees their agreement. Marx concurs with Proudhon in that they both stand for the 'demolition' of the contemporary machinery of government. This common ground of Marxism with Anarchism (both with Proudhon and with Bakunin), neither the Opportunists nor the Kautskians wish to see, for on this point they have themselves diverged from Marxism. Marx does differ both from Proudhon and Bakunin on the point of Federalism (not to speak of the dictatorship of the proletariat). Federalism is a direct fundamental outcome of the anarchist petty middle-class ideas. Marx is a centralist; and in the above cited quotation of his speculations there is no withdrawal from the central position. Only people full of middle-class 'superstitious faith' in the State can mistake the destruction of the bourgeois State for the destruction of centralism.

But will it not be centralism if the proletariat and poorest peasantry take the power of the State into their own hands, organize themselves quite freely into communes, and co-ordinate the action of all the communes for the purpose of striking at Capital, for the purpose of crushing the resistance of the capitalists, in order to accomplish the transference of private property in railways, factories, land, and so forth to the nation, to the whole of society? Will that not be the most consistent democratic centralism? And proletarian centralism at that?

Bernstein simply cannot conceive the possibility of voluntary centralism, of a voluntary union of the communes into a nation, a voluntary fusion of the proletarian communes in the business of destroying capitalist supremacy and the capitalist machinery of government. Like all philistines, Bernstein can imagine centralism only as something from above, to be imposed and maintained solely by means of bureaucracy and militarism.

Marx, as though he foresaw the possibility of the distortion of his ideas, purposely emphasizes that the accusation against the Commune that it desired to destroy the unity of the nation, to do away with a central authority, was a deliberate falsehood. He purposely uses the phrase 'to organize the unity of the nation,' so as to oppose the conscious, democratic, proletarian centralism to the capitalist, military, official centralism.

But none so deaf as those who will not hear. And the Opportunists of modern Social-Democracy do not, on any account, want to hear of the destruction of the State, of the removal of the parasite.

5 THE DESTRUCTION OF THE PARASITE-STATE

We have already quoted the words of Marx on this subject, and must now supplement them.

'It is generally the fate of new creations of history [wrote Marx], to be mistaken for any old and even defunct forms of social life to which the new institutions may bear a sort of likeness. Thus, this new Commune, which is breaking up (*bricht*) the modern State, was regarded as the resurrection of the mediaeval communes . . . as a federation of small States (Montesquieu, the Girondins), as an exaggerated form of the ancient struggle against over-centralization. . . . The Communal constitution would have restored to the social body all those forces hitherto devoured by the parasitic excrescence called "the State," feeding upon society and hindering it from moving forward freely. By this one act the regeneration of France would have been advanced. . . .

'The Communal constitution would have brought the rural producers under the intellectual leadership of the chief towns of each district, and would have secured for them there, in the persons of the town workers, the natural representatives of their interests. The very existence of the Commune would have involved, as a matter of course, local self-government, but no longer as a balance to the power of the State, which now becomes superfluous. . . .'

'The annihiliation of the power of the State,' which was a 'parasitic excrescence,' its 'amputation,' its 'destruction'; 'the power of the State now becomes superfluous'—these are the expressions used by Marx regarding the State when appraising and analysing the experience of the Commune.

All this was written a little less than half a century ago; and now one has to excavate, as it were, in order to bring uncorrupted Marxism to the knowledge of the masses. The conclusions drawn from the observation of the last great revolution, through which Marx lived, have been forgotten just at the moment when the time has arrived for the next great proletarian revolutions.

'The variety of interpretations to which the Commune has been subjected, and the multiplicity of interests which found their expression in it, proves that it was a thoroughly flexible political form, whereas all previous forms of Government have been, in their essence, repressive. Its true secret was this. It was essentially *the government of the working class*, the result of the struggle of the producing against the appropriating class; it was the political form, at last discovered, under which Labour could work out its economic emancipation. . . .'

'Without this last condition the Communal constitution would have been an impossibility and a delusion.'

The Utopians had busied themselves with the 'discovery' of the political forms under which the Socialist reconstruction of society could take place. The Anarchists turned away from the question of political forms of any kind. The Opportunists of modern Social-Democracy have accepted the capitalist political forms of a parliamentary democratic State as the limit which cannot be overstepped; they have broken their foreheads praying before this idol, and they have denounced as Anarchism every attempt to destroy these forms.

Marx deduced from the whole history of Socialism and of political struggle that the State was bound to disappear, and that the transitional form of its disappearance (the transition from the political State to the non-State) would be the 'proletariat organized as the ruling class.' But Marx did not undertake the task of 'discovering' the political 'forms' of this future stage. He limited himself to an exact observation of French history, its analysis and the conclusion to which the year 1851 had led, viz., that matters were moving towards the destruction of the capitalist machinery of the State.

And when the mass revolutionary movement of the proletariat burst forth, Marx, in spite of the failure of that movement, in spite of its short life and its patent weakness, began to study what political forms it had disclosed.

The Commune was the form 'discovered at last' by the proletarian revolution, under which the economic liberation of Labour can proceed. The Commune was the first attempt of a proletarian revolution to *break up* the bourgeois State, and constitutes the political form, 'discovered at last,' which can and must take the place of the broken machine. We shall see below that the Russian revolutions of 1905 and 1917, in different surroundings and under different circumstances, have been continuing the work of the Commune and have been confirming Marx's brilliant analysis of history.

CHAPTER IV

Continuation. Supplementary Explanations by Engels

MARX gave us the fundamentals on the subject of the meaning of the Commune. Engels returned to the same question repeatedly, elucidating Marx's analysis and conclusions, sometimes explaining so clearly and forcibly *other* sides of the question that we must stop expressly to consider these explanations.

I THE HOUSING QUESTION

Already in his work on the Housing Question (1872) Engels took into account the experience of the Commune, dwelling several times on the problems of the Revolution in relation to the State. It is interesting to note that in the treatment of this concrete question we are shown clearly, on the one hand, those features of the proletarian State which resemble features of the present State —features which give us ground for speaking of a State in both cases; and, on the other hand, the features which differentiate them and mark the transition to the destruction of the State.

'How can the housing problem be solved? In modern society this question is solved, like every other social question, by a gradual economic equalization of supply and demand. This, however, is a kind of solution which itself constantly creates the problem anew, that is, it gives no solution. How the Social Revolution will solve this question depends not only on circumstances of time and place but it is bound up with questions which go much further, amongst which one of the most important is the abolition of the distinction between town and country. As we are not interested in utopian speculations on the structure of future society, it would be more than a waste of time to dwell upon this point. One thing is certain; even now there are sufficient habitable buildings in the large towns materially to relieve the real shortage of accommodation, if sensible use were made of them. This, of course, could only be brought about by the expropriation of their present possessors, and by settling in them the homeless workers or the workers who are now living in over-crowded homes. And as soon as the workers win political power, such a measure, based on the best interests of society, will be as easily carried out as all other expropriations and commandeerings by the modern State.' (German Edition, 1887, p. 22.)

Here it is not the change in the form of the State which is considered, but only the character of its activity. Expropriations and the occupation of houses take place by direction even of the present State. The proletarian State, from the formal point of view, will also 'direct' the occupation of houses and the expropriation of buildings. But it is clear that the old executive apparatus, the bureaucracy, connected with the bourgeoisie, would simply be useless for the carrying out of the orders of the proletarian State.

'It is necessary to state that the actual seizure of all the means of labour and of all industry by the labouring masses of the nation is the direct antithesis to the Proudhonist "buying out." Under the Proudhonist system the individual worker becomes the owner of a house, of a small-holder's plot of land, of necessary tools. In the other case, however, the "labouring people" becomes the collective owner of houses, factories and tools. The use of these houses, factories and so forth, will hardly be offered, at any rate, during the transition period, to single individuals or to companies without covering the expenses. In the same way, the abolition of the private ownership of land does not presuppose the abolition of rent, but its handing over, although in a different form, to the whole of society. The actual appropriation of all the means of labour by the labouring masses does not exclude in any way, therefore, the preservation of the right to rent or let' (p. 69).

In the next chapter we shall discuss the question touched on here, namely, the economic reasons for the 'withering away' of the State. Engels expresses himself most cautiously here, saying that the proletarian State will 'hardly' allot houses without pay, 'at any rate, during the period of transition'. The letting of

houses, belonging to the whole nation, to separate families for
rent presupposes the collection of this rent, a certain amount of
control, and some standard or other to guide the allotment of the
houses. All this demands a certain form of State, but it does not
at all involve a special military and bureaucratic apparatus, with
officials occupying privileged positions. But a transition to a state
of affairs when it will be possible to let houses without rent is
bound up with the complete 'withering away' of the State.

Speaking of the conversion of the Blanquists after the Commune, and under the influence of its experience, to the Marxist
point of view, Engels, it so happens, formulates it as

'The necessity for political action by the proletariat and for
proletarian dictatorship, as the transition towards the abolition
of classes and, together with them, of the State. . . .' (p. 55.)

Those who are addicted to hair-splitting or bourgeois 'exter-
minators of Marxism', will perhaps see a contradiction between
this admission of the 'abolition of the State' and the repudiation
of a formula like that of the anarchists, contained in the quotation
from the *Anti-Dühring*, given above. It would not be surprising
if the Opportunists wrote down Engels, too, as an 'Anarchist',
for the Socialist-Chauvinists are now more and more adopting
the fashion of accusing the Internationalists of Anarchism.

That, together with the abolition of classes, the State will also
be abolished—this Marxism has always taught. The well-known
passage on the 'withering away of the State' in the *Anti-Dühring*
does not accuse the Anarchists merely of being in favour of the
abolition of the State, but of spreading the theory that it is possible to accomplish this 'within twenty-four hours'. In view of
the complete distortion, by the present predominating 'Social-
Democratic' doctrine concerning the relation of Marxism to
Anarchism, of the question of the abolition of the State, it will be
particularly useful to recall one particular controversy of Marx
and Engels with the Anarchists.

2 THE DISPUTE WITH THE ANARCHISTS

This dispute occurred in 1873. Marx and Engels then contributed articles against the Proudhonist 'Autonomists' or 'Anti-
Authoritarians' to an Italian Socialist review, and it was only in

1913 that these articles appeared in German in the *Neue Zeit*.

'If the political struggle of the working class [wrote Marx, ridiculing the Anarchists for their repudiation of political action] assumes a revolutionary form; if the workers, in place of the dictatorship of the bourgeoisie, set up their own revolutionary dictatorship, then they commit a terrible crime and offer an insult to principle; because, forsooth, the workers, in order to meet the miserable, gross requirements of the moment, in order to crush the resistance of the capitalist class, cause the State to assume a revolutionary and transitional form, instead of laying down their arms and abolishing the State.' (*Neue Zeit*, 1913-4, Year 32, Vol. I., page 40.)

This alone is the kind of 'abolition' of the State, against which Marx protested, refuting the Anarchists. He protested not against the theory of the disappearance of the State when classes disappear, or of its abolition when classes have been abolished, but only against the proposition that the workers should deny themselves the use of arms, the use of organized force, that is, *the use of the State*, for the purpose of 'breaking the resistance of the capitalist class'. Marx purposely emphasizes, in order that the true sense of his contentions against the Anarchists might not be perverted, 'the revolutionary *and transitional form*' of the State necessary for the proletariat. The proletariat only needs the State *temporarily*. We do not at all disagree with the Anarchists on the question of the abolition of the State as a *final aim*. But we affirm that, for the attainment of this aim, we must make temporary use of the weapons and methods of the State *against* the exploiters, just as the temporary dictatorship of the oppressed class is necessary for the annihilation of all classes. Marx chooses the sharpest and clearest mode of stating the position against the Anarchists. Having cast off the yoke of the capitalists, ought the workers 'to lay down their arms', or should they use them against the capitalists in order to break their resistance? And the systematic employment of arms by one class against the other, what is that if not a 'transitional form of the State'?

Let every Social-Democrat ask himself whether *that was the way* in which he examined the question of the State in his discussions with the Anarchists? *Was* that the *way* in which the vast majority of the official Social-Democratic parties of the Second International treated it?

Engels develops these same ideas in even greater detail and more simply. He first of all ridicules the muddled ideas of the Proudhonists, who called themselves 'Anti-Authoritarians,' that is, they denied every form of authority, of subordination, of power. Take a factory, a railway, a vessel on the open seas, said Engels; is it not clear that not one of these complex technical concerns, based on the use of machines and the ordered co-operation of many people, could function without a certain amount of subordination, and, consequently, of authority or power? 'When I use these arguments,' writes Engels, 'against the most hopeless Anti-Authoritarians, they can only give me the following answer, "Ah, that is true, but the question is not of the authority we confer on our delegates, *but of a certain commission.*" These people think that a thing can be altered by merely changing its name.'

Having shown in this way that authority and autonomy are relative terms, that the sphere of their application varies with the various phases of social development, that it is absurd to regard them as absolute terms; after adding that the domain of the application of machinery and production on a large scale is ever extending, Engels passes from a general discussion of authority to the question of the State.

'If the Autonomists [he writes] merely meant to say that the social organization of the future would admit authority only within those limits which the conditions of industry inevitably dictate, then it would be possible to come to an understanding with them. But they are blind in respect of all the facts which make authority necessary, and they fight passionately against a mere word.

'Why do not the Anti-Authoritarians limit themselves to shouting against the *political* authority, against the State? All Socialists agree that the State, and together with it, also political authority, will vanish as the result of the future Socialist Revolution, i.e. that public functions will lose their political character and will be transformed into simple administrative functions, concerned with social interests. But the Anti-Authoritarians demand that the political State should be abolished at one blow, even before those social relations which gave birth to the State

are themselves abolished. They demand that the first act of the
Social Revolution shall be the abolition of all authority.

'These gentlemen, have they ever seen a Revolution? Revolution is undoubtedly the most authoritative thing possible.
Revolution is an act in which part of the population forces its
will on the other part by means of rifles, bayonets, cannon,
i.e. by most authoritative means. And the conquering party is
inevitably forced to maintain its supremacy by means of that fear
which its arms inspire in the reactionaries. Had the Paris
Commune not relied on the authority of the armed people against
the bourgeoisie, would it have lasted longer than a single day?
May we not rather censure the Commune for not having made
sufficient use of this authority? And so, either the Anti-Authoritarians themselves do not know what they are talking about, in
which case they merely sow confusion; or they do know what they
are talking about, in which case they are betraying the proletariat.
In either case they serve only the interests of reaction.' (p. 39.)

In this discussion questions are touched on, which must be
investigated in connection with the subject of the correlation of
politics and economics during the withering away of the State.
(The next chapter treats of this subjec .) Such are the problems
of the transformation of the nature of public functions, from political to simply administrative, and of the 'political State'. This
last term, particularly liable to cause misunderstanding, indicates
the process of the withering away of the State: The dying State,
at a certain stage of its decay, can be called a non-political State.
The most remarkable point in our quotation from Engels' work
is, again, the way he puts the position against the Anarchists.
Social-Democrats, desiring to be disciples of Engels, have disputed with the Anarchists thousands of times since 1873, but
they have not disputed at all as Marxists can and should. The
Anarchist idea of the abolition of the State is muddled and *non-
revolutionary*—that is how Engels put it. It is precisely the
Revolution, in its rise and development, with its specific problems
in relation to violence, authority, power and the State, that the
Anarchists do not wish to see. The usual criticism of the
Anarchists by the modern Social-Democrats has been reduced to
the purest middle-class triviality:—'We, forsooth, recognize the
State, whereas the Anarchists do not.' Naturally such trivialities

cannot but repel any revolutionary working men who think at all. Engels says something quite different. He emphasizes that all Socialists recognize the disappearance of the State as a result of the Socialist Revolution. He then deals with the concrete question of the Revolution—that very question which, as a rule, the Social-Democrats, because of their opportunism, evade, leaving it, so to speak, exclusively for the Anarchists 'to work out'. And in thus formulating the question Engels takes the bull by the horns. Ought not the Commune to have made *more* use of the *revolutionary* power of the *State*, that is, of the proletariat armed and organized as the ruling class?

The modern predominating official Social-Democracy has generally dismissed the concrete problems facing the proletariat during the revolution, either by some inane philistine jeers, or, at the best, by the evasive sophism, 'Wait and see'. And the Anarchists have thus gained the right to reproach such Social-Democrats with betraying their mission of educating the working class in revolution. Engels makes use of the experience of the last proletarian revolution for the direct purpose of drawing from it concrete conclusions as to what and how the proletariat should do and act concerning both banks and the State.

3 THE LETTER TO BEBEL

One of the most remarkable, if not *the* most remarkable, reasoning in the works of Marx and Engels on the State is contained in the following passage in Engels' letter to Bebel on March 18-28, 1875. This letter, we may remark in passing, was first published, so far as we know, by Bebel, in the second volume of his memoirs (*My Life*), published in 1911, that is, thirty-six years after the writing and despatch of the letter.

Engels wrote to Bebel, criticizing that same draft of the Gotha programme which Marx criticized in his famous letter to Bracke, and, referring particularly to the question of the State, said:—

'The Free People's State has been transformed into a Free State. According to the grammatical meaning of the words, the Free State is one in which the State is free in relation to its citizens, that is, a State with a despotic government. It would be well to throw overboard all this nonsense about the State, especially after the Commune, which was already no longer a State in the proper sense of the word.

'The Anarchists have too long been able to throw into our teeth this "People's State," although already, in Marx's works against Proudhon, and then in the *Communist Manifesto*, it was stated quite plainly that with the introduction of the Socialist order of society, the State will dissolve of itself (*sich auflöst*), and will disappear. As the State is only a transitional institution which we are obliged to use in the revolutionary struggle in order forcibly to crush our opponents, it is a pure absurdity to speak of a Free People's State. During the period when the proletariat still *needs* the State, it does not require it in the interests of freedom, but in the interests of crushing its antagonists; and when it becomes possible really to speak of freedom, than the State, as such, ceases to exist. We should, therefore, suggest that everywhere the word *State* be replaced by *Gemeinwesen* (Commonwealth), a fine old German word, which corresponds to the French word "Commune" ' (p. 322, German Edition).

One should bear in mind that this letter refers to the Party programme which Marx criticized in his letter dated only a few weeks later than the above (Marx's letter of May 5, 1875), and that Engels was living at the time with Marx in London. Consequently, when he says 'we' Engels undoubtedly suggests to the leader of the German working class party, both in his own and in Marx's name, that the word 'State' should be struck out of their programme and exchanged for 'Commonwealth'.

What a howl about 'Anarchism' would be raised by the leaders of present-day 'Marxism', adulterated to meet the requirements of the Opportunists, if such an alteration in their programme were suggested to them. Let them howl. The capitalist class will pat them on the back for it.

In the meantime, however, we shall go on with our work. In revising the programme of our party, Engels' and Marx's advice must undoubtedly be taken into consideration in order to come nearer to the truth, to re-establish Marxism, to purge it from distortion, to direct the struggle for freedom of the working class into the right channels. Among the Bolsheviks there will certainly be none opposed to the advice of Engels and Marx. Difficulties may, perhaps, crop up regarding terminology. In German there are two words meaning 'Commonwealth', of which Engels used the one which does not denote a single community, but the sum of all, a system of communities. In Russian there is no such word, and perhaps we may have to choose the French word 'Commune', although this also has its drawbacks.[1]

'The Commune was no longer a State in the proper sense of the word.' Here is Engels' most important theoretical proposition. After what has been said above, this statement is quite intelligible. The Commune *ceased* to be a State in so far as it had to repress, not the majority, but a minority, of the population (the exploiters); it had broken the bourgeois machinery of government, and, in the place of a *special* repressive force, the whole population itself was coming on the scene. All this is a departure from the State in its proper sense. And had the Commune become consolidated, the relics of the State would of themselves have 'withered away' within it; there would have been no need for the State to 'abolish' its institutions, they would have ceased to function in proportion as less and less was left for them to do.

'The Anarchists throw into our teeth the "People's State".' In saying this, Engels has in mind especially Bakunin and his attacks on the German Social Democrats. Engels admits these attacks to be justified *in so far* as the 'People's State' is as senseless and as far removed from Socialism as the '*Free* People's State'. Engels tries to alter the character of the controversy of the German Social-Democrats with the Anarchists, to make it true to principle, and to clear it from opportunist prejudice concerning the 'State'. Alas! Engels' letter has been stowed away for thirty-six years. We shall see below that, even after the publication of Engels' letter, Kautsky still obstinately continues to repeat those very mistakes against which Engels gave his warning.

Bebel replied to Engels in a letter, dated September 21, 1875, in which, amongst other things, he wrote that he 'fully agreed' with Engels' criticism of the projected programme, and that he had reproached Liebknecht for his readiness to make concessions (Bebel's *Memoirs*, German Edition, Vol. II., p. 304). But if we

---

[1] It will be seen that the English language possesses just the equivalent of the German *Gemeinwesen*, which the Russian lacks. It is even probable that the German term was suggested to Engels by the English word—Trans.

take Bebel's pamphlet, *Our Aims*, we shall find there absolutely wrong views of the State. 'The State must be transformed from one based on *class supremacy* to a *people's State*.' (*Unsere Ziele*, 1886, p. 14.) This is printed in the *ninth* edition of Bebel's pamphlet. Small wonder that such constantly repeated opportunist views of the State have been absorbed by the German Social-Democracy, especially as the revolutionary interpretations by Engels were safely stowed away, and all the conditions of life have been such as to wean them from Revolution.

4 CRITICISM OF THE DRAFT OF THE ERFURT PROGRAMME

In a discussion of the doctrines of Marxism regarding the State, the criticism of the Erfurt Programme sent by Engels to Kautsky on June 29, 1891, and only published ten years later in the *Neue Zeit*, cannot be passed over; for this criticism is mainly concerned with the *opportunist* views of Social-Democracy on the questions of State organization.

In passing, we may note that Engels also raises an exceedingly valuable point of economics, which shows how attentively and thoughtfully he followed the various phases of the latest development of Capitalism, and how he was able, in consequence, to foresee to a certain extent the problems of our own, the Imperialist, epoch. Here is this point. Touching on the words used in the draft of the programme, 'the want of ordered plan' as characteristic of Capitalism, Engels writes:

'If we pass from joint stock companies to trusts, which get hold of and monopolize whole branches of industry, not only private production, but also the want of ordered plan disappears.' (*Neue Zeit*, year 20, Vol. I., 1901-2, p. 8).

Here we have what is most essential in the theoretical appreciation of the latest phase of Capitalism, that is Imperialism, viz., that Capitalism becomes *monopolistic* Capitalism. This fact must be emphasized because the 'Reformist' middle-class view that monopolistic capitalism, whether private or State, is no longer Capitalism, but can already be termed 'State Socialism', or something of that sort, is one of the most widespread errors. The trusts, of course, have not given us, and, indeed, cannot give us, full and complete order and system in production. But, however much of an ordered plan they may yield, however closely capitalist magnates may estimate in advance the required extent of production on a national and even international scale, and, however carefully and systematically they may regulate it, we still remain under Capitalism—Capitalism, it is true, in its latest phase, but still, undoubtedly, Capitalism. The nearness of such Capitalism to Socialism should be, in the mouth of real representatives of the proletariat, an argument for the nearness, ease, feasibility and urgency of the Socialist Revolution, and not at all one for tolerating a repudiation of such a revolution, or the attempts to make Capitalism look attractive, in which the Reformists are habitually engaged.

But to return to the question of the State. Engels makes here three valuable suggestions: in the first place, on the question of a Republic; secondly, on the connection between the problems of nationalities and the form of the State; and thirdly, on local self-government.

With regard to the question of a Republic, Engels made this point the gravamen of his criticism of the draft of the Erfurt programme; and when we remember what an important part the Erfurt programme has played in International Social-Democracy, how it became the model for the whole of the Second International, it may, without exaggeration, be said that Engels criticized in this connection the opportunism of the whole Second International. 'The political demands of the draft,' Engels writes, 'are vitiated by a great fault. *They do not mention* (Engels' italics) what ought certainly to have been said.'

And, later on, he makes it clear that the German constitution is but a copy of the reactionary constitution of 1850, that the Reichstag is only, as Wilhelm Liebknecht put it, 'the fig-leaf of Absolutism', and that to 'wish to make all the means of production public property' on the basis of a constitution which has legalized the existence of petty States and the federation of petty German States, is an 'obvious absurdity.'

'It is dangerous to touch on this subject,' Engels adds, knowing full well that it was impossible for police reasons to include in the programme a demand for a republic in Germany. But Engels does not simply rest content with this obvious consideration which satisfies 'everybody'. He continues:

'But the matter must, in one way or another, be pressed forward. To what an extent this is essential is shown particularly just now by the way opportunism is gaining ground in the Social-Democratic press. Fearing a renewal of the anti-Socialist Laws, or remembering some premature declarations made when those Laws were in force, some people desire now that the party should recognize the present legal order in Germany as sufficient for the peaceful realization of all its demands.'

Engels brings out as of prime importance the fact that German Social-Democracy was acting in fear of the renewal of the Exceptional Laws, and, without hesitation, calls this Opportunism, declaring that just because of the absence of a Republic and freedom in Germany, the dreams of a 'peaceful' path were quite absurd. Engels is sufficiently careful not to tie his hands in advance. He admits that in republican or very free countries 'one can conceive' (only 'conceive'!) a peaceful development towards Socialism, but in Germany he repeats:—

'In Germany, where the Government is almost omnipotent, and the Reichstag and all other representative bodies have no real power, to proclaim anything of that sort, and that without any need, is to take off the fig leaf from Absolutism and to screen its nakedness by one's own body. . . .'

The great majority of official leaders of German Social-Democracy, who 'stowed away' this advice, have indeed proved the screen of Absolutism.

'Such a policy can only, in the end, lead the party on to a false road. General abstract political questions are pushed to the foreground, and in this way all the immediate concrete problems which arise automatically on the order of the day at the first approach of important events, during the first political crisis, are hidden from sight. What else can result from this than that the party may suddenly, at the first critical moment, prove helpless, that on decisive questions confusion and division will arise within the party because these questions had never been discussed?

'This neglect of great fundamental considerations for the sake of the momentary interests of the day, this chase after momentary successes, and this race after them without account of ultimate results, this sacrifice of the future movement for the present, is, perhaps, the result of "honest" motives, but is and remains, none the less, Opportunism, and "honest" Opportunism is, perhaps, more dangerous than any other. . . . If there is anything about which there can be no doubt, it is that our party and the working class can only gain supremacy under a political regime like a democratic republic. This latter is, indeed, the specific form for the dictatorship of the proletariat, as has been demonstrated by the great French Revolution. . . .'

Engels repeats here in a particularly emphatic form the fundamental idea which, like a red thread, runs throughout all Marx's work, viz., that the Democratic Republic is the nearest jumping-board to the dictatorship of the proletariat. For such a republic, without in the least setting aside the domination of capital, and, therefore, the oppression of the masses and the class struggle, inevitably leads to such an extension, intensification and development of that struggle that, as soon as the chance arises for satisfying the fundamental interests of the oppressed masses, this chance is realized inevitably and solely in the form of the dictatorship of the proletariat, of the guidance of these masses by the proletariat. These also have been, for the whole of the Second International, 'forgotten words' of Marxism, and their neglect was demonstrated with particular vividness by the history of the Menshevik party during the first half year of the Russian Revolution of 1917.

On the question of a Federal Republic, in connection with the national composition of the population, Engels wrote:—

'What ought to arise in the place of present-day Germany (with its reactionary monarchist constitution and the equally reactionary division into small States, a division which perpetuates the peculiarities of "Prussianism" instead of submerging them in Germany as a single whole)? In my opinion the proletariat can only make use of the form of a one and indivisible republic. A federal republic is still, as a whole, a necessity in the enormous territory of the United States, but even so it is already becoming an impediment in the Eastern States. It would be a progressive step in England, where four nationalities live on the two islands, and where, in spite of one Parliament, three systems of legislation exist side by side. It has long since become a hindrance in little

Switzerland, and if there the Federal Republic can still be tolerated, it is only because Switzerland is content with the rôle of an entirely passive member of the European State system. For Germany, a federalization on the Swiss model would be an enormous step backward. Two points differentiate a federated State from a unitary State, viz., that each individual State within the union has its own civil and criminal legislation, its own particular judicial system; and then this: that, side by side with the popular chamber, there is a chamber of representatives from the States in which every Canton votes as such, irrespective of its size.'

In Germany the Federated State is the transition to the complete unitary State, and the 'revolutions from above' of 1866 and 1870 must not be turned backwards, but must be completed by a 'movement from below'.

Engels not only shows no indifference to the question of the form of the State, but, on the contrary, analyses with the greatest possible care the transitional forms, in order to establish, from the concrete historical peculiarities of each separate case, *from what and to what* the given transitional form is evolving.

Engels, like Marx, insists, from the point of view of the proletariat and the proletarian revolution, on democratic centralism, on the one and indivisible republic. The Federal Republic is considered by him to be either an exception and a hindrance to development, or a transitional form between a monarchy and a centralized republic, a 'progressive step' in certain definite conditions. And amongst these definite conditions arises the problems of nationalities.

With Engels, as with Marx, in spite of their pitiless criticism of the reactionary nature of the small States, often, in certain concrete cases, hidden from the eye under the cloak of the national question, there is nowhere a trace of any desire to ignore the national question—a desire of which the Dutch and Polish Marxists are often guilty, as a result of their most justifiable opposition to the narrow, middle-class nationalism of 'their' little States.

Even in England, where the geographical conditions, the common language, and the history of many centuries would seem to have put an end to the national question of the separate small divisions in England—even here Engels is cognisant of the patent fact that the national question has not yet been overcome, and recognizes, in consequence, that the establishment of a federal republic would be a 'progressive' step. Of course, there is no trace here of a renunciation of criticism of the defects of the Federal Republic or of the most determined propaganda and fight for a unitary and democratically-centralized republic.

But Engels' conception of a centralized democracy is not of that bureaucratic order with which middle class ideologists (including Anarchists) identify it. Centralism does not, with Engels, in the least exclude a wide local autonomy, which combines a voluntary defence of the unity of the State by the communes and districts with the absolute abolition of all bureaucracy and all 'ordering about' from above.

'And so we want a unitary Republic [writes Engels, setting out the programmatic views of Marxism on the State] but not in the sense of the present French Republic, which is neither more nor less than the Empire established in 1798 without the Emperor. From 1792 to 1798 each French department, each municipality, enjoyed complete self-government on the American model, and this is what we, too, ought to have. How local self-government should be organized and how it is possible to do without a bureaucracy has been demonstrated to us by America and the first French Republic, and is still being demonstrated by Canada, Australia, and other British Dominions. Such a provincial and communal self-government is a far freer institution than, for instance, the Swiss Federation under whch, it is true, the Canton is very independent of the *Bund* [that is, of the Federal State as a whole] but is also independent of the district and the commune. The cantonal governments appoint the district state-holders and prefects, a feature which is quite absent in the English-speaking countries, and which we, in our own country, must in the future abolish as completely as the Prussian *Landräte, Regierungsräte*' [that is, all officials appointed from above].

In accordance with this, Engels suggests the following wording for the clause in the programme regarding self-government: 'Complete self-government for the provinces, districts and communes through officials elected by universal suffrage, the abolition of all local and provincial authorities appointed by the State.'

In the *Pravda* of May 28, 1917, suppressed by the Government of Kerensky and other 'Socialist' Ministers, I had already occasion to point out how in this connection (not by any means in this alone), our sham Socialist representatives of the sham-revolutionary sham-democracy, have scandalously departed from democracy. Naturally people who have allied themselves with the Imperialist capitalist class remained deaf to this criticism.

It is particularly important to note that Engels, armed with precise facts, disproves by a telling example the superstition very widespread, among especially the lower middle class democracy, that a Federal Republic necessarily means a larger amount of liberty than a centralized republic. This is not true. The facts cited by Engels regarding the centralized French Republic of 1792-98 and Federal Switzerland disprove this. The really democratic centralized republic gave more liberty than the federal republic—in other words, the *greatest* amount of local freedom known in history was granted by a centralized republic, and not by a Federal Republic.

Insufficient attention has hitherto been paid to this fact, as, indeed, to the whole question of federal and centralized republics and local self-government, in our party literature and agitation.

5 THE PREFACE OF 1891 TO MARX'S *CIVIL WAR IN FRANCE*

In his preface to the third edition of the *Civil War in France* (this preface is dated March 18, 1891, and was originally published in the *Neue Zeit*) Engels, side by side with many other interesting questions in connection with the State, gives a remarkably striking *resumé* of the lessons of the Commune. This *resumé*, confirmed by all the experience of the period of twenty years separating the author from the Commune, and directed particularly against the 'superstitious faith in the State' so widely diffused in Germany, can, quite justly, be called the *last word* of Marxism on the question here dealt with.

In France, Engels notes, the workers were armed after every revolution. 'Consequently the first commandment for every bourgeois at the head of the State was the disarmament of the workers. Accordingly, after every revolution won by the workers, a new struggle arose which ended with their defeat. . . .

This is a summing up of the experience of bourgeois revolutions, which is as short as it is expressive. The essence of the whole matter—also, by the way, of the question of the State—viz., *has* the oppressed class arms? is here wonderfully well expressed. It is just this essential thing which, more often than not, is ignored both by professors under the influence of capitalist ideology and by the lower middle-class democrats. In the Russian Revolution of 1917 it was to the 'Menshevik,' a so-called 'Marxist,' Tseretelli, that the Cavaignac honour fell of babbling out this secret of bourgeois revolutions. In his 'historic' speech of June 9th (22nd) Tseretelli blundered out the decision of the bourgeoisie to disarm the Petrograd workers—referring, of course, to this decision as his own, and as a vital necessity for the State.

Tseretelli's historic speech of June 9th (22nd) will certainly constitute for every historian of the Revolution of 1917 one of the clearest illustrations of how the *block* of Socialist-Revolutionaries and Mensheviks, led by Mr Tseretelli, went over to the side of the capitalist class *against* the revolutionary proletariat.

Another incidental remark of Engels', also connected with the question of the State, dealt with religion. It is well-known that German Social-Democracy, in proportion as it began to decay and to become more and more opportunist, slid down more and more frequently to the philistine misinterpretation of the celebrated formula, that 'religion is a private matter'. That is, this formula was twisted to mean that even for the party of the revolutionary proletariat the question of religion was a private matter. It was against this complete betrayal of the revolutionary programme of the proletariat that Engels revolted. In 1891 he only saw the *very feeble* beginnings of Opportunism in his party, and therefore he expressed himself on the subject most cautiously:—

'Corresponding with the fact that in the Commune there sat, almost without exception, only workmen or the recognized representatives of the workers, its decisions were distinguished by their resolute proletarian character. These decisions either decreed such reforms as the republican bourgeoisie had rejected only out of base cowardice, but which formed a necessary foundation for the free activity of the working class. Such, for instance, was the adoption of the principle that in *relation to the State* religion is simply a private matter. Or the Commune promulgated decrees directly in the interests of the working class and, to a certain extent, inflicting deep wounds on the old body social.'

Engels deliberately emphasized the words 'in relation to the State,' not as a mere hint, but as a straight thrust at German Opportunism which had declared religion to be a private matter in *relation to the party;* thus lowering the party of the revolutionary proletariat to the level of the most superficial 'free-thinkers' of the middle class, ready to admit a non-religious State, but renouncing all *party* struggle against the religious opium which stupifies the people.

The future historian of German Social-Democracy investigating the root causes of its shameful collapse in 1914, will find no little material of interest on this question, beginning with the evasive declarations in the articles of the intellectual leader of the party, Kautsky, opening the door wide to Opportunism, and ending with the attitude of the party towards the *Los-von-Kirche Bewegung* (the movement for the disestablishment of the Church) in 1913.

But let us pass on to the manner in which, twenty years after the Commune, Engels summed up its lessons for the struggling proletariat.

Here are the lessons to which Engels attached prime importance:

'It was just this oppressive power of the former centralized Government, the army, the political police, the bureaucracy which Napoleon created in 1798, and which, from that time onwards, every new Government had taken over as a desirable weapon for use against its opponents—it was just this power which should have fallen throughout France as it had fallen in Paris.

'The Commune was compelled to recognize from the very first that the working class, having obtained supremacy, could no longer carry on the business of government by means of the old machinery; that, in order that the working class might not lose again its newly-won supremacy, it must, on the one hand, sweep aside the whole of the old machine of oppression which had hitherto been used against it, and on the other, secure itself against its own deputies and officials by declaring them all without exception, revocable at any time.'

Engels emphasizes again and again that not only in a Monarchy, *but also in a democratic republic*, the State remains the State, that is, it retains its fundamental and characteristic feature, viz., the transformation of officials—'the servants of society'—and of its organs into the rulers of society.

'Against this inevitable feature of all systems of government that have existed hitherto, viz., the transformation of the State and its organs from servants into the lords of society, the Commune used two unfailing remedies. First, it appointed to all posts, administrative, legal, educational, persons elected by universal suffrage; introducing at the same time the right of recalling those elected at any time by the decision of their electors. Secondly, it paid all officials, both high and low, only such pay as was received by any other worker. The highest salary paid by the Commune was 6,000 francs (about £240).[1]

'Thus was created an effective barrier to place-hunting and career-making, even apart from the imperative mandates of the deputies in representative institutions introduced by the Commune over and above this.'

Engels touches here on the interesting boundary where a consistent democracy is, on the one hand, *transformed* into Socialism, and, on the other, Socialism. For, in order to destroy the State, it is necessary to convert the functions of the public service into such simple operations of control and book-keeping as are within the reach of the vast majority of the population, and, ultimately, of every single individual. And, in order to do away completely with the political adventurer, it must be made impossible for an 'honourable', though unsalaried, sinecure in the public service to be used as a jumping-off ground for a highly

---

[1] Nominally this means about 2,400 roubles per annum. According to the present rates of exchange in Russia this would be equal to 6,000 roubles. Those Bolsheviks are making quite an unpardonable error who are proposing a salary of 9,000 roubles for members of the Town Duma, for instance, instead of suggesting a maximum salary of 6,000 roubles *for the whole of the State*—a sum quite sufficient for anybody. [As a matter of fact, the salaries of Peoples' Commissioners after the Bolshevik Revolution were fixed at 500 roubles per month. Since then, however, the value of the rouble decreased still further, so the salaries had to be raised.—Trans.]

profitable post in a bank or a joint-stock company, as happens *constantly* in the freest capitalist countries.

But Engels does not make the mistake made, for instance, by some Marxists on the question of the right of a nation to self-determination, viz., that, forsooth, this is impossible under Capitalism and will be unnecessary under Socialism. Such an apparently clever, but really incorrect statement might be repeated of *any* democratic institution, amongst others, of the payment of moderate salaries to officials; for, during the lifetime of capitalism a completely consistent democracy is impossible, whilst under Socialism all political democracy *disappears*.

This is a sophism, comparable to the old humorous problem of at what point a man will become bald if he loses his hair one by one.

The development of democracy to its logical conclusion, the investigation of the *forms* of this development, testing them by *practice*, and so forth—all this is part of the objects in the struggle for the Social Revolution. Taken separately, no kind of Democracy will yield Socialism. But in actual life Democracy will never be 'taken by itself;' it will be 'taken together' with other things, it will exert its influence also on economics, helping on its reorganisation; it will be subjected, in its turn, to the influence of economic development, and so on. That is the dialectical process of actual living history. Engels continues:—

'This disruption (*Sprengung*) of the old machinery of government and its replacement by a new and really democratic one, is described in detail in the third part of the *Civil War*. But it was necessary to dwell once more in brief on this point, that is, on one or two features of this replacement, because in Germany the superstitious faith in the State has left the realm of philosophy and passed into the general consciousness of the bourgeoisie and even of many workers. According to the teaching of the philosophers, the State is the "realization of Idea," or, translated into theological language, the Kingdom of God on earth; the State is the field in which is, or should be, realized eternal Truth and Justice. And from this follows a superstitious reverence for the State and for everything appertaining to the State—a superstitious reverence which takes root the more readily as people are accustomed, from their childhood, to think that the affairs and interests common to the whole of society cannot be carried out

and protected in any other way than in the one in existence—
that is, by means of the State and its well-paid officials. People
think they are making an extraordinarily big step forward if they
rid themselves of faith in a hereditary Monarchy and become
partisans of a democratic republic. Whereas, in reality, the State
is nothing more than an apparatus for the oppression of one class
by another, in a democratic Republic, not a whit less than in a
Monarchy. At best the State is an evil inherited by the proletariat after coming out victorious in the struggle for class
supremacy. The victorious proletariat, just like the Commune,
will be obliged immediately to amputate the worst features of
this evil, until such time as a new generation, brought up under
new and free social conditions, will prove capable of throwing on
the dust-heap all the useless old rubbish of State organization.'

Engels cautioned the Germans, in the event of the Monarchy
being replaced by a Republic, not to forget the fundamentals of
Socialism on the question of the State in general. His warnings
now read like a direct lesson to Messrs. Tseretelli and Tchernoff,
who revealed in their coalition tactics a superstitious faith in,
and respect towards, the State!

Two more points. (1) When Engels says that in a democratic
republic, 'not a whit less' than in a Monarchy, the State remains
an 'apparatus for the oppression of one class by another', this by
no means signifies that the *form* of oppression is a matter of
indifference to the proletariat, as some Anarchists 'teach'. A
wider, more free and open form of the class struggle and class
oppression enormously assists the proletariat in its struggle for
the annihilation of all classes. (2) Why only a new generation will
be able completely to scrap the ancient lumber of the State—this
question is bound up with the question of the supersession of
Democracy, to which we now turn.

6 ENGELS ON THE SUPERSESSION OF DEMOCRACY

Engels had occasion to speak on this subject in connection with
the question of the 'scientific' incorrectness of the term 'Social-
Democrat'.

In the introduction to his edition of his articles of the 'seventies
on various subjects, mainly on international questions (*'Inter-*

nationales aus dem Volksstaat'), dated January 3, 1894 (that is, a year and a half before his death) Engels wrote that in all his articles he used the word 'Communist', not 'Social-Democrat'; because at that time it was the Proudhonists in France and the Lassalleans in Germany who called themselves Social-Democrats.

'For Marx and for me [Engels continues] it was therefore quite impossible to use such an elastic term to describe our particular point of view. At the present time things are different, and this word ("Social-Democrat") may, perhaps, pass muster, although it remains inexact (*unpassend* literally "unsuitable") for a party whose economic programme is not simply a general Socialist one, but definitely Communist—for a party whose final political aim is the supersession of the whole State and, therefore, also of Democracy. But the names of *real* (the italics are Engels') political parties never completely correspond with fact: the party develops, the name remains.'

The dialectician Engels remains true to dialectics to the last day of his life. Marx and I, he says, had a splendid, scientific, exact name for the party, but there was no real party, that is, no mass-proletarian party. Now, at the end of the nineteenth century, there is a real party; but its name is scientifically incorrect. Never mind, 'it will pass muster', only let the party grow, only let not the scientific inexactitudes of its name be hidden from it, and let it not hinder its development in the right direction.

Perhaps, indeed, some humorist might comfort us Bolsheviks *à la* Engels: we have a real party, it is developing splendidly; even such a meaningless and barbarous term as 'Bolshevik' 'will pass muster', although it expresses nothing but the purely accidental fact that at the Brussels-London Conference of 1903 we had a majority (*Bolshinstvo*). Perhaps now, when the July and August persecutions of our party by the Republican and 'revolutionary' middle-class democracy have made the word 'Bolshevik' such a universally respected name; when, in addition, these persecutions have signalized such a great historical step forward made by our party in its *actual* development, perhaps now even I should hesitate to repeat my April suggestion to change the name of our party. Perhaps I would propose a 'compromise' to our comrades, to call ourselves the Communist Party, but to retain 'Bolsheviks' in brackets.[1] . . . But the question of the name of the party is incomparably less important that the question of the relation of the revolutionary proletariat to the State.

In the usual debates about the State the mistake is constantly made against which Engels cautions us here, and which we have indicated above. Namely, it is constantly forgotten that the destruction of the State involves also the destruction of democracy; that the withering away of the State also means the withering away of Democracy. At first sight such a statement seems exceedingly strange and incomprehensible. Indeed, perhaps some one or other may begin to fear lest we be expecting the advent of such an order of society in which the principle of majority rule will not be respected—for is not a Democracy just the recognition of this principle ?

No, Democracy is not identical with majority rule. No, Democracy is a *State* which recognizes the subjection of the minority to the majority, that is, an organization for the systematic use of *violence* by one class against the other, by one part of the population against another.

We set ourselves, as our final aim, the task of the destruction of the State, that is, of every organized and systematic violence, every form of violence against man in general. We do not expect the advent of an order of society in which the principle of the submission of the minority to the majority will not be observed. But, striving for Socialism, we are convinced that it will develop further into Communism, and, side by side with this, there will vanish all need for force, for the *subjection* of one man to another, of one section of society to another, since people will *grow accustomed* to observing the elementary conditions of social existence *without force and without subjection*.

In order to emphasize this element of habit, Engels speaks of a *new* generation, 'brought up under new and free social conditions which will prove capable of throwing on the dustheap all the useless old rubbish of State Organization'—*every* sort of State, including even the democratic republican State.

For the elucidation of this, we must examine the question of the economic foundations of the withering away of the State.

[1] This was actually done after the November Revolution: The Bolshevik party then officially styled itself: 'Communist Party (of the Bolsheviks').—Trans.

CHAPTER V

The Economic Foundation of the Withering Away of the State

A MOST detailed elucidation of this question is given by Marx in his *Criticism of the Gotha Programme* (letter to Bracke, May 15, 1875, printed as late as 1891 in the *Neue Zeit*, ix. 1). The polemical part of this remarkable work consisting of a criticism of Lassalleanism has, so to speak, overshadowed its positive part, namely the analysis of the connection between the development of Communism and the withering away of the State.

I THE FORMULATION OF THE QUESTION BY MARX

From a superficial comparison of the letter of Marx to Bracke (May 15, 1875) with Engels' letter to Bebel (March 28, 1875), discussed above, it might appear that Marx was much more of an upholder of the State than Engels, and that the difference of opinion between them on the question of the State is very considerable.

Engels suggests to Bebel that all the chatter about the State should be thrown overboard; that the word 'State' should be eliminated from the programme and replaced by 'Common wealth'; Engels even declares that the Commune was really no longer a State in the proper sense of the word. Whereas Marx even speaks of the 'future State in Communist society', that is, apparently recognizing the necessity of a State even under Communism.

But such a view would be fundamentally incorrect; and a closer examination shows that Marx's and Engels' views on the State and its decay were completely identical, and that Marx's expression quoted above refers merely to the *decaying* State.

It is clear that there can be no question of defining the exact moment of the *future* 'withering away'—the more so as it must obviously be a prolonged process. The apparent difference between Marx and Engels is due to the different subjects they dealt with, the different aims they were pursuing. Engels set forth the problem in a plain, bold, and large outline in order to show Bebel all the absurdity of the current superstitions concerning the State, shared to no small degree by Lassalle himself. Marx only touches upon *this* question in passing, being interested mainly in another subject—the *evolution* of Communist society. The whole theory of Marx is an application of the theory of evolution—in its most consistent, complete, well-thought-out and fruitful form—to modern Capitalism. Naturally, for Marx there arose the question of the application of this theory both to the *coming* crash of Capitalism and to the *future* development of *future* Communism.

On what foundation of facts can the future development of future Communism be based? It can be based on the fact that *it has its origin* in Capitalism, that it develops historically from Capitalism, that it is the result of the action of social forces to which Capitalism *has given birth*. There is no shadow of an attempt on Marx's part to fabricate a Utopia, idly to guess that which cannot be known. Marx treats the question of Communism in the same way as a naturalist would treat the question of the development of, say, a new biological variety, if he knew that such and such was its origin, and such and such is the direction in which it changes its form.

Marx, first of all, brushes aside the confusion which is introduced by the Gotha programme into the question of the mutual relations of State and of Society.

'Contemporary society [he writes] is capitalist society, which exists in all civilized countries, freed, to a greater or lesser extent, from admixture of mediaevalism, more or less varying in type according to the peculiar historical conditions of development of each country, more or less fully developed. The "contemporary State," on the contrary, varies with every State boundary. In the Prusso-German Empire it is quite a different thing from that in Switzerland; in England quite different from that in the United States. The "contemporary State" is, therefore, a fiction.

'However, in spite of the motley variety of their forms, the

different forms of the State in the different civilized cou.
have this in common—they are all based on contempo
bourgeois society, more or less capitalistically developed. T.
have, therefore, certain fundamental traits in common. In this
sense one can speak of the "contemporary State" in contradistinction to that future time when its present root, namely,
capitalist society, will have perished.

'The question is then put thus: To what transformation will
the forms of government be subjected in communist society? In
other words, what social functions will there remain, then,
analogous to the present functions of the State? This question
can only be answered with the help of the scientific method; and
however many thousands of times the word "people" is combined
with the word "State," this will not bring us one iota nearer its
solution. . . .'

Having thus ridiculed all the talk of a 'People's State', Marx
formulates the question and warns us, as it were, that for a
scientific answer to it one can only rely on firmly established
scientific facts.

The first fact that has been established with complete exactness
by the whole theory of evolution, indeed, by the whole of science
—a fact which the utopians forgot, however, and which is now
forgotten by the present Opportunists, afraid of the Socialist
revolution—is that, historically, there must undoubtedly be a
special stage or epoch of *transition* from Capitalism to Communism.

2 THE TRANSITION FROM CAPITALISM TO COMMUNISM

'Between capitalist and communist society [Marx continues]
there lies a period of revolutionary transformation from the
former to the latter. A stage of political transition corresponds to
this period, and the State during this period can be no other than
the *revolutionary dictatorship of the proletariat*.'

This conclusion Marx bases on an analysis of the rôle played by
the proletariat in modern capitalist society, on the facts of the
development of this society and on the irreconcilability of the
antagonistic interests of the proletarian and the capitalist class.

Earlier the question was put thus: To attain its emancipation the proletariat must overthrow the capitalist class, conquer political power and establish its own revolutionary dictatorship. Now the question is put somewhat differently: The transition from capitalist society developing towards Communism, to a Communist Society, is impossible without a period of 'political transition', and the State in this period can only be the revolutionary dictatorship of the proletariat.

What, then, is the relation of this dictatorship to democracy?

We saw that the *Communist Manifesto* simply places side by side the two ideas: the 'conversion of the proletariat into the ruling class' and the 'conquest of Democracy'. On the basis of all that has been said above, one can define more exactly how democracy changes in the transition of Capitalism to Communism.

In capitalist society, under the conditions most favourable to its development, we have a more or less complete democracy in the form of a democratic republic. But this democracy is always bound by the narrow framework of capitalist exploitation, and, consequently, always remains, in reality, a democracy only for the minority, only for the possessing classes, only for the rich. Freedom in capitalist society always remains more or less the same as it was in the ancient Greek republics, that is, freedom for the slave owners. The modern wage-slaves, in virtue of the conditions of capitalist exploitation, remain to such an extent crushed by want and poverty that they 'cannot be bothered with democracy', have 'no time for politics'; that, in the ordinary peaceful course of events, the majority of the population is debarred from participating in public political life.

The accuracy of this statement is perhaps most clearly proved by Germany, just because in this State constitutional legality has lasted and remained stable for a remarkably long time—for nearly half a century (1871-1914); and Social-Democracy during this time has been able, far better than has been the case in other countries, to make use of 'legality' in order to organize into a political party a larger proportion of the working class than has occurred anywhere else in the world.

What, then, is this highest proportion of politically conscious and active wage-slaves that has so far been observed in capitalist society? One million members of the Social-Democratic Party

out of fifteen millions of wage-workers! Three millions industrially organized out of fifteen millions!

Democracy for an insignificant minority, democracy for the
rich—that is the democracy of capitalist society. If we look more
closely into the mechanism of capitalist democracy, everywhere
—in the so-called 'petty' details of the suffrage (the residential
qualification, the exclusion of women, etc.), in the technique of
the representative institutions, in the actual obstacles to the right
of meeting (public buildings are not for the 'poor'), in the purely
capitalist organization of the daily press, etc., etc.—on all sides
we shall see restrictions upon restrictions of Democracy. These
restrictions, exceptions, exclusions, obstacles for the poor, seem
slight—especially in the eyes of one who has himself never known
want, and has never lived in close contact with the oppressed
classes in their herd life, and nine-tenths, if not ninety-nine
hundredths, of the bourgeois publicists and politicians are of this
class! But in their sum these restrictions exclude and thrust out
the poor from politics and from an active share in democracy.
Marx splendidly grasped the *essence* of capitalist democracy,
when, in his analysis of the experience of the Commune, he said
that the oppressed are allowed, once every few years to decide
which particular representatives of the oppressing class are
to represent and repress them in Parliament!

But from this capitalist democracy—inevitably narrow,
stealthily thrusting aside the poor, and therefore to its core,
hypocritical and treacherous—progress does not march along a
simple, smooth and direct path to 'greater and greater democracy',
as the Liberal professors and the lower middle-class Opportunists
would have us believe. No, progressive development—that is,
towards Communism—marches through the dictatorship of the
proletariat; and cannot do otherwise, for there is no one else who
can *break the resistance* of the exploiting capitalists, and no other
way of doing it.

And the dictatorship of the proletariat—that is, the organization
of the advance-guard of the oppressed as the ruling class, for the
purpose of crushing the oppressors—cannot produce merely an
expansion of democracy. *Together* with an immense expansion of
democracy—for the first time becoming democracy for the poor,
democracy for the people, and not democracy for the rich folk

—the dictatorship of the proletariat will produce a series of restrictions of liberty in the case of the oppressors, exploiters and capitalists. We must crush them in order to free humanity from wage-slavery; their resistance must be broken by force. It is clear that where there is suppression there must also be violence, and there cannot be liberty or democracy.

Engels expressed this splendidly in his letter to Bebel when he said, as the reader will remember, that 'the proletariat needs the State, not in the interests of liberty, but for the purpose of crushing its opponents; and, when one will be able to speak of freedom, the State will have ceased to exist'.

Democracy for the vast majority of the nation, and the suppression by force—that is, the exclusion from democracy—of the exploiters and oppressors of the nation: this is the modification of democracy which we shall see during the *transition* from Capitalism to Communism.

Only in Communist Society, when the resistance of the capitalists has finally been broken, when the capitalists have disappeared, when there are no longer any classes (that is, when there is no difference between the members of society in respect of their social means of production), *only then* 'does the State disappear *and one can speak of freedom*'. Only then will be possible and will be realized a really full democracy, a democracy without any exceptions. And only then will democracy itself begin to wither away in virtue of the simple fact that, freed from capitalist slavery, from the innumerable horrors, savagery, absurdities and infamies of capitalist exploitation, people will gradually *become accustomed* to the observation of the elementary rules of social life, known for centuries, repeated for thousands of years in all sermons. They will become accustomed to their observance without force, without constraint, without subjection, without the *special apparatus* for compulsion which is called the State.

The expression 'the State withers away', is very well chosen, for it indicates the gradual and elemental nature of the process. Only habit can, and undoubtedly will, have such an effect: for we see around us millions of times how readily people get accustomed to observe the necessary rules of life in common, if there is no exploitation, if there is nothing that causes indignation, that calls forth protest and revolt and has to be suppressed.

Thus, in capitalist society, we have a democracy that is curtailed, wretched, false; a democracy only for the rich, for the minority. The dictatorship of the proletariat, the period of transition to Communism, will, for the first time, produce a democracy for the people, for the majority, side by side with the necessary suppression of the minority constituted by the exploiters. Communism alone is capable of giving a really complete democracy, and the fuller it is the more quickly will it become unnecessary and wither away of itself. In other words, under Capitalism we have a State in the proper sense of the word: that is, a special instrument for the suppression of one class by another, and of the majority by the minority at that. Naturally, for the successful discharge of such a task as the systematic suppression by the minority of exploiters of the majority of exploited, the greatest ferocity and savagery of suppression is required, and seas of blood are needed, through which humanity has to direct its path, in a condition of slavery, serfdom and wage labour.

Again, during the *transition* from Capitalism to Communism, suppression is *still* necessary; but in this case it is the suppression of the minority of exploiters by the majority of exploited. A special instrument, a special machine for suppression—that is, the 'State'—is necessary, but this is now a transitional State, no longer a State in the ordinary sense of the term. For the suppression of the minority of exploiters, by the majority of those who were *but yesterday* wage-slaves, is a matter comparatively so easy, simple and natural that it will cost far less bloodshed than the suppression of the risings of the slaves, serfs or wage labourers, and will cost the human race far less. And it is compatible with the diffusion of democracy over such an overwhelming majority of the nation that the need for any *special machinery* for suppression will gradually cease to exist. The exploiters are unable, of course, to suppress the people without a most complex machine for performing this duty; but *the people* can suppress the exploiters even with a very simple 'machine'—almost without any 'machine at all, without any special apparatus—by the simple *organization of the armed masses* (such as the Councils of Workers' and Soldiers' Deputies, we may remark, anticipating a little).

Finally, only under Communism will the State become quite unnecessary, for there will be *no one* to suppress—'no one' in the sense of a *class*, in the sense of a systematic struggle with a definite section of the population. We are not utopians, and we do not in the least deny the possibility and inevitability of excesses by *individual persons*, and equally the need to suppress such excesses. But, in the first place, for this no special machine, no special instrument of repression is needed. This will be done by the armed nation itself, as simply and as readily as any crowd of civilized people, even in modern society, parts a pair of combatants or does not allow a woman to be outraged. And, secondly, we know that the fundamental social cause of excesses which violate the rules of social life is the exploitation of the masses, their want and their poverty. With the removal of this chief cause, excesses will inevitably begin to 'wither away'. We do not know how quickly and in what stages, but we know that they will be withering away. With their withering away, the State will also wither away. Marx, without plunging into Utopia, defined more fully what can *now* be defined regarding this future epoch: namely, the difference between the higher and lower phases (degrees, stages) of Communist society.

3 THE FIRST PHASE OF COMMUNIST SOCIETY

In the *Criticism of the Gotha Programme* Marx disproves in detail the Lassallean idea of the receipt by the workers under Socialism of the 'undiminished' or 'full product of their labour'. Marx shows that out of the whole of the social labour of society, it will be necessary to deduct a reserve fund, a fund for the expansion of industry, the replacement of 'worn-out' machinery, and so on; then, also, out of the collective product a fund for the expenses of management, for schools, hospitals, homes for the aged, and so forth.

Instead of the hazy, obscure, general phrase of Lassalle —'the full product of his labour for the worker'—Marx gives a sober estimate as to how exactly a Socialist society will have to manage its affairs. Marx takes up a *concrete* analysis of the conditions of life of a society in which there will be no capitalism, and says: 'We have to deal here' (analysing the programme of the

Party), 'not with a communist society which has *developed* on its own foundations, but with one which has just *issued* actually from capitalist society, and which, in consequence, in all respects—economic, moral, and intellectual—still bears the stamp of the old society, from the womb of which it came.' And it is this communist society—a society which has just come into the world out of the womb of Capitalism, and which, in all respects, bears the stamp of the old society—that Marx terms the first, or lower, phase of communist society.

The means of production are now no longer the private property of individuals. The means of production belong to the whole of society. Every member of society, performing a certain part of socially-necessary labour, receives a certificate from society that he has done such and such a quantity of work. According to this certificate, he receives from the public stores of articles of consumption a corresponding quantity of products. After the deduction of that proportion of labour which goes into the public fund, every worker, therefore, receives from society as much as he has given it.

'Equality' seems to reign supreme. But when Lassalle, having in view such a social order (generally called 'Socialism', but termed by Marx the first phase of Communism), speaks of this as 'just distribution', and says that this is 'the equal right of each to an equal share of the products of labour', Lassalle is mistaken, and Marx explains his error.

'Equal right [says Marx] we indeed have here; but it is *still* a "bourgeois right," which, like every right, *presupposes inequality*. Every "right" is an application of the *same* measure to *different* people who, as a matter of fact, are not similar and are not equal one to another; and, therefore, "equal right" is really a violation of equality, and an injustice. In effect, every man having done as much social labour as every other, receives an equal share of the social products (with the above-mentioned deductions). Notwithstanding this, different people are not equal to one another. One is strong, another is weak; one is married, the other is not. One has more children, another has less, and so on.

'With equal labour [Marx concludes], and therefore with an equal share in the public stock of articles of consumption, one will, in reality, receive more than another, will find himself richer, and so on. To avoid all this, "rights," instead of being equal, should be unequal.'

The first phase of Communism, therefore, still cannot produce justice and equality; differences, and unjust differences, in wealth will still exist, but the *exploitation* of one man by many, will have become impossible, because it will be impossible to seize as private property the *means of production*, the factories, machines, land, and so on. While tearing to tatters Lassalle's small bourgeois, confused phrase about 'equality' and 'justice' *in general*, Marx at the same time shows the *line of development* of communist society, which is forced at first to destroy *only* the 'injustice' that the means of production are in the hands of private individuals. *It is not capable* of destroying at once the further injustice which is constituted by the distribution of the articles of consumption according to 'work performed' (and not according to need).

The vulgar economists, including the bourgeois professors (such as 'our' Tugan-Baranowsky), constantly reproach the Socialists with forgetting the inequality of mankind and with 'dreaming' of destroying this inequality. Such a reproach, as we see, only proves the extreme ignorance of the bourgeois ideologists.

Marx not only, with the greatest care, takes into account the inevitable inequalities of men; he also takes cognisance of the fact that the mere conversion of the means of production into the common property of the whole of society—'Socialism' in the generally accepted sense of the word—*does not remove* the short-comings of distribution and the inequality of 'bourgeois justice', which continue to exist as long as the products are divided according to the quantity of 'work performed'.

'But these defects [Marx continues] are unavoidable in the first phase of communist society, in the form in which it comes forth, after the prolonged travail of birth, from capitalist society. Justice can never be in advance of its stage of economic development, and of the cultural development of society conditioned by the latter.'

And so, in the first phase of communist society (generally called Socialism), 'bourgeois justice' is *not* abolished in its entirety, but only in part, only in proportion to the economic transformation so far attained, that is, only in respect of the means of production. 'Bourgeois law' recognizes them as the private property of separate individuals. Socialism converts them into common property, and to that extent, and only to that extent, does 'bourgeois law' die out. But it continues to live as far as its other part is concerned, in the capacity of regulator or adjuster dividing labour and allotting the products amongst the members of society.

'He who does not work neither shall he eat'—this Socialist principle is *already* realized. 'For an equal quantity of labour an equal quantity of products'—this Socialist principle is also already realized. Nevertheless, this is not yet Communism, and this does not abolish 'bourgeois law', which gives to unequal individuals, in return for an unequal (in reality) amount of work, an equal quantity of products.

This is a 'defect', says Marx, but it is unavoidable during the first phase of Communism; for, if we are not to land in Utopia, we cannot imagine that, having overthrown Capitalism, people will at once learn to work for society *without any regulations by law*; indeed, the abolition of Capitalism does not *immediately* lay the economic foundations for such a change.

And there is no other standard yet than that of 'bourgeois law'. To this extent, therefore, a form of State is still necessary, which, whilst maintaining the public ownership of the means of production, preserves the equality of labour and equality in the distribution of the products. The State is withering away in so far as there are no longer any capitalists, any classes, and, consequently, any *class* whatever to suppress. But the State is not yet dead altogether, since there still remains the protection of 'bourgeois law', which sanctifies actual inequality. For the complete extinction of the State complete Communism is necessary.

4 THE HIGHEST PHASE OF COMMUNIST SOCIETY

Marx continues:—

'In the highest phase of communist society, after the disappearance of the enslavement of man caused by his subjection to the principle of division of labour; when, together with this, the opposition between brain and manual work will have disappeared; when labour will have ceased to be a mere means of supporting

\d will itself have become one of the first necessities of life; , with the all-round development of the individual, the productive forces, too, will have grown to maturity, and all the forces of social wealth will be pouring an uninterrupted torrent —only then will it be possible wholly to pass beyond the narrow horizon of bourgeois laws, and only then will Society be able to inscribe on its banner: "From each according to his ability; to each according to his needs".'

Only now can we appreciate the full justice of Engels' observations when he mercilessly ridiculed all the absurdity of combining the words 'freedom' and 'State'. While the State exists there can be no freedom. When there is freedom there will be no State.

The economic basis for the complete withering away of the State is that high stage of development of Communism when the distinction between brain and manual work disappears; consequently, when one of the principal sources of modern *social* inequalities will have vanished—a source, moreover, which it is impossible to remove immediately by the mere conversion of the means of production into public property, by the mere expropriation of the capitalists.

This expropriation will make it possible gigantically to develop the forces of production. And seeing how incredibly, even now, Capitalism *retards* this development, how much progress could be made even on the basis of modern technique at the level it has reached, we have a right to say, with the fullest confidence, that the expropriation of the capitalists will result inevitably in a gigantic development of the productive forces of human society. But how rapidly this development will go forward, how soon it will reach the point of breaking away from the division of labour, of the destruction of the antagonism between brain and manual work, of the transformation of work into a 'first necessity of life' —this we do not and *cannot* know.

Consequently, we are right in speaking solely of the inevitable withering away of the State, emphasizing the protracted nature of this process, and its dependence upon the rapidity of development of the *higher phase* of Communism; leaving quite open the question of lengths of time, or the concrete forms of this withering away, since material for the solution of such questions is not available.

The State will be able to wither away completely when Society has realized the formula:'From each according to his ability; to each according to his needs'; that is, when people have become accustomed to observe the fundamental principles of social life, and their labour is so productive, that they will voluntarily work *according to their abilities*. 'The narrow horizon of bourgeois law', which compels one to calculate, with the pitilessness of a Shylock, whether one has not worked half an hour more than another, whether one is not getting less pay than another—this narrow horizon will then be left behind. There will then be no need for any exact calculation by Society of the quantity of products to be distributed to each of its members; each will take freely 'according to his needs'.

From the capitalist point of view, it is easy to declare such a social order a 'pure Utopia', and to sneer at the Socialists for promising each the right to receive from society, without any control of the labour of the individual citizens, any quantity of truffles, motor cars, pianos, and so forth. Even now, most bourgeois '*savants*' deliver themselves of such sneers, but thereby they only display at once their ignorance and their material interest in defending Capitalism. Ignorance—for it has never entered the head of any Socialist 'to promise' that the highest phase of Communism will actually arrive, while the *anticipation* of the great Socialists that it *will* arrive, assumes *neither the present* productive powers of labour, *nor the present* unthinking 'man in the street' capable of spoiling, without reflection, the stores of social wealth and of demanding the impossible. As long as the 'highest' phase of Communism has not arrived, the Socialists demand the *strictest* control, *by Society and by the State*, of the quantity of labour and the quantity of consumption; only this control must *start* with the expropriation of the capitalists, with the control of the workers over the capitalists, and must be carried out, not by a Government of bureaucrats, but by a Government of the *armed workers*.

The interested defence of Capitalism by the capitalist ideologists (and their hangers-on like Tseretelli, Tchernoff and Co.) consists just in that they *substitute* their disputes and discussions about the far future for the essential, imperative questions *of the day*: the expropriation of the capitalists, the conversion of *all* citizens into workers and employees of *one* huge 'syndicate'—the whole State—and the complete subordination of the whole of the work of this syndicate to a really democratic State—to the *State consisting of the Councils of Workers' and Soldiers' Deputies*. In reality, when a learned professor, and in his train, some philistine, and in his wake Messrs Tseretelli and Tchernoff, talk of unreasonable Utopias, of the demagogic promises of the Bolsheviks, of the impossibility of 'bringing in' Socialism, it is the highest stage or phase of Communism which they have in mind, and which no one has not only promised, but ever even thought of trying to 'bring in', because, in any case, it is altogether impossible to 'bring it in'.

And here we come to that question of the scientific difference between Socialism and Communism, upon which Engels touched in his discussion cited above on the incorrectness of the name 'Social Democrat'. The political difference between the first, or lower, and the higher phase of Communism will in time, no doubt, be tremendous; but it would be ridiculous to emphasize it now, under Capitalism, and only, perhaps, some isolated Anarchist could invest it with primary importance—that is, if there are still people amongst the Anarchists who have learnt nothing from the Plekanoff-like conversion of the Kropotkins, the Graves, the Cornelisens, and other 'leading lights' of Anarchism to Social-Chauvinism or Anarcho-*Jusquauboutism* as one of the few Anarchists still preserving their honour (Gay) has expressed it.

But the scientific difference between Socialism and Communism is clear. That which is generally called Socialism is termed by Marx the first or lower phase of Communist society. In so far as the means of production become public property, the word Communism is also applicable here, providing that we do not forget that it is not full Communism. The great importance of Marx's explanation is this: that here, too, he consistently applies materialist dialectics, the theory of evolution, looking upon Communism as something which evolves *out of* Capitalism.

Instead of artificially elaborate and scholastic definitions and profitless disquisitions on the meanings of words ('what Socialism is', 'what Communism is'), Marx gives us an analysis of what may be called the stages in the economic growth of Communism.

In its first phase or first stage Communism *cannot* as yet be economically mature and quite free of all tradition and of all taint of Capitalism. Hence we see the interesting phenomenon of the first phase of Communism retaining 'the narrow horizon of bourgeois law'. Bourgeois law, in respect of the distribution of articles of consumption, presupposes inevitably the capitalist State, for law is nothing without the organization for *forcing* people to obey it. Consequently, for a certain time not only bourgeois law, but even the capitalist State may remain under Communism without the capitalist class.

This may appear to some a paradox, a piece of intellectual subtlety, of which Marxism is often accused by people who would not put themselves out to study its extraordinarily profound teachings. But, as a matter of fact, the Old surviving in the New confronts us in life at every step in nature as well as in Society. It is not Marx's own sweet will which smuggled a scrap of bourgeois law into Communism; he simply indicated what is economically and politically inevitable in a society issuing from the *womb of Capitalism*.

Democracy is of great importance in the working-class struggle for freedom against the capitalists. But Democracy is not a limit one may not overstep; it is merely one of the stages in the course of development from Feudalism to Capitalism, and from Capitalism to Communism.

Democracy implies equality. The immense significance of the struggle of the proletariat for equality and the power of attraction of such a battle-cry are obvious, if we but rightly interpret it as meaning the *annihilation of classes*. But the equality of Democracy is *formal* equality—no more; and immediately after the attainment of the equality of all members of society in respect of the ownership of the means of production, that is, of equality of labour and equality of wages, there will inevitably arise before humanity the question of going further from equality which is formal to equality which is real, and of realizing in life the formula 'From each according to his ability; to each according to his needs.' By what stages, by means of what practical measures humanity will proceed to this higher aim—this we do not and cannot know. But it is important that one should realize how infinitely mendacious is the usual capitalist representation of

Socialism as something lifeless, petrified, fixed once for all. In reality, it is *only* with Socialism that there will commence a rapid, genuine, real mass advance, in which first the majority and then the *whole* of the population will take part—an advance in all domains of social and individual life.

Democracy is a form of the State—one of the varieties of the State; and, consequently, like every State, it stands as an organized, systematic application of force against mankind. That is its one aspect. But, on the other hand, it is the formal recognition of the equality of all citizens, the equal right of all to determine the structure and administration of the State. Out of this formal recognition there arises, in its turn, a stage in the development of Democracy, when it first rallies the proletariat as a revolutionary class against Capitalism, and gives it an opportunity to crush, to break to atoms, to wipe off the face of the earth the capitalist government machine—even the republican variety: the standing army, police, and bureaucracy. Second, it enables it to substitute for all this a more democratic, but still a *State* machinery in the shape of armed masses of the working class, which then become transformed into a universal participation of the people in a militia.

Here 'quantity passes into quality'. Such a degree of Democracy carries with it the abandonment of the framework of capitalist society, and the beginning of its Socialist reconstruction. If *everyone* really takes part in the administration of the State, Capitalism cannot retain its hold. As a matter of fact, Capitalism, as it develops, itself prepares the ground for everyone to be able really to take part in the administration of the State.

We may class as part of this preparation of the ground the universal literacy of the population, already realized in most of the more progressive capitalist countries; then the education and discipline inculcated upon millions of workers by the huge, complex, and socialized apparatus of the post, railways, big factories, large-scale commerce, banking, and so on, and so forth.

With such an *economic* groundwork it is quite possible, immediately, within twenty-four hours, to pass to the overthrow of the capitalists and bureaucrats, and to replace them, in the control of production and distribution, in the business of apportioning labour and products, by the armed workers, or the people in arms. The question of control and book-keeping must not be confused with the question of the scientifically educated staff of engineers, agriculturists, and so on. These gentlemen work today owing allegiance to the capitalists: they will work even better tomorrow, owing it to the armed workers. Book-keeping and control—these are the chief things necessary for the smooth and correct functioning of the *first phase* of communist society. *All* the citizens are here transformed into the hired employees of the State, which then is the armed workers. *All* the citizens become the employees and workers of *one* national State 'syndicate'. It simply resolves itself into a question of all working to an equal extent, of all carrying out regularly the measure of work apportioned to them, and of all receiving equal pay.

The book-keeping and control necessary for this have been simplified by capitalism to the utmost, till they have become the extraordinarily simple operations of watching, recording, and issuing receipts, within the reach of anybody who can read and write and knows the first four arithmetical rules.[1] When the majority of the citizens themselves begin everywhere to keep such accounts and maintain such control over the capitalists, now converted into employees, and over the intellectual gentry, who still retain capitalist habits, this control will, indeed, become universal, pervading, rational: it will be ubiquitous, and there will be no way of escaping it.

The whole of society will have become one office and one factory, with equal work and equal pay. But this 'factory' discipline, which the proletariat will extend to the whole of society on the defeat of Capitalism and the overthrow of the exploiters, is by no means our ideal, and is far from our final aim. It is but a foothold as we press on to the radical cleansing of society from all the brutality and foulness of capitalist exploitation: we leave it behind as we move on.

When all, or be it even only the greater part of society, have learnt how to govern the State, have taken this business into their own hands, have established a control over the insignificant

[1] When most of the functions of the State are reduced to this book-keeping and control by the workers themselves it ceases to be a 'political' State. Then 'the public functions are converted from political into simple administrative functions' (cf. above, chap. iv., par. 2, on the dispute of Engels with the Anarchists).

minority of capitalists, over the gentry with capitalist leanings, and workers thoroughly demoralized by capitalism—from this moment the need for any government begins to vanish. The more complete the Democracy, the nearer the moment when it ceases to be necessary. The more democratic the 'State' consisting of armed workers, which is 'no longer really a State in the ordinary sense of the term', the more rapidly does every form of the State begin to decay. For when all have learnt to manage, and really do manage, socialized production, when all really do keep account and control of the idlers, gentlefolk, swindlers, and suchlike 'guardians of capitalist traditions', the escape from such general registration and control will inevitably become so increasingly difficult, so much the exception, and will probably be accompanied by such swift and severe punishment (for the armed workers are very practical people, not sentimental intellectuals, and they will scarcely allow anyone to trifle with them), that very soon the *necessity* of observing the simple, fundamental rules of any kind of social life will become a habit. The door will then be wide open for the transition from the first phase of Communist society to its second higher phase, and along with it to the complete withering away of the State.

CHAPTER VI

The Vulgarization of Marx by the Opportunists

THE question of the relation of the State to the Social Revolution, and of the Social Revolution to the State, like the question of Revolution generally, occupied very little the best known theoreticians of the Second International (1889-1914). But the most characteristic thing in that process of the gradual growth of Opportunism, which led to the collapse of the Second International in 1914, is this, that even when they actually came into contact with this question they did their best to evade it or else passed it by unnoticed.

It may, in general, be said that the evasiveness on this question of the relation of the proletarian revolution to the State, an evasiveness which was both convenient to the Opportunists and bred and fed them—resulted in a distortion of Marxism and in its complete vulgarization.

To characterize, if only in brief, this lamentable process, let us take the best-known theoreticians of Marxism: Plekhanoff and Kautsky.

I THE CONTROVERSY BETWEEN PLEKHANOFF AND THE ANARCHISTS

Plekhanoff devoted a special pamphlet to the question of the relation of Socialism to Anarchism entitled *Anarchism and Socialism*, published in German in 1894. He managed somehow to treat this question without touching on the most vital, controversial point, the essential point *politically*, in the struggle with the Anarchists: the relation of the Revolution to the State, and the question of the State in general. His pamphlet may be divided into two parts: one, historico-literary, containing valuable material for the history of the ideas of Stirner, Proudhon, and others; the second, ignorant and narrow-minded, containing a clumsy disquisition on the theme 'that an Anarchist cannot be distinguished from a bandit', an amusing combination of subjects and most characteristic of the entire activity of Plekhanoff on the eve of Revolution and during the revolutionary period in Russia. Indeed, in the years 1908 to 1917 Plekhanoff showed himself to be half doctrinaire and half philistine, walking, politically, in the wake of the bourgeoisie.

We saw how Marx and Engels, in their polemics against the Anarchists, explained most thoroughly their views on the relation of the Revolution to the State. Engels, when editing in 1891 Marx's *Criticism of the Gotha Programme*, wrote that 'we'— that is, Engels and Marx—'were then in the fiercest phase of our battle with Bakunin and his Anarchists: hardly two years had then passed since the Hague Congress of the International' (the First). The Anarchists had tried to claim the Paris Commune as their 'own', as a confirmation of their teachings, thus showing that they had not in the least understood the lessons of the Commune or the analysis of those lessons by Marx. Anarchism has given nothing approaching a true solution of the concrete political problems: are we to *break* up the old State machine, and what shall we put in its place?

But to speak of 'Anarchism and Socialism', leaving the whole question of the State out of account and taking no notice at all of the whole development of Marxism before and after the Commune—that meant an inevitable fall into the pit of Opportunism. For that is just what Opportunism wants—to keep these two questions in abeyance. To secure this is, in itself, a victory for Opportunism.

2 KAUTSKY'S CONTROVERSY WITH THE OPPORTUNISTS

Undoubtedly an immeasurably larger number of Kautsky's works have been translated into Russian than into any other language. It is not without some justification that German Social-Democrats sometimes make the joke that Kautsky is more read in Russia than in Germany—and we may say, in parentheses, that there is deeper historical significance in this joke than those who first made it suspected. For in 1905 the Russian workers manifested an extraordinarily strong, an unexampled demand for the best works, the best Social-Democratic literature in the world, and translations and editions of these works appeared in quantities unheard of in other countries. Thereby with one sweep the immense experience of the neighbouring, more advanced, country, was transplanted on to the almost virgin soil of our proletarian movement.

Besides his popularization of Marxism, Kautsky is particularly well known in our country by his controversies with the Opportunists, with Bernstein at their head. But one fact is almost unknown, which, however, cannot be passed over if we are to apply ourselves to the task of investigating how it was that Kautsky rolled down into the disgraceful morass of confusion and defence of Social Chauvinism at the time of greatest crisis in 1914-15. This fact is that before he came forward against the best-known representatives of Opportunism in France (Millerand, Jaurès), and Germany (Bernstein), Kautsky had shown very great vacillation.

The Russian Marxist journal, *The Dawn*, which was published at Stuttgart in 1901-2, and advocated revolutionary proletarian doctrines, had to call Kautsky to account, denouncing his resolution at the Paris International Socialist Congress of 1900 as a 'piece of elastic', because of its evasive, temporising and conciliatory attitude towards the Opportunists. Letters have been published from Kautsky's pen in Germany revealing no less hesitancy before he took the field against Bernstein. Of immeasurably greater importance, however, is the circumstance that, in his very debates with the Opportunists, in his formulation of the question and his method of treating it, we can observe, now that we are investigating the *history* of his latest betrayal of Marxism, his systematic gravitation towards Opportunism, and that precisely on this question of the State.

Let us take Kautsky's first big work against Opportunism: *Bernstein and the Social-Democratic Programme.* Kautsky refutes Bernstein in detail; but the characteristic thing about it is this:

Bernstein, in his famous, or infamous, *Socialist Fundamentals*, accuses Marxism of Blanquism, an accusation since repeated thousands of times by the Opportunists and Liberals of Russia against the representatives of revolutionary Marxism, the Bolsheviks. In this connection Bernstein dwells particularly on

Marx's *Civil War in France*, and tries—as we saw, quite un-
successfully—to identify Marx's view of the lessons of the
Commune with that of Proudhon. He also pays particular attention to Marx's conclusion, emphasized by him in his preface of
1872 to the *Communist Manifesto* to the effect that 'the working
class cannot simply lay hold of the ready-made State machine, and
set it going for its own purposes'. The dictum pleased Bernstein
so much that he repeated it no less than three times in his book—
interpreting it in the most distorted Opportunist sense. We have
seen what Marx means—that the working class must *shatter*,
break, *blow up* (*sprengen*, explode, is the expression used by
Engels) the whole State machine; whereas, according to Bernstein, it would appear as though Marx by these words warned the
working class *against* excessive revolutionary zeal when seizing
power.

One cannot imagine a more vulgar and discreditable perversion
of Marx's ideas. How, then, did Kautsky act in his detailed
refutation of Bernsteinism?

He avoided the examination of the entire enormity of the perversion of Marxism on this point. He cited the above-quoted
passage from Engels' preface to Marx's *Civil War in France*,
saying that, according to Marx, the working class cannot *simply*
take possession of the ready-made State machine, but, generally
speaking, it *can* take possession of it—and that is all. . . . As for
the fact that Bernstein attributed to Marx the direct opposite of
the latter's real views, and that the real task of the proletarian
revolution, as formulated by Marx ever since 1852, was the
shattering of the State machine—not a word of all this is to be
found in Kautsky. The result was that the most important distinction between Marxism and Opportunism on the question of
the proletarian revolution was glossed over! 'The solution of the
problem of the proletarian dictatorship,' wrote Kautsky 'in
opposition' to Bernstein, 'we can safely leave to the future' (p.
172, German Edition).

This is not a polemic *against* Bernstein, but really a concession
to him, a surrender of the position to Opportunism: for at
present the Opportunists ask nothing better then 'safely to leave
to the future' all the fundamental questions of the proletarian
revolution.

Marx and Engels, from 1852 to 1891—for forty years—had taught the proletariat that it must *break* the State machine; but Kautsky, in 1899, confronted on this point with the complete betrayal of Marxism by Opportunists, fraudulently substitutes the question as to the concrete forms of the destruction of the State machine in the place of the more general one about the necessity of destroying it, and then saves himself behind the screen of the 'indisputable'—and barren—truth, that concrete forms cannot be known in advance. . . .

Between Marx and Kautsky, between their respective attitudes to the problem before the proletarian party as to how to prepare the working class for Revolution, there is a wide abyss.

Let us take the next, more mature, work by Kautsky, also devoted to a large extent, to a refutation of Opportunist errors. This is his pamphlet on the *Social Revolution*. The author chose here as his special theme the question of 'the proletarian revolution' and the 'proletarian régime.' He gave us here much valuable matter; but just this question of the State was *ignored*. Throughout the pamphlet the author speaks of the conquest of the power of the State—and that is all. That is to say, the question is so formulated as to constitute a concession to Opportunism, since the possibility of the conquest of power is admitted *without* the destruction of the State machine. The very thing which Marx, in 1872, had declared to be out of date in the programme of the *Communist Manifesto* is revived by Kautsky in 1902!

The pamphlet also contains a special paragraph on 'the forms and weapons of the Social Revolution'. Here he treats of the general political strike, of the question of civil war, and of 'the instruments of force at the disposal of the modern large States such as the bureaucracy and the Army; but of that which the Commune had already taught the workers, not a syllable. Evidently Engels had issued no idle warning, for the German Social-Democrats particularly, against 'superstitious reverence' for the State.

Kautsky propounds the matter thus: the victorious proletariat 'will realise the democratic programme', and he formulates its clauses; but of what the year 1871 has taught us about the middle-class democracy being replaced by a proletarian one—not a word. He disposes of the question by such plausible banalties as: 'It is obvious that we shall not attain supremacy under the present order of things. Revolution itself presupposes a prolonged and far-reaching struggle which, as it proceeds, will change our political and social structure.'

'Obvious' this undoubtedly is: as much as that horses eat oats, or the Volga flows into the Caspian Sea. The only pity is that he should use this empty and bombastic phrase 'far-reaching' to slur over the essential question for the revolutionary proletariat as to *wherein* exactly lies this 'far-reaching' nature of its revolution in respect of the State and Democracy, as distinguished from the non-proletarian revolutions of the past?

Here is a most important point, by ignoring which Kautsky, in point of fact, gives over the whole position to the Opportunists, whilst declaring war against them in awe-inspiring words, emphasizing the importance of the 'idea of revolution'—how much is this 'idea' worth, if one is afraid to propagate it among the workers?—or 'Revolutionary idealism above all . . .' declaring that the English workers represent now little more than a lower middle-class. . . .

'In a Socialist society [Kautsky writes] there can exist, side by side, the most varied forms of industrial undertakings—bureaucratic [? ?], trade unionist, co-operative, individual.' 'There are, for instance, such enterprises as cannot do without a bureaucratic [? ?] organization: such are the railways. Here democratic organization might take the following form:—The workers elect delegates, who form something in the nature of a parliament, and this parliament determines the conditions of work, and superintends the management of the bureaucratic apparatus. Other enterprises might be handed over to the workers' unions, which again could be organized on a co-operative basis.'

This view is erroneous, and represents a step backward by comparison with the deductions of Marx and Engels in the 'seventies from the example of the Commune.

So far as this assumed necessity of 'bureaucratic' organization is concerned, there is no difference whatever between railways and any other form of big industry, any factory, great commercial undertaking or extensive capitalist farm. The conduct of all such enterprises requires the strictest discipline, the nicest accuracy in the apportionment of the work, under peril of damage to mechanism or product, or even the confusion and stoppage of the whole business. In all such enterprises the workers will, of course, 'choose delegates who will form something in the nature of a parliament'.

But herein lies the crux: this 'something in the nature of a parliament' will not be a parliament in the middle-class sense. Kautsky's ideas do not go beyond the boundaries of middle-class parliamentarism. 'This something in the nature of a parliament' will not merely 'determine the conditions of work, and superintend the management of the bureaucratic apparatus', as imagined by Kautsky. In a Socialist society, this 'something in the nature of a parliament', consisting of workers' delegates, will determine the conditions of work, and superintend the management of the 'apparatus'—but this apparatus will not be 'bureaucratic'. The workers, having conquered political power, will break up the old bureaucratic apparatus, they will shatter it from its foundations up, until not one stone is left standing upon another; and the new machine which they will fashion to take its place will be formed out of these same workers and employees themselves. To guard against their transformation into bureaucrats, measures will be taken at once, which have been analysed in detail by Marx and Engels:—(1) Not only will they be elected, but they will be subject to recall at any time. (2) They will receive payment no higher than that of ordinary workers. (3) There will be an immediate preparation for a state of things when *all* shall fulfil the functions of control and superintendence, so that *all* shall become 'bureaucrats' for a time, and no one should therefore have the opportunity of becoming 'bureaucrats' at all.

Kautsky has not reflected at all on Marx's words: 'The Commune was not a parliamentary, but a working corporation, at one and the same time making the laws and executing them.' He has not in the least understood the difference between a middle-class parliament combining democracy (not for the people) with bureaucracy (against the people), and proletarian democracy, which will take immediate steps to cut bureaucracy down at the roots, and which will be able to carry out measures to their logical conclusion, to the complete destruction of bureaucracy, and the final establishment of democracy for the people. Kautsky reveals here again the same old 'superstitious respect' for the State, and 'superstitious faith' in bureaucracy.

Let us pass to the last and best of Kautsky's works against the Opportunists, his pamphlet, *The Road to Power*, published in 1909. This pamphlet constitutes a considerable step in advance, inasmuch as it does not treat of the revolutionary programme in general (as in the book of 1899 against Bernstein), nor of the problems of a social revolution independently of the time of its occurrence (as in the pamphlet *The Social Revolution*, of 1902), but of the concrete conditions which compel us to recognize that the revolutionary era is *approaching*.

The author distinctly points out the intensification of class antagonisms in general and the growth of Imperialism, which plays a particularly important part in this connection. After the 'revolutionary period of 1789-1871' in Western Europe an analogous period begins for the East in 1905. A world-war is coming nearer with threatening rapidity. 'The proletariat can no longer talk of a premature revolution.' 'We have entered upon a revolutionary period.' 'The revolutionary era is beginning.'

These declarations are perfectly clear. The pamphlet offers us a measure of comparison between the high promise of German Social-Democracy before the Imperialist war and the depth of degradation to which it fell—carrying with it Kautsky himself—when the war broke out. 'The present situation,' Kautsky wrote in the pamphlet under review, 'contains this danger, that we, German Social-Democracy, may easily be considered more moderate than we are in reality.' But when it came to the test, the German Social-Democratic Party turned out even more moderate and opportunist than it had seemed. It is the more characteristic that, side by side with such definite declarations regarding the revolutionary era already upon us, Kautsky, in the pamphlet which he says himself is devoted to precisely the '*political* revolution', again quite passes over the question of the State.

The sum total of these evasions of the subject, omissions and shufflings inevitably led to that complete surrender to opportunism of which we shall soon have to speak.

German Social-Democracy, as it were, in the person of Kautsky, declared: I still uphold revolutionary views (1899); I recognize, in particular, the inevitability of the social revolution of the proletariat (1902); I recognize that a new revolutionary era is upon us (1909); still I disavow that which Marx said so early as 1852—if once the question is definitely raised as to the tasks confronting a proletarian revolution in respect to the State (1913).

It was precisely in this bald form that the question was put in the debate with Pannekoek.

3 THE DEBATE BETWEEN KAUTSKY AND PANNEKOEK

Pannekoek came out against Kautsky as one of the representatives of the 'Left Radical' group, which counted in its ranks Rosa Luxemburg, Karl Radek, and others, which, while upholding revolutionary tactics, was united in the conviction that Kautsky was passing over to a 'central' position, wavering, without principle, between Marxism and Opportunism. The correctness of this view has been fully proved by the war, when this 'central' current of Kautskianism, wrongly called Marxist, revealed itself in all its pitiful helplessness.

In an article touching on the question of the State, entitled 'Mass Action and Revolution' (*Neue Zeit*, 1912, xxx.2), Pannekoek characterized Kautsky's position as an attitude of 'passive radicalism', as 'a theory of inactive expectancy'. 'Kautsky does not want to see the process of revolution' (p. 616). In treating this subject, Pannekoek approached the problem which interests us, the tasks of a proletarian revolution in relation to the State.

'The struggle of the proletariat [he wrote] is not merely a struggle against the capitalist class to control the State, but a struggle against *the State*. . . . The essence of a proletarian revolution is the destruction of the organized forces of the State, and their forcible suppression (*ablösung*) by the organized forces of the proletariat. . . . Until the entire State organization is destroyed, the struggle will not end. That is its aim. The organization of the majority demonstrates its superiority by destroying the organized force of the ruling minority' (p. 548).

Pannekoek did not expound his ideas very skilfully, but the ideas are sufficiently clear; and it is interesting to note how Kautsky combated them. 'Up till now,' he wrote, 'the difference between Social-Democrats and Anarchists has consisted in this: the first desired to conquer the State authority, while the Anarchists' aim was to destroy it: Pannekoek wants to do both'

(p. 724). If Pannekoek's exposition lacks precision and concreteness—not to speak of other defects which have no bearing on the present subject—Kautsky seized on just that one point in Pannekoek's article which is the essence of the whole matter; and *on this fundamental question of principle* Kautsky forsakes the Marxian position entirely and surrenders himself without reserve to the Opportunists. His definition of the difference between Social-Democrats and Anarchists is absolutely wrong; and Marxism is finally vulgarized and distorted.

This is what the difference between the Marxists and Anarchists is: (1) The Marxists aim at the complete destruction of the State, but recognize that this aim is only attainable after the extinction of classes by a Socialist revolution as the result of the establishment of Socialism, leading to the withering away of the State. The Anarchists, on the other hand, want the complete destruction of the State within twenty-four hours, and do not understand the conditions under which alone such a destruction can be carried out. (2) The Marxists recognize that when once the proletariat has won political power it must utterly break up the old machinery of the State, and substitute for it a new machinery of organized armed workers, after the type of the Commune. Anarchists, on the other hand, while advocating the destruction of the State, have no clear idea as to *what* the proletariat will put in its place and how it will use its revolutionary power; they even deny that the revolutionary proletariat has any necessity to make use of the State and to establish its revolutionary dictatorship. (3) Marxists insist upon making use of the modern State as a means of preparing the workers for revolution; Anarchists reject all this.

In this controversy it is Pannekoek, not Kautsky, who represents Marxism, seeing that it was Marx himself who taught that the mere transference of the old State machine into new hands is no conquest of power at all: the proletariat must smash up this apparatus and replace it by something altogether new. Kautsky rats from Marxism to the Opportunists, because, under his hands, this destruction of the State, which is utterly repugnant to the Opportunists, completely disappears. Nothing remains but an opportunist loophole in his interpretation of 'conquest' as the gaining of a majority.

In order to cover up his distortion of Marxism Kautsky radiates erudition, offering us 'quotations' from Marx himself. Marx wrote in 1850 of the necessity of 'a decisive centralization of force in the hands of the State'; and Kautsky triumphantly asks: 'Does Pannekoek want to destroy "Centralism"?' This is nothing but a conjuring trick. It is the same sort of thing as Bernsteins's identification of the views of Marx and Proudhon on Federation *versus* Centralism.

Kautsky's 'quotation' is neither here nor there. The new form of the State admits Centralism as much as the old; if the workers voluntarily unify their armed forces, this will be centralism: but it will be based on the complete destruction of centralized government apparatus—the army, police, bureaucracy. Kautsky's behaviour is certainly not honest here; the well-known dissertations of Marx and Engels on the Commune are ignored in favour of a quotation which has no relevance at all.

'Perhaps Pannekoek wants to destroy the State functions of the officials? [Kautsky continues] But we cannot do without officials even in our party and trade-union organizations, much less in the State administration. For State officials our programme demands, not annihilation, but election by the people. It is not a question as to the precise form which the administrative apparatus will take in the future State, but as to whether our political struggle destroys (literally: dissolves, *auflöst*) the State *before we have conquered it* [Kautsky's italics]. What Ministry with its officials, could be destroyed? [Here follows an enumeration of the Ministries of Education, Justice, Finance and War.] No, not one of the present Ministries will be abolished in our political struggles against the Government. . . . I repeat, to avoid misunderstanding, it is not here a question as to what form a victorious Social-Democracy will give to the "future State," but as to how our opposition changes the present State' (p. 725).

This is an obvious trick: *Revolution* was the question Pannekoek raised. Both the title of his article and the passages quoted above clearly enough show that. But Kautsky shifts and changes the point of view from one of revolution to one of Opportunism, when he jumps over to the question of 'opposition'. According to him, we must for the present confine ourselves to opposition; *after* we have won power we can have a talk about other things.

The Revolution has vanished: that is precisely what the Opportunists wanted.

Opposition and general political struggle is beside the point; we are concerned with the *Revolution*. And Revolution is when the administrative apparatus and the whole machinery of government are destroyed, and a new proletarian power of the armed workers has filled their place.

Kautsky reveals a 'superstitious respect' for the Ministries: but why cannot they be replaced, say by committees of specialists working under sovereign all-powerful councils of workers' and soldiers' delegates ? The essence of the matter is not at all whether the Ministries shall remain or be turned into committees of specialists or any other kind of institution; all this is quite unimportant. The main thing is, whether we are still to have the old machinery of government, saturated through and through with routine and inertia, and connected by thousands of threads with the capitalist class; or shall it be broken up and replaced by something altogether new ? The essence of revolution is not that a new class shall govern by means of the old governmental machinery, but that it shall smash up this machinery and govern by means of a new machine.

This is a fundamental idea of Marxism, which Kautsky either conceals or has not understood at all. This question of his about officials makes it plain how little he has understood the lessons of the Commune or the teachings of Marx. 'We cannot do without officials even in our party and trade-union organization'—we cannot do without officials under *Capitalism*, the domination of the middle class. The proletariat is oppressed, the labouring masses are enslaved by Capitalism; democracy is narrowed, crushed, curtailed, mutilated by Capitalism, wage-slavery, the poverty and misery of the masses. It is precisely the conditions of life under Capitalism which are the cause, and there is no other, why the officials of our political parties and trade unions are corrupt—or, rather, have the tendency to become corrupt, to become bureaucrats, that is, privileged persons detached from the masses, *and standing above it*. That is just the essence of bureaucracy, and until the capitalists have been expropriated and the bourgeoisie overthrown, nothing can prevent even workers' officials from being to some extent 'bureaucratized'.

From what Kautsky says, one might think that a Socialism with elected employees would still tolerate bureaucrats and bureaucracy. That is the grand falsehood. Marx took the example of the Commune to show that under Socialism the workers' employees will cease to be 'bureaucrats' and 'officials'—especially when election is supplemented by the right of immediate recall; still more, when their pay is brought down to the level of the pay of the average worker; and still more again, when parliamentary institutions are replaced by 'working bodies which both make and apply the laws'.

All Kautsky's arguments against Pannekoek, and particularly his triumphant point that we cannot do without officials even in our parties and trade unions, show nothing so much as that Kautsky has adopted the old 'arguments' of Bernstein against Marxism itself. Bernstein's renegade book, *Socialist Fundamentals*, is an attack on 'primitive' democracy—'doctrinaire democracy,' as he calls it—on imperative mandates, functionaries who receive no remuneration, impotent central representative bodies, and so on. British trade union experience, as interpreted by the Webbs, is Bernstein's proof of how untenable 'primitive democracy' is. Seventy odd years of development 'in absolute freedom' (p. 137, German Edition), have, forsooth, convinced the trade unions that primitive democracy is useless, and led them to replace it by ordinary parliamentarism combined with bureaucracy.

But the 'absolute freedom' in which the trade unions developed was in reality *complete capitalist enslavement* under which—what more natural?—'one cannot do without' concessions to the evil power of force and falsehood by which the 'lower' orders are excluded from the affairs of the 'higher' administration.

Under Socialism much of the primitive democracy will inevitably be revived. For the first time in the history of civilized nations, the *mass* of the population will rise, beyond voting and elections, to a direct control of the every-day administration of the affairs of the nation. Under Socialism, *all* will take a turn in management, and will soon become accustomed to the idea of no managers at all.

Marx's wonderful critico-analytical mind perceived that the practical measures of the Commune contained that revolutionary departure of which the Opportunists are afraid, and which they do not want to recognize, out of cowardice, out of reluctance to break irrevocably with the bourgeoisie; and which the Anarchists do not want to perceive either through haste or a general want of comprehension of the conditions of great social transformations. 'One must not even think of such a thing as the break-up of the old machinery of government, for how shall we do without Ministeries and without officials?'—thus argues the Opportunist, saturated through and through with philistinism, and in reality not merely bereft of faith in revolution, in the creative power of revolution, but actually in deadly fear of it (like our Social-Revolutionaries and Mensheviks). 'One must *only* think of the destruction of the old machinery of government: never mind searching for concrete lessons in earlier proletarian revolutionary movements, or analysing *by what and how* to replace what has been destroyed':—thus argues the Anarchist: that is, the best of the Anarchists, not those who follow, with Kropotkin & Co., in the train of the bourgeoisie; and consequently, the tactics of the Anarchist become the tactics of despair instead of a revolutionary grappling with concrete problems— ruthless, courageous, and, at the same time, cognisant of the conditions under which the masses progress.

Marx teaches us to avoid both classes of error. He teaches us dauntless courage to destroy the old machinery of government, and at the same time shows us how to put the question concretely: The Commune was able, within a few weeks, to *start* the building of a new proletarian State machinery by introducing the measures indicated above to secure a wider democracy, in which bureaucracy should be uprooted. Let us learn revolutionary courage from the Communards. In their practical measures we can see *an indication* of practical, every-day and immediately possible measures; it is along such a path that we shall arrive at the complete destruction of bureaucracy.

It can be destroyed. When Socialism has shortened the working day, raised the masses to a new life, created such conditions for the majority of the population as to enable everybody, *without exception*, to perform the functions of government, then every form of the State will completely wither away.

'To destroy the State [Kautsky wrote] can never be the object of a general strike, but only to wring concessions from the Government on some particular question, or to replace a hostile Government by one willing to meet the proletariat half way. . . . But never, under no conditions, can it [a proletarian victory over a hostile Government] lead to the destruction of the State. It can lead only to a certain rearrangement (*Verschiebung*) of forces *within the State*. . . . The aim of our political struggle, then, remains as before, the conquest of power within the State by the gaining of a majority in Parliament, and the conversion of Parliament into the master of the Government' (pp. 726, 727, 732).

This is nothing but the most vulgar Opportunism: a repudiation of revolution in deeds, whilst upholding it in words, Kautsky's imagination goes no further than a 'Government willing to meet the proletariat half way'—further backwards towards philistinism than we were in 1874, when the *Communist Manifesto* proclaimed 'the organization of the proletariat as the ruling class'. Kautsky will have to realize his beloved 'unity' with the Scheidemanns, Plekhanoffs and Vanderveldes: all the lot will agree to fight for a Government 'meeting the proletariat half way'.

But we shall go forward to a break with these traitors to Socialism. We are working for a complete destruction of the old machinery of government, in such a way that the armed workers themselves *shall be the Government*, which will be a very different thing. Kautsky may enjoy the pleasant company of the Legiens, Davids, Plekhanoffs, Potressoffs, Tseretellis and Tchernoffs, who are quite willing to work for the 'rearrangement of forces within the State . . . the gaining of a majority in Parliament, and the supremacy of Parliament over the Government'. A most worthy object, wholly acceptable to the Opportunists, in which everything remains within the framework of a middle-class parliamentary republic.

We, however, shall go forward to a break with the Opportunists. And the whole of the class-conscious proletariat will be with us—not for a 're-arrangement of forces', *but for the overthrow of the capitalist class*, the *destruction* of bourgeois parliamentarism, the building up of a democratic republic after the type of the Commune or a republic of Soviets (Councils) of workers' and soldiers' deputies—the revolutionary dictatorship of the proletariat.

.   .   .   .

Further to the 'right' of Kautsky there are, in international Socialism, such tendencies as the *Socialist Monthly* (*Sozialistische Monatshefte*) in Germany (Legien, David, Kolb, and many others, including the Scandinavians, Stauning and Branting); the followers of Jaurès and Vandervelde in France and Belgium; Turati, Treves, and other representatives of the right wing of the Italian party; the Fabians and 'Independents' (the Independent Labour Party, dependent, as a matter of fact, always on the Liberals) in England; and similar sections. All these gentry, while playing a great, very often a predominant rôle, in parliamentary work and in the journalism of the party, decisively reject the dictatorship of the proletariat and carry out a policy of unconcealed Opportunism. In the eyes of these gentry, the dictatorship of the proletariat 'contradicts' democracy! There is really nothing seriously to distinguish them from lower middle-class democrats.

Taking these circumstances into consideration, we have a right to conclude that the Second International, in the persons of the overwhelming majority of its official representatives, has completely sunk down into Opportunism. The experience of the Commune has been not only forgotten, but distorted. So far from making vivid in the workers' minds the near approach of the time when they are to smash the old machinery of the State and substitute a new one, thereby making their political domination the foundation for a Socialist reconstruction of society, they have actually taught the workers the direct opposite of this, and represented the 'conquest of power' in a way that left thousands of loopholes to Opportunism.

It was a fateful thing to have confused and hushed up the question of the relation of a proletarian revolution to the State at a time when the States, with their swollen military apparatus in a whirlwind of Imperialist rivalry, had became monstrous military beasts devouring the lives of millions of people, in order to decide whether England or Germany—this or that group of financial capitalists—should dominate the world.

AFTERWORD

THIS little book was written in August and September, 1917. I had already drawn up the plan for the next, the seventh chapter, on the experiences of the Russian Revolutions of 1905 and 1917. But, apart from the title, I had not succeeded in writing a single line of the chapter, being prevented therefrom by a political crisis—the eve of the November Revolution of 1917. Such a hindrance can only be welcomed. However, this final part of the book, devoted to the lessons of the Russian Revolutions of 1905 and 1917, will probably have to be put off for a long time. It is more pleasant and more useful to live through the experience of a revolution than to write about it.

THE AUTHOR

PETROGRAD
  (*Nov.* 30*th*) *Dec.* 12, 1917